CM0092O7748

Žižek

Žižek
A Critical Introduction

Sarah Kay

Polity

First published in 2003 by Polity Press in association with Blackwell Publishing Ltd

Editorial office:
Polity Press
65 Bridge Street
Cambridge CB2 1UR, UK

Marketing and production:
Blackwell Publishing Ltd
108 Cowley Road
Oxford OX4 1JF, UK

Distributed in the USA by
Blackwell Publishing Inc.
350 Main Street
Malden, MA 02148, USA

A catalogue record for this book is available from the British Library.

Library of Congress Cataloging-in-Publication Data

Kay, Sarah.
Žižek : a critical introduction / Sarah Kay.
p.   cm. – (Key contemporary thinkers)
Includes bibliographical references and index. ISBN 0-7456-2207-0 (alk. paper) – ISBN 0-7456-2208-9 (pbk. : alk. paper)
1. Žižek, Slavoj.   I. Title.   II. Key contemporary thinkers (Cambridge, England)
B4870.Z594 K39 2003
199'.4973 – dc21
                                                  2002012055

Typeset in 10½ on 12 pt Palatino
by SNP Best-set Typesetter Ltd., Hong Kong
Printed and bound in Great Britain by MPG Books Ltd, Bodmin, Cornwall

For further information on Polity, visit our website: http://www.polity.co.uk

Key Contemporary Thinkers

Published

Jeremy Ahearne, *Michel de Certeau: Interpretation and its Other*

Peter Burke, *The French Historical Revolution: The* Annales *School 1929–1989*

Michael Caesar, *Umberto Eco: Philosophy, Semiotics and the Work of Fiction*

M. J. Cain, *Fodor: Language, Mind and Philosophy*

Rosemary Cowan, *Cornel West: The Politics of Redemption*

Colin Davis, *Levinas: An Introduction*

Simon Evnine, *Donald Davidson*

Edward Fullbrook and Kate Fullbrook, *Simone de Beauvoir: A Critical Introduction*

Andrew Gamble, *Hayek: The Iron Cage of Liberty*

Nigel Gibson, *Fanon: The Postcolonial Imagination*

Graeme Gilloch, *Walter Benjamin: Critical Constellations*

Karen Green, *Dummett: Philosophy of Language*

Espen Hammer, *Stanley Cavell: Skepticism, Subjectivity, and the Ordinary*

Phillip Hansen, *Hannah Arendt: Politics, History and Citizenship*

Sean Homer, *Fredric Jameson: Marxism, Hermeneutics, Postmodernism*

Christopher Hookway, *Quine: Language, Experience and Reality*

Christina Howells, *Derrida: Deconstruction from Phenomenology to Ethics*

Fred Inglis, *Clifford Geertz: Culture, Custom and Ethics*

Simon Jarvis, *Adorno: A Critical Introduction*

Sarah Kay, *Žižek: A Critical Introduction*

Douglas Kellner, *Jean Baudrillard: From Marxism to Post-Modernism and Beyond*

Valerie Kennedy, *Edward Said: A Critical Introduction*

Chandran Kukathas and Philip Pettit, *Rawls: A Theory of Justice and its Critics*

James McGilvray, *Chomsky: Language, Mind, and Politics*

Lois McNay, *Foucault: A Critical Introduction*

Philip Manning, *Erving Goffman and Modern Sociology*

Michael Moriarty, *Roland Barthes*

Harold W. Noonan, *Frege: A Critical Introduction*

William Outhwaite, *Habermas: A Critical Introduction*

Kari Palonen, *Quentin Skinner: History, Politics, Rhetoric*

John Preston, *Feyerabend: Philosophy, Science and Society*
Chris Rojek, *Stuart Hall*
Susan Sellers, *Hélène Cixous: Authorship, Autobiography and Love*
Wes Sharrock and Rupert Read, *Kuhn: Philosopher of Scientific Revolutions*
David Silverman, *Harvey Sacks: Social Science and Conversation Analysis*
Dennis Smith, *Zygmunt Bauman: Prophet of Postmodernity*
Nicholas H. Smith, *Charles Taylor: Meaning, Morals and Modernity*
Geoffrey Stokes, *Popper: Philosophy, Politics and Scientific Method*
Georgia Warnke, *Gadamer: Hermeneutics, Tradition and Reason*
James Williams, *Lyotard: Towards a Postmodern Philosophy*
Jonathan Wolff, *Robert Nozick: Property, Justice and the Minimal State*

Forthcoming

Maria Baghramian, *Hilary Putnam*
Sara Beardsworth, *Kristeva*
James Carey, *Innis and McLuhan*
George Crowder, *Isaiah Berlin: Liberty, Pluralism and Liberalism*
Thomas D'Andrea, *Alasdair MacIntyre*
Maximilian de Gaynesford, *John McDowell*
Reidar Andreas Due, *Deleuze*
Eric Dunning, *Norbert Elias*
Jocelyn Dunphy, *Ricoeur*
Matthew Elton, *Daniel Dennett*
Chris Fleming, *René Girard: Violence and Mimesis*
Paul Kelly, *Ronald Dworkin*
Carl Levy, *Antonio Gramsci*
Moya Lloyd, *Judith Butler*
Nigel Mapp, *Paul de Man*
Dermot Moran, *Edmund Husserl*
Jim Murray, *C. L. R. James: Ideas in Social Movement*
James O'Shea, *Wilfrid Sellars*
Nicholas Walker, *Heidegger*

Contents

Preface

I want to start this preface with a tribute to Elizabeth and Edmond Wright. A psychoanalyst-and-critic and a philosopher respectively, they were the ideal trail-blazers – if there is to be such a discipline – of 'Žižek studies'. Their *Žižek Reader* and their edited volume of *Paragraph* on Žižek have inaugurated this field-in-waiting with insight and authority.

When Polity asked me to contribute a volume on Žižek to the Key Contemporary Thinkers series, I was struck, by contrast, with a sense of incongruity. A French medievalist by profession, I might seem the last person in the world to take it on. Which is precisely why, on reflection, I did so. Citing the words of a courtier to his Queen in Shakespeare's *Richard II*, Žižek frequently asserts the value of 'looking awry':

> Like perspectives, which rightly gaz'd upon
> Show nothing but confusion; ey'd awry
> Distinguish form. (Act II, scene ii)

I hope my seemingly inappropriate vantage-point may also turn out to be a good one from which to 'distinguish the form' in Žižek's work.

As a medievalist, it has been an especial pleasure for me to write on someone who is not dead. I fear, though, that the very act of writing a book such as this is mortifying to its subject. Lacan resisted all attempts to arrest and thereby stultify his insights. Žižek's thought is not as difficult to formulate as Lacan's, but it still relies on movement as its life force: both development over time and the constant switches of perspective to which his riotous assembly of materials gives rise. I have tried to conserve a sense of the former, but it has tended to be at the expense of the latter, except in my opening and closing chapters. Žižek's writing is a distinctively hectic *omnium gatherum*, but this makes it difficult for readers to pursue particular themes. Mindful of the different interests with which they will approach him, I have marshalled his volatile swarms of ideas into something more resembling single-file traffic.

The fields to which Žižek's *oeuvre* contributes most are psychoanalysis and philosophy. These are both conceptually elaborate disciplines, and as such have evolved technical vocabularies that should not be dismissed as 'jargon'. I have set out to explain this terminology rather than avoid it. In the expectation that readers will want to read this book selectively, I have tried to make each chapter self-contained and self-explanatory (though there are occasional cross-references); a selective glossary is also provided to mop up remaining terminological difficulties. I have followed Žižek's usage in most respects. Unlike him, however, I avoid the use of upper-case initial letters in spelling the three Lacanian registers (or orders) of symbolic, real and imaginary, and most other terms of art (event, substance, truth, etc.); I retain it only to distinguish the big Other and the Thing. References to Žižek's writings, and to those of other authors cited, are included in the text, using shortened forms of titles. Lacan's *Seminar* is cited by volume and page numbers. 'Ibid.' is used only to refer to the same page of the same work as the immediately preceding reference.

Psychoanalysis is a subject capable of provoking derision and hostility. For some, the imputation that they have an unconscious is gratuitously offensive. They view the claims of psychoanalysis as hovering uncertainly between personal outrage and unsubstantiated nonsense. Such readers will not find a defence of psychoanalysis in this book, except in so far as Žižek's claims regarding its relevance to other fields are explored. In my view, the outrageousness of psychoanalysis is one of its more obvious strengths, and provides vital leverage against the dead weight of common sense. Moreover, while this book is introductory, it is not an introduction to psychoanalytic theory *as such*, but to Žižek's use of it, and I present here only areas that seem to me to be relevant to his work.

Acknowledgements

I should like to acknowledge help in writing this book from many sources. It was written during a period of leave financed by the University of Cambridge, for which I am grateful. Encouragement and valuable advice on individual chapters were provided by Bill Burgwinkle, Colin Davis and Sylvia Huot. The Polity reader's report was a model of balance between reservations and tolerant good humour. If acknowledgements could confer immortality, then Christopher Cannon should be immortalized for reading the whole book in draft and commenting so fully and helpfully on the experience. The impetus to work on Žižek was born in the Medieval Reading Group in Cambridge, to whose members I am indebted for sustaining an intellectual environment of such high quality. In addition to the colleagues I have already named, Mark Chinca, Marilynn Desmond, Elizabeth Edwards, Simon Gaunt, Jane Gilbert, Miranda Griffin, David Hult, Francesca Nicholson, Simon Pender, Benjamin Ramm, Nicolette Zeeman and others are all at risk of finding their own ideas distorted or merely plagiarized in this book. Finally, I should like to thank Slavoj Žižek himself for reading the typescript and putting me right on a lot of points in a generous and stimulating conversation.

1

Introduction: Thinking, Writing and Reading about the Real

Slavoj Žižek is the most vital interdisciplinary thinker to emerge in recent years. He has become so influential across the whole range of the humanities and social sciences that his importance can be compared with that of Foucault in the 1970s and 1980s; but he is much more fun to read. His publishers like to include in the blurb on the back of his books the claim that he 'provides the best intellectual high since *Anti-Oedipus*'; but he is a lot more entertaining than Deleuze and Guattari too. Reading Žižek is like taking an exhilarating ride on a roller-coaster through anecdote, Kant, popular film, science, religion, Marx, opera, smut, current affairs, modern art, Derrida, political correctness, canonical literature, cyberspace, etc. etc., being constantly buffeted as you do so in the twists and turns of Hegelian dialectic and Lacanian theory. A riveting speaker, Žižek is also his own best publicist, and even if, when you hear him, you may have the feeling that you've heard it before, the experience is still irresistibly energizing.

At the core of Žižek's work is a vigorous reactivation of Lacanian psychoanalysis in the service of a project at once political and philosophical. His main philosophical contention is that Lacan's thought is heir to the Enlightenment, but represents a seismic shift forwards. For Žižek, Lacan both continues and radicalizes the trajectory of European transcendental metaphysics: that is, of the quest to achieve true understanding of the nature of being that starts with Plato and is then decisively reoriented by Kant and Hegel. Žižek contrasts Lacan with the deviations from this tradition represented by Heidegger and post-structuralism (initially Žižek identifies Lacan as 'postmodern', but not for long).

Žižek is a leading thinker, but he does not work in isolation.[1] Born in 1949 in what was then Yugoslavia and is now Slovenia, he is one of a group of Slovenian Lacanians based at the Institute of Philosophy in Ljubljana, Slovenia. The characteristics of this group are their shared background in Continental philosophy (Descartes, Kant, Hegel, Marx), their fascination with Lacanian psychoanalysis, and a relentless urge to explain each in the terms of the other. A true pedagogic passion drives their writings. They are also united by their interest in ideology and popular culture. Several of the volumes edited by Žižek contain examples of work by his fellow Slovenians. They are formidable linguists, who, like Žižek himself, seem at home in several European vernaculars, capable of reading Hegel and Lacan in the original German or French; their culture is cosmopolitan, and much of their work, like Žižek's own, is available in a range of languages. Like him, they originally published in Slovenian, principally in the journal *Problemi* and the book series *Analecta* which they had founded.

With a doctorate in philosophy from Ljubljana, and a first book on Heidegger, Žižek studied for a second doctorate in Paris with Lacan's son-in-law and principal disciple, Jacques-Alain Miller. His thesis with Miller, on Hegel and Lacan, provided much of the substance for his first two books in English, *The Sublime Object of Ideology* (1989) and *For They Know Not What They Do: Enjoyment as a Political Factor* (1990); the latter was published in French in the same year. Another early book, a collection of essays produced in collaboration with several other Slovenian Lacanians and entertainingly entitled *Everything You Wanted to Know about Lacan (But Were Afraid to Ask Hitchcock)* (1992), first appeared in French, and *Enjoy Your Symptom!* (likewise 1992) also gave rise to a French version. The French psychoanalytical film theorist Michel Chion is a significant collaborator and reference point at this time. Another theorist who was interested in Žižek and the other Slovenian Lacanians at this early date was the influential American Marxist critic Fredric Jameson. Ernesto Laclau, a political theorist working in the UK, also recognized Žižek's work and contributed a supportive explanatory preface to *The Sublime Object of Ideology*. His greater exposure than the other Slovenian Lacanians on the international lecture circuit, particularly in the USA, where he has held a succession of visiting professorships, has led Žižek to pull away from them somewhat. For a period he maintained a vigorous debate with the American philosopher and theorist of gender Judith Butler. Among his major interlocutors now is the French philosopher Alain Badiou, a student of the French Marxist Althusser and a vehement anti-capitalist.

Since the early 1990s Žižek has published at a hectic pace, with an increasing number of titles coming out each year. Faced with this abundance, where should one start? Among his most accessible books are the ones on popular culture, especially *Looking Awry* (1991); more specialized, but also pretty readable, is his recent study of the film director Kieślowski, *The Fright of Real Tears* (2001). Another good starting point is the comic self-interview in which he obligingly asks himself to outline his views to himself (published in *The Metastases of Enjoyment* of 1994). Probably his best books are *The Sublime Object of Ideology* (1989), *Tarrying with the Negative* (1993) and *The Ticklish Subject* (1999), but many of the ideas developed in these works are also contained in a more accessible form in *Enjoy Your Symptom!*. That this last may, in some sense, be the key Žižekian text is suggested by the fact that he has published it twice, in 1992 and again in expanded form in 2001.

Like other intellectual superstars, Žižek is at risk of writing faster than he can read, and at times faster even than he can think. A certain dilution, repetitiveness[2] and inattention to detail[3] are the price of success. But his energy seems unabated as he continues to find new areas of debate and new partners *in* debate. Indeed, since this book was drafted, a further book has appeared, co-written with Mladen Dolar, called *Opera's Second Death*; a collection of Lenin's writings flanked by an Introduction and Afterword, *Revolution at the Gates*, appeared as it went to press; a revised edition, with a new Introduction, of *For They Know Not What They Do* has been announced; and a further book on cognitive psychology, Christianity and other matters is in hand.

Thinking about the Real

What holds these various philosophical, political and cultural strands together in Žižek's writing is his sustained interrogation of what Lacan calls the 'real'. Since this difficult concept is, in a sense, what all of his books revolve around (and indeed, most of the later writings of Lacan too), it is not possible to provide a snappy definition of what it means, but I shall start by offering a few pointers. (See also the entry REAL in the Glossary.)

The real must not for a moment be confused with what, through discourse, we represent to ourselves as 'reality'; it is, by definition, that which discourse cannot include. Whereas Foucault's *oeuvre* turns around the problem of discourse and how we are positioned in and by it, Žižek's concern is thus with the exact obverse. The real is more akin to the mad machines and terrifying inertia evoked in the opening pages of the *Anti-Oedipus*, but instead of constituting – as these do for Deleuze and Guattari – a material reality analogous to the various historical modes of production, the real for Žižek is far more elusive and far less amenable to description. This does not mean, however, that it is not all around us. On the contrary, it dogs our every step – as though stuck to the sole of our shoe, as Lacan humorously put it.[4] Lacan's remark brings to mind the joke told about Sir Thomas Beecham, who when asked if he had ever conducted music by Stockhausen replied, 'No, but I trod in some once.' The real is the disgusting, hidden underside of reality which we cannot fail but step on, however much we imagine that our minds are set on higher things. Indeed, the more we keep our heads in the air, the more it clings to our feet. And just as we can't keep ourselves from sniffing at it – whether with titillation or revulsion – so it fills us with *jouissance*, or enjoyment: the thrill of the real. This enjoyment can never be directly experienced or acknowledged, but it colours our responses in the guise of an obscene smear, an opaque, contaminating stain. Or, to take a rather different and less unsavoury tack, the real can be thought of as the limit of language, and thus as everything we lose by becoming speaking beings. This limitation is just that: a cut-off point so absolute as to be invisible to us as language-users. If we attempt to trace it, it wraps back into the heart of language, just as the hole in the middle of a doughnut is a continuation of the space that surrounds it. Thanks to the hole, the doughnut is a doughnut, even though, in a sense, the hole is precisely what is not in it; analogously, the real is what shapes our sense of reality, even though it is excluded from it. Conversely, the real may be represented as something unremittingly resistant, a 'hard kernel' that our thoughts keep glancing off and that no mental light can illumine. The words most commonly used by Žižek to gesture towards the real include 'antagonism', 'traumatic', 'impossible', 'kernel' and 'deadlock'; others that belong (some of them surprisingly) in this field are 'act', 'death', 'drive', 'ethical', 'freedom', 'forced choice' and 'love' (see the Glossary for an elaboration of some of these terms).

Žižek's concept of the real will be explored from many angles in this book. The panoramic range of topics he discusses, from smutty anecdotes to religious faith and from science fiction movies to quantum physics, all interest him because of the way they simultaneously exclude and engage it. For now, in this summary of the main lines of Žižek's thought, it is enough to say that Žižek places Lacan in the tradition of post-Enlightenment metaphysics because he sees Lacan as a philosopher of the real. However elusive the real may be, it insinuates its effects upon us; however negative, it remains a point of anchorage to which we are bound by enjoyment. Post-structuralism, then, is criticized for distancing itself from metaphysics and casting itself adrift from the real. Likewise, the real lies at the heart of Žižek's political project because, for him, ideology relies upon the social organization of enjoyment, and it is through enjoyment that political compliance is secured. By means of what he calls 'the act', however, we erupt into non-compliance, disturb ideology, and loosen its hold on us. In Žižek's terms, we accomplish the political equivalent of 'traversing the fantasy' – a phrase referring to the outcome of Lacanian therapy, in which we glimpse that what we had taken for reality was all along an illusion masking the space of the real, and so have an opportunity to build 'reality' afresh. The philosophical and political dimensions of his project are thus inseparable, even if what connects them (the real) is precisely that which, in a sense, is not there. Their conjunction is brought out most clearly in his most ambitious book to date, *The Ticklish Subject*, whose subtitle declares it as addressing 'the absent centre of political ontology'.

This 'absent centre' takes on different coloration in different phases of Žižek's philosophy. Most pervasive (and from a Lacanian standpoint most orthodox) is the identification of the real with sexual difference. The real is also explored in terms of the negative in Hegel's dialectic. From *The Indivisible Remainder* (1996) onwards, the negativity of the real is discovered in the resistance offered to thought by material reality. This 'materialist' account leads Žižek (in *The Ticklish Subject* of 1999 and subsequent writings) to identify the unshakeable monolith of capital as a manifestation of the real. His recent writings on Christianity also lead to a new and original purchase on the real as the domain of grace, by contrast with that of law.

Where political thought is concerned, there are likewise major changes between the earlier and later Žižek. In works prior to *The*

Indivisible Remainder, his principal stance is anti-totalitarian, and his main subject matter is the critique of ideology, especially national- ist and racist ideology. His next books (most notably *The Ticklish Subject*) mount an impassioned attack on capitalism, and plead for a return to universality as the only means of opposing capitalist globalization. Most recently, the wheel seems almost to have come full circle as Žižek critiques liberalism and queries the very category of 'totalitarianism'. A constant of Žižek's political writing through- out, however, has been his opposition to cynicism and his promo- tion of what he calls 'the act', a violent disruption of the *status quo* that might make it possible to puncture the prevailing ideology and effect political change.

Writing about the Real

Žižek's writing can be quite hard going. In part this is because philosophical thought is inevitably demanding, especially when, like Žižek's, it is conceived in response to thinkers who are them- selves notoriously difficult. Even when he is in pedagogic vein, his determination to illumine a difficulty in one writer (typically Hegel) in the light of a difficulty in another (typically Lacan) can prove as much intimidating as enlightening. In part, too, it is because the boundary between exposition and critique is blurred in his writing, as it is in much recent theory and philosophy. Žižek tends to expli- cate the thought of any writer with whom he disagrees in terms that anticipate the intended corrective; his exposition 'always already' contains the germs of the ensuing critique, and thus tends to be couched in his prevailing (Hegelianized) Lacanese. The aim of this book is to facilitate access to Žižek's thought, and I start in chapter 2 with the fundamental Lacan–Hegel exchange.

There is, however, another reason why Žižek's writing can be baf- fling, which I shall address in this Introduction. At the local level, his writing is enormous fun. His materials are so lively and varied, and his raconteur's art so seductive, that the ideas seem to come to life. One has the sense of being presented with a succession of nuggets which are individually fascinating and which, squirrelled away, would make a veritable storehouse of insights into Lacanian and philosophical apothegms ('the Other does not exist', 'there is no sexual relation', 'the Spirit is a bone', etc.). But at the level of the chapter, and still more of the book, his writing can seem utterly chaotic. The principal moves of his argument are often hard to make

out, and its overall thrust can be unclear. This is the more disconcerting since a good deal of care has evidently gone into the construction of the books themselves. They exhibit, for instance, a
marked concern for balance and symmetry; they often follow an
elegant tripartite plan, and the individual chapters of any given
work are remarkably similar in length. So why does what appears,
from one point of view, to be so carefully orchestrated seem, from
another, to be so utterly shapeless?

The answer I propose is that Žižek's challenge to his readers
to find coherence in his writing is the way he personally has evolved
of writing around the real. Žižek teases at the limits of our understanding at the level of the chapter or the book in a way practised
by Lacan from the level of the sentence upwards. Syntactically tortuous and laden with puns, circumlocutions, obscure allusions and
foreign terms, Lacan's prose is a tireless (if fatiguing) testimony to
the gaps that haunt our speech.[5] As Žižek puts it, 'the only way to
comprehend Lacan is to approach his work . . . as a succession of
attempts to seize the same persistent traumatic kernel' (*Metastases*,
173). Although Žižek's style seems, by contrast with Lacan's, to be
a model of clarity, the construction of his writing overall is illu-
mined by this comment. Such coherence as can be ascribed to it will
come from the reader's own willingness to 'seize the . . . traumatic
kernel' that emerges as a counter-effect of the text's loose-knit and
disorienting structure. Žižek's manner of composition, that is, provokes the reader to acknowledge the real *as* an effect *of* writing and
in its effect *on* writing. The next section traces a reader's experience
of reading about the real and offers some strategies for coping with
Žižek's texts.

Reading about the Real

In this necessarily selective account, I shall look at three features of
Žižek's writing which disconcert the reader initially: his oblique
approach to a topic, his sometimes surprising use of exemplification, and his inconsistent persona and personal style.[6]

The oblique approach

The way Žižek broaches an argument often appears to bear a scant
relationship to what then appears to be its main content. The first
chapter of *Tarrying with the Negative* is a challenging review of the

conception of the subject from Descartes to Lacan ('subject' being used here in the philosophical sense to refer to the nature of the agency that says 'I'). But it opens with Žižek lofting in sideways an apparently innocuous inquiry into the relation between *noir* and *neo-noir* films. It is only once this inquiry has focused on the similarities between two *neo-noir* films, *Angel Heart* and *Blade Runner*, that the point emerges, as if by chance, that both films present a 'radical undermining of self-identity' (*Tarrying*, 10). The paradox of *Blade Runner* is that memory, usually the prop and guarantee of identity, is precisely what makes the identity of the hero (Harrison Ford) forfeit. Because what seem like 'his' memories have in all likelihood been fabricated (he is probably not a human being but a 'replicant'), the 'I' he thinks he is cannot avoid the suspicion that he is not that 'I' after all. It is only in retrospect, when we have read a good deal more of the chapter, that we see, as it were, the point of this point. *Blade Runner* illustrates in the register of popular culture the traumatic split between the subject available to consciousness, a prey to the fictions of the symbolic order, and the transcendental or unconscious subject, a split which (Žižek contends) runs through post-Cartesian philosophy, and is the manifestation in it of the real. The relation of *noir* to *neo-noir* films was the feint or detour by which the real of this split was approached. The obliqueness of Žižek's approach enables the reader to see that the real cannot be approached directly, but is always stumbled upon in a way that is at once contingent and unavoidable.

Because the real is experienced as much as absence as troubling excess, form rather than content may provide a means of approaching it. Content may mesmerize and mislead, but if we can look at things in such a way as to make the content recede from view and instead bring the formal parallels into focus, then the gaps that emerge *between* them may prove a source of insight. An instance of an argument that is introduced obliquely through form rather than content is the opening chapter of *The Sublime Object of Ideology*, in which we are invited to understand how Marx's concept of commodity fetishism has the same formal properties as Freud's theory of dreams.[7] For Marx, the commodity is an entity that effaces its own origins. The human effort of manufacturing it is what determines its value as an object of exchange; yet it presents itself to the consumer not as a product of labour but as an object that is valuable in so far as it can be made use of. The commodity, as a result, possesses a pseudo-magical value that derives from the way in which it conceals from those who use it the actual economic relations that produced it. Likewise, what Freud calls the 'dreamwork' is the operation whereby the desire which gave rise to the dream is repressed and displaced on to its form. The point of comparison between the dream and the commodity, then, is not some tangible content, but something which is lost in our conscious perception of both. This formal analogy between the two opens up, in the rest of the chapter, a brilliant revision of Marx's notion of ideology in which the unconscious plays a central role.

Žižek's interest in form is focused not just on the gap that holds open a particular structure, but on the way it is also deposited as a presence on the manifest content, inflecting or 'staining' it. In *The Sublime Object* this inflection is especially far reaching. The initial comparison between society's symptoms (the commodity) and those of the clinic (the patient reporting his dreams to the analyst) has its own repressed content, which then adheres to the form of the whole book. This content, which is never made explicit, is that the capitalist world is pathological; and the form taken by the book is that of a psychoanalytic therapy. Part I is about the symptom, Part II is very largely about the fantasy, and Part III is about our subjection to the real. This progression parallels that of the clinic, from the patient's initial complaints about his symptoms, to the way he privately represents his condition to himself, through to his disturbing and 'traversing' this fantasy in order to expose its contingent and fabricated nature. Thus, although Freud's account of the dreamwork is innocently introduced as a merely fleeting comparison, its evocation of the clinical encounter is also deposited on the book as a whole.[8] In negotiating the indirection of a book such as this, Žižek's readers may well feel baffled and frustrated, but these very feelings may help to draw them into the analytical process and provoke acknowledgement of the real.

The excess in the example

Žižek's examples do not just replicate the theoretical point which they are introduced to exemplify. Just as his entry into an argument can be confusingly oblique, likewise what was seemingly a mere illustration can lead to unexpected departures.

The instance that I will discuss here comes from chapter 2 of *Tarrying with the Negative*, where Žižek draws out the implications of Lacan's responses to Descartes's famous *cogito*, 'I think, therefore I am'. Because Lacan believes that there is an irresolvable split between the conscious and the unconscious, he experiments with various ways of recasting Descartes's formula in order to mark how, for psychoanalysis, its two halves must necessarily be sundered: we cannot consciously command both thinking and being. Žižek takes Lacan's speculations further, distinguishing between a 'masculine' and a 'feminine' variant of the formula. (The reasons for this, too complex to go into here, are examined below, pp. 87–90). I will concentrate on the feminine variant, 'I think, therefore it is',[9] which results from breaking apart Descartes's formula in such a way that *cogito* ('I think') stays in the conscious mind, but *ergo sum* ('therefore I am') is relegated to the unconscious. *Ergo sum* must now be recast as 'therefore *it* is', '*it*' being equivalent to Freud's *id* or Lacan's *ça*, terms used to refer to the dimension of the real in the unconscious.[10] The subject is rent, its 'being' confined to the real, and its capacity for 'thinking' defined by its severance from being. Žižek expounds all this, and then proceeds to illustrate it using examples from popular culture. Disconcertingly, however, this so-called feminine subjectivity turns out to be exemplified by one female and two male characters: Sigourney Weaver in *Alien*, Mr Valdemar in Poe's story of the same name, and James Stewart in *It's a Wonderful Life* (*Tarrying*, 62–4). Why?

The point of the examples, it seems to me, is twofold: to bring out the horrific nature of the '*it*' in all cases, and to underline how gender is separate from sex. Either way, the excess which flows out from the examples relates to the problem of the real.

The revision of Descartes's formula to 'I think, therefore it is' underlines the extent to which we are mutilated and off balance as a result of our 'I' being severed from the real of our being. The formula runs the risk, however, of being purely cerebral. It risks, that is, performing what it says: recoiling from the real it has expelled, much as, when Sigourney Weaver recoils from the monstrous figure of the alien, 'the subject constitutes itself by rejecting the slimy substance of *jouissance*' (*Tarrying*, 62). Žižek uses this phrase again in citing 'The Facts in the Case of Mr Valdemar'. Poe's tale recounts how the protagonist, who had lain for a long time in suspended animation, woke up and said 'I am dead', whereupon his body instantly liquefied 'into a pure, formless, slimy substance of *jouissance*' (ibid.). The final example, *It's a Wonderful Life*, is the most telling of the three. Its ostensible point is to show how the 'I' of George Bailey (James Stewart) is likewise sundered from its being in the real. Žižek's interest thus centres on the scene in which George is about to commit suicide and his guardian angel conducts him back over his life 'reduced to a nonexistent gaze, i.e. . . . paradoxically entitled to observe the world in which [he does] not exist' (*Tarrying*, 64). However, this point is reached only after Žižek has lingered over the substance of what the angel shows to George. If George hadn't existed, the consequences would have been night-marish for his family and community. Here the true point of com-parison with the other examples emerges: 'We see him encounter the real in the filmic dream, and it is precisely in order to escape this traumatic real that the hero takes refuge within the (diegetic) "reality", i.e. the ideological fantasy of an idyllic town community' (*Tarrying*, 63). The common ground between all three examples, then, is that they emphasize the traumatic (slimy, nightmarish) quality of the real *'it'* from which the 'I think' of each character recoils.

Secondly, the examples suggest that 'masculine' and 'feminine' are not inherent gender identities, but incompatible positions linked only by their different ways of fielding (or failing to field) this trau-matic *it*. Gender difference relies not on physical or social differen-tiation, but on differing subject positions in relation to this real. Thus it is not the anatomical body but the position of the psyche that is gendered for psychoanalysis. To serve mixed-sex examples in illustration of 'femininity' helps insinuate this point (which I develop in chapter 4).

The apparent misfit between the theoretical context and the illus-trative instance provokes Žižek's readers to work out the reason for it. In the passage just discussed, this working out leads us to the problematic at the core of his writing: that of our relation to the real. By the same token, for the reader, a relation to the real, both as some-thing lost to conscious thought and as a fearsome threat, is conjured in the very effort of trying to understand his text.

Žižek's personal style

Uncertainty as to how to read Žižek's persona introduces the posi-tion(s) from which this relation to the real might be broached. The personal style of his writing may enthuse or irritate readers, but it is unlikely to leave them cold.[11] Emphatic and flamboyant, it is peppered with instances of 'of course', 'ultimately' and 'crucially', and long stretches in italics. The progress of interpretation is a the-atrical performance in which he will proffer an opinion tolerantly proffered as banal ('one usually thinks'), before brandishing a much cleverer one ('what this leaves out of account, of course'), only to proceed with a flourish to its dramatic reversal ('but ultimately, of course').[12] Connections between ideas are gestured at with a lordly tone ('suffice it to recall in this context'; 'it is against this background that one has to conceive'; 'the temptation to be avoided here').

Readers may find all this annoying. I think, nevertheless, that there is as much self-conscious bravado and self-mockery in these procedures as self-conceit. Caught in the glare of self-awareness, flamboyance and impudence can quickly transform into self-parody, and Žižek abounds in self-puncturing moments that cut the ground from under his grandiloquence. In *Tarrying with the Negative* he characterizes himself as an obsessional neurotic who can avoid feeling guilty about watching so many idiotic films only by subsequently sacrificing himself on the altar of theory and writing mind-bendingly complex commentaries on them (*Tarrying*, 73). Another *piquant* instance of self-parody comes at the start of *Everything You Wanted to Know*, where he imagines a postmodern theorist (himself) in dialogue with a lower mortal: 'You think what you see is a simple melodrama even your senile granny would have no difficulty in following? Yet without taking into account . . ./the difference between symptom and *sinthom* [*sic*]; the structure of the Borromean knot; the fact that Woman is one of the Names-of-the-Father; etc., etc./ you've totally missed the point!' (*Everything*, 2). The self-mockery of these moments is confirmed by the more openly self-deprecating humour of Žižek's personal reminiscences in his writings – his experiences of military service, the disapproval he encounters from his relatives, the minefield of negotiation with one's in-laws.[13] The result is that, in Žižek's writing, what we think of as 'serious' thought constantly threatens to dissolve into derision, a threat which it is difficult for the reader to locate, and consequently impossible to parry. If Žižek, not I, were writing this section, he might choose as his title, 'Theorist or Impostor? Yes, Please!' What is the reader to make of all this?

I am going to focus my discussion on an anecdote which Robert Boynton (in 'Enjoy Your Žižek!') records Žižek as telling about his analysis by Jacques-Alain Miller. Like Lacan, Miller uses the technique of the variable session with his patients in place of the traditional '50-minute hour':

'It was my strict rule, my sole ethical principle, to lie consistently: to invent all symptoms, fabricate all dreams,' [Žižek] reports of his treatment. 'It was obsessional neurosis in its absolute purest form. Because you never knew how long it would last, I was always prepared for at least two sessions. I have this incredible fear of what I

might discover if I really went into analysis. What if I lost my frenetic theoretical desire? What if I turned into a common person?'
Eventually, Žižek claims, he had Miller completely taken in by his
charade: 'Once I knew what aroused his interest, I invented even
more complicated scenarios and dreams. One involved the Bette
Davis movie *All About Eve*. Miller's daughter is named Eve, so I told
him that I had dreamed about going to a movie with Bette Davis in
it. I planned every detail so that when I finished he announced
grandly, "This was your revenge against me!"'

The ostensible butt of this anecdote is Miller. But once someone
admits to being a prankster, then he could be pulling your leg at
any time – and Žižek loves this kind of intellectual practical joke.[14]
If we take his stories at face value, we risk becoming the butt of the
hoax ourselves. Whatever the truth of this anecdote, however, it is
revealing that Žižek should cast himself in the role of trickster on
the analytical couch and thus associate psychoanalysis, theory and
theatrical pretence.

Lacan's account, in his *Seminar* XVII, of four interlocking discourses – those of the master, the university, the analyst and the
patient – enables us to take this discussion further, and to see
that Žižek's tale deliberately confuses the reader as to which dis-
course(s) he aspires to.[15] Like Lacan, he actively distances him from
the first two. The discourse of the master lays claim to uncontested
authority (but betrays inner anxiety at its own deficiency); it
addresses itself to control over knowledge, but the real eludes it.
The discourse of the university affirms control over knowledge (but
rests on an ultimately arbitrary authority); it wants to address itself
to the real, but produces anxious, deficient subjects. What remain,
then, are the discourses of the analysand (or patient) and the
analyst. The analysand presents as a hysterical subject, preoccupied
by her[16] lack of some inner substance, and thus condemned to theatricality. She addresses herself to the analyst, whom she invests
with magisterial authority, hoping to gain from him knowledge of
what this mysterious treasure is. The way the analyst responds is
by himself posing as this object, and revealing it to her in all its
vacuity. The analyst's task, then, is to be abject and unlovely in order
that the patient should realize that the authority she is looking for
in him does not exist, and that it is the nature of the subject to be
an empty performance, lacking a central core. In this way, the
analyst produces knowledge of a different order from that of any
of the other discourses: the knowledge that there is no such thing
as one's inner treasure, except as the object of one's desire. Eventu-

ally the analysand is drawn, through glimpsing this worthlessness, to renounce belief in mastery and see it as imposture; in this way, the analyst becomes a waste product of the analytical scene.[17] By thus 'traversing the fantasy' the subject accepts the vacuity of subjectivity, the fact that, in its lack, it is subject to the real.

With this in mind, we can go back to Žižek's anecdote about his analysis with Miller. Clearly, one thing he is doing is staging a bravura performance of 'the discourse of the hysteric'. He couples a frenzied desire for knowledge ('What if I lost my frenetic theoretical desire?') with the conviction that he is the repository of some secret treasure ('What if I turned into a common person?'). But he has also appropriated the role of the analyst. Not only does he pre-empt the analyst's terms of art ('invent all symptoms, fabricate all dreams') and anticipate his diagnosis ('obsessional neurosis in its absolute purest form'), he also effects Miller's elimination from the scene, wickedly branding him as having erroneously assumed the position of the master ('he announced grandly, "This was your revenge against me!" ') and assuming his position himself. In this way, Žižek monopolizes both halves of the analytical script, combining in his own person the theatricality and restless search for knowledge of the neurotic and the deflating derision of the analyst.

This anecdote suggests that a way of accounting for Žižek's often disconcerting writing style is that it conflates two interlocking positions. As analysand-theorist, he enthuses over his theoretical treasure with a histrionic glee that tips into self-parody, his performance being further undermined by the laconic derision he displays as analyst. This combination is well illustrated by *Enjoy Your Symptom!*. Ostensibly, it proceeds in the discourse of the patient; each of its chapters frames a question that insists on a troublesome Lacanian term: 'Why Does a *Letter* Always Arrive at Its Destination?', 'Why Is *Woman* a Symptom of Man?', and so on. However, the injunction which provides the book's title can be spoken only from the perspective of the analyst, who, recognizing that the patient is wedded to his symptom, encourages him to embrace it as his identity. What the patient took to be 'the worst', the hindrance to his being, is actually 'the best', the form of his subjection to the real.

More generally, I suggest that this anecdote about Miller and himself serves as a figure of the way Žižek's readers are precipitated into the thick of the analytical scene with all its tensions, passions and potential for exposure to the real. This is confirmed by my earlier remarks about *The Sublime Object of Ideology*, which, as I said, has the form of a therapy. A clinical outline is also discernible in chapter 4 of *Looking Awry* and in *The Abyss of Freedom*. The Introduction to *For They Know Not What They Do*, a book which began life as a series of lectures delivered in Slovenia in 1989 in the run-up to the country's first democratic elections, also presents the book as a psychoanalysis, though in this case Žižek confines himself to the role of analysand and identifies the public – ourselves – as the analyst (*For They Know Not*, 3).

One of the commonplaces about the Slovenian Lacanians is that they do not practise psychoanalysis in the clinic.[18] However, Žižek treats the world as a textual clinic in which the writer's task is to speak for and to social pathology.[19] As his readers, *we* are that world, and in requiring us to make sense of his writings for ourselves, Žižek enjoins on us the difficulty of 'traversing the fantasy' and recognizing our subjection to the real. In this way, his writings perform the intellectual equivalent of his concept of 'the act', provoking us as reader-agents to rid ourselves of complacency towards the symbolic order, a provocation which is bound to be as uncomfortable as it is challenging.[20]

Conclusion and the Way Ahead

Often Žižek's observations about other writers can just as illuminatingly be applied to himself, and the following comments on Derrida suggest that it is precisely the capacity for disconcerting elusiveness which confers unity on his own texts:

> The kernel of unreadability that resists and belies every interpretative appropriation – that is, the very feature which makes a text forever 'non-identical to itself', the unappropriable foreign ingredient-body on account of which a text always eludes and defers its being comprehended – is the ultimate guarantee of its identity; without this unassimilable kernel, the text would lack any proper consistency, it would be a transparent medium, a mere appearance of *another* essential identity. (*Indivisible Remainder*, 26, emphasis original)

Žižek's own 'kernel of unreadability', I have argued, reflects the 'unassimilable kernel' in his writing which in turn points to how, for him, thought is also hollowed out by the 'unassimilable kernel' of the real.

Obviously, then, the reading I have offered is my own way of making sense of what, I am also claiming, eludes sense. Each reader must find his or her own way of grappling with the gaps, and will never come up with the same account twice. As with Lacan, every reading of a Žižek text is only a possible trajectory – which is not to say that it is not true. In the one offered here, I have placed a lot of weight on the experience of difficulty, irritation, frustration and so forth, as provoking us to engage with the 'kernel of unreadability' in his writings. But it is equally the case that, in his unstinting efforts to address this 'unassimilable kernel', Žižek's harnessing of popular culture, jokes, cyberpunk, etc. generates a constant stream of enjoyment. Although Žižek never disguises the sombre side of *jouissance*, the effervescent excitement with which it bursts out from his reflections is also a perpetual source of joking and amusement. Another, but just as valid, introduction to his thought could be written through the optic of the insubstantiality of humour and its converse, the real of laughter.

In the chapters that follow I shall do Žižek a disservice in taking to pieces what he has so exuberantly hurtled together. Each pursues a Žižekian theme – not in isolation, since that would be impossible, but nevertheless in an attempt to focus on one issue at a time. Chapter 2 is about Žižek's controversial conjuncture of Lacan and Hegel, which provides the framework for all his other work. Chapter 3 focuses on culture and the way in which works of art articulate a sense of 'reality'. Chapter 4 addresses the problematic of gender and sexual difference, and Žižek's interaction with Judith Butler. Chapter 5 looks selectively at the vast range of philosophical reference in Žižek, concentrating on his view of human nature as filtered through theology and psychoanalysis. The final chapter is about what I take to be his central preoccupation – politics – a domain so all embracing that something of the richness and variety of Žižek's thinking is, I hope, represented in it.

2

Dialectic and the Real: Lacan, Hegel and the Alchemy of après-coup

The twin themes of 'Lacan with Hegel' and 'Hegel through Lacan' are pretty much omnipresent in Žižek's writings. The purpose of this chapter is not to offer a beginner's guide to either of these thinkers (there are in any case already several excellent ones available[1]) but to introduce and comment on their extraordinary conjunction in Žižek's work. My presentation of both Lacan and Hegel will therefore be partial – fortunately, given how much each of them wrote – and concerned less with either thinker in himself than with the relationship Žižek sees between them.[2] The core of this relationship is the negativity at the heart of dialectic which Žižek discerns in the thought of both Hegel and Lacan, and which he identifies with the real. This chapter, then, outlines the philosophical scaffolding with which, as I wrote in the Introduction, Žižek thinks about the real.

The main lines of my argument are these. Lacan developed his ideas in response to Freud, and disparaged the legacy of Hegel; Žižek, by contrast, largely neglects Freud, and substitutes Hegel as the vital precursor of, and reference point for, Lacan's thought. This results in Žižek's reading Hegel, against the grain of standard practice, as a philosopher of the symbolic and the real in the Lacanian sense; which in turn has implications for the way in which the symbolic and the real are understood in Lacan. In particular, while Žižek transforms Hegel into a psychoanalytic philosopher, he also reads psychoanalysis as a rationalist metaphysics. This convergence between Lacan and Hegel enables Žižek to develop a number of important themes that draw on both simultaneously, and I devote sections to his treatment of 'substance and subject' and 'universal and particular'. The last part of the chapter assesses Žižek's thinking about the Lacan–Hegel coupling and the possibility that its importance is now beginning to wane.

Lacan and *après-coup*

Lacan presents his life's work as renewing psychoanalysis through a return to Freud. This paradoxical formula, whereby progress is secured by looking back, is central to psychoanalytic thinking. For Freud, the psyche does not follow a linear development in which the present is heir to its past. Rather, since the subject revisits and reworks its past in response to its successive experiences, it is as true to say that the past is heir to the present. This is not to say that the past is merely a fabrication of the present; without its past, the present would not be as it is; but the past nevertheless assumes meaning only as reconfigured in the present. For example, a hysterical symptom is a patient's response to the reactivation of a childhood trauma which assumes content and significance only when triggered retrospectively. This phenomenon of retrospection, called *Nachträglichkeit* by Freud, is termed *après-coup* by Lacan, and provides the most obvious meaning of his well-known apothegm that 'A letter always arrives at its destination'. It is the fact that a recipient recognizes himself as its addressee which retrospectively determines a discourse as a message, sent to him, that has now arrived.[3]

Lacan's return to Freud is a paradigmatic instance of *après-coup*. What 'arrives' is Freud read *à la lettre* in all his resistant difficulty. This troublesome, even traumatizing, Freud had been eliminated from the practices of his so-called followers, but his message, thanks to structural linguistics and anthropology having obligingly installed a post-box in Lacan's head, can at last now be 'delivered'. The result is that the 'true' Freud turns out to be, at the same time, a Freud reworked almost beyond recognition. To understand Freud is not to repeat him – that would be the highway to *misunderstanding* – but to reconfigure him in one's own present. As Lacan puts it, 'One never goes beyond Freud.... Nor does one attempt to measure his contribution quantitatively.... One uses him. One moves around in him. One takes one's bearings from the direction he points in' (*Seminar* VII, 206).

Žižek's work is dictated by this same temporal paradox. Lacan's concept of *après-coup* provides him with both a favoured theme and a recurrent argumentative strategy.[4] But the progress he achieves by 'returning' to Lacan involves, as its corollary, a different 'return' from that taken by Lacan. Žižek pays relatively little attention to Freud. Instead, he leaps into a more distant past, to the writings of the German Enlightenment philosopher G. F. W. Hegel (1770–1831), whose ambitious and demanding works encompass a vast range from logic to aesthetics, and who is most widely known as the author of *The Phenomenology of Spirit* (first published in 1807), a remarkable account of the evolution of self-consciousness through reason.

Of course, the point of *après-coup* is that it does not seek to repeat the past, but to release its significance for the present. Nevertheless, Žižek's is a courageous, not to say contentious, move given that Lacan is quite explicit that Freud is a far more relevant reference point for his own thought than Hegel.[5] It will be useful to sketch something of Lacan's position on Hegel before looking more closely at how Žižek reconfigures it.

Lacan on Hegel

Lacan's relationship to Hegel is complex and contains many positive elements.[6] He frequently refers to the processes he describes as 'dialectic' (as in 'the dialectic of desire'), and, despite the influence of structuralism, with its privileging of binary opposition, he cultivates triadic schemes such as characterize Hegel's thought (preeminently in his three registers, or orders, of symbolic, imaginary and real; see Glossary, REGISTER). It is also striking to what extent the dynamic and economic metaphors which predominate in Freud (repression, investment, etc.) are replaced, in Lacan, by anthropological terms like 'subject', 'other' and 'alienation', that owe much to Hegel. The way such terms are articulated in Lacan's thought signals another debt to Hegel: namely the process of 'reflection', the movement of exchange and return that characterizes Hegelian argument. Reflection unfolds in three stages which can be described, somewhat simplistically, in these terms (I give a fuller account in the section below entitled 'Subject and substance').[7] An entity is first manifested in its own appearance ('positing reflection'). It is then registered, for example as an object, in the reflection of this appearance by something external to it, for example the subject ('external reflection'). The third stage comes with the union of the preceding two and the recognition that subject and object each mirror the other, each being posited in itself and externalized from without (determining reflection). A psychoanalytical example of this process is provided by Lacan's account of subjectivity as a function of mutual recognition. I position myself as a result of the way I am already recognized *by the other*, while the other who recognizes me is himself in a position to do so because he is already recognized *by me*. One of Lacan's often repeated sayings, that 'all desire is the desire of the Other', is also an instance of reflection, since the desire in question is both *my* desire *for* the Other and the desire that arises *in* the Other, whether for me or for something else. The mirroring movement of 'determinate reflection' produces inversion, as in another phenomenon described by Lacan: that of 'receiving one's own message in inverted form'. If I say, for example, 'You are my man', what this implies for communication to take place is that you already unconsciously recognize yourself as the one whom I recognize as my man. Unconsciously you return my own message to me in an inverted form, as if saying to me, 'I am the one who is recognizable to you as your man because you are recognizable to me as my woman' (cf. *Seminar* III, 36–7).

Lacan, while acknowledging his debt to Hegel, is severe in his criticisms of him. His important paper 'The Subversion of the Subject and the Dialectic of Desire in the Freudian Unconscious' is a polemical depreciation of Hegel in favour of Freud.[8] Lacan's target in this paper is the *Phenomenology*, and his objections to Hegel are these:

1 In Hegel, all antinomies are resolved, that is, discovered in advance to have been imaginary; the point of Hegel's dialectic is to found a new symbolic on an imaginary basis ('Subversion', 296). This is a damaging allegation, since for Lacan the imaginary register is primarily a decoy luring us away from the more significant register of the symbolic. Rereading Hegel's dialectic of master and slave,[9] Lacan argues that their imaginary struggle to the death needs to be re-situated within the symbolic horizon where another death, that of the symbolic itself, can be envisaged ('Subversion', 307–9). The fact that the Hegelian dialectic is confined to the imaginary has the further implication for Lacan, not spelled out here, that he sees Hegel as deludedly adopting philosophical idealism, whereas Lacan identifies himself as a materialist.[10] (By 'idealism' is meant a philosophical system which maintains that reality as we understand it is a reflection of mental processes, such as ideas, as opposed to

'materialist' doctrines which insist that all entities, including the mind, are to be understood in terms of material processes.)

2 Hegel's dialectic results in the production of a self-identical, perfected subject of self-consciousness ('Subversion', 296), whereas Lacan contends that there is a misrecognition (*méconnaître*) that is essential to self-knowledge (*me connaître*) ('Subversion', 306), and that the subject is inwardly split by the 'opacity of the signifier' ('Subversion', 307–8). Later (*Seminar* XI, session v), Lacan will be still more explicit that in his view consciousness is subordinate to the unconscious, and not the other way round.

3 Hegel's dialectic of thesis, antithesis, synthesis (Lacan's terms[11]) folds in on itself and suffers from 'immanentism' ('Subversion', 296). In the psychoanalytical dialectic inspired by Freud, the imaginary and symbolic registers are at odds, and the paradoxes to which this disjunction gives rise point to a 'gap' (*béance*) between them ('Subversion', 318), so that, unlike in Hegel, there is no immanent totality and Lacan's account of the subject is transcendent ('Subversion', 307).

4 Hegel's explanation of suffering is inferior to Freud's, because he takes no account of sexuality ('Subversion', 297); the whole of Lacan's essay is given over to charting, by means of the graphs of desire, how the space of the subject is carved out by the trajectories of (real) drive and (symbolic) desire. (See Glossary for the antinomy between DRIVE and DESIRE in Lacan's thought.)

5 Hegel posits the unity of truth and knowledge which are disjoined by Freud ('Subversion', 301). In psychoanalysis, truth is an effect of speech and has the structure of a fiction; it is quite distinct from reality ('Subversion', 305–6). Our knowledge of the real is denied us by 'castration'. Our only access to the real of *jouissance* is indirect and *après-coup*, mediated (in the form of 'surplus enjoyment') and 'fictionalized' by the symbolic order: 'Castration means that *jouissance* must be refused, so that it can be reached on the inverted ladder (*l'échelle renversée*) of the Law of desire' ('Subversion', 324).

For Lacan, in short, Hegel's thought is marred by its aspiration to imaginary wholeness; he takes insufficient account of the symbolic order that institutes difference, splitting and desire, and none at all of the real which impels drive, *jouissance* and lack; he is thus condemned as an idealist, by contrast with Lacan's professed materialism.

Lacan and Hegel United

Although a Hegelian dimension to Lacan is widely acknowledged, no one before Žižek has set out so forcefully to dislodge Freud as Lacan's primary reference point and substitute Hegel in his place. I quoted above Lacan's account of his debt to Freud: 'One never goes beyond Freud. . . . Nor does one attempt to measure his contribution quantitatively. . . . One uses him. One moves around in him. One takes one's bearings from the direction he points in' (*Seminar* VII, 206). Similarly, Žižek reads Hegel in a way that rarely 'goes beyond' Lacan but 'uses him, . . . moves around in him, . . . takes [his] bearings from the direction he points in'. That is, there is never any question that Lacan, not Hegel, is the primary reference point. Hegel may be envisaged as a philosopher best read through a Lacanian lens, or as key to a proper understanding of Lacan; but as Grigg rightly says, 'the essential aspect of Žižek's work is clearly Lacanian' ('Absolute Freedom', 112).

Taking his cue, then, from Lacan, the framework within which Žižek 'moves around' is pre-eminently that of the Lacanian *après-coup*, and the 'direction in which he [takes Lacan to] point' is that indicated in a throwaway remark in *Seminar* XVII, 38:

> Where is one to place [knowledge] in the [discourse of the analyst]? In the place which, in the discourse of the Master, Hegel, the most sublime of hysterics, designates as that of truth.
>
> For indeed, one cannot say that the *Phenomenology of Spirit* consists in setting out from so-called self-consciousness grasped at the most immediate level of sensation, as though to imply that all knowledge is known from the outset. What would be the point of all this phenomenology, unless it was about something else?[12]

There must, Lacan is saying here, be more to Hegel's *Phenomenology* than meets the eye. Referring to his account of the four discourses, which is developed in this *Seminar* and at which we glanced in the Introduction, Lacan identifies Hegel as the patient, a hysterical or split subject ($) desperate to acquire knowledge of his hidden treasure (see above, pp. 13–14, and Glossary, DISCOURSE). This $ is the truth hidden beneath the master's discourse, where it occupies the position that, in the discourse of the analyst, is taken by knowledge (S2). Historically, of course, analytical knowledge *was* developed by Freud through his reflections on the treatment of hysteria; but Lacan can also be taken as meaning that he, as a psycho-

analyst, may have much to learn from Hegel's philosophy once it
has been recognized as a form of hysteria. (It is important to remem-
ber that, for Lacan, hysteria is not a pathology but a structure; Lacan
is not casting aspersions on Hegel's mental health, but acknowledging that he poses radical questions about the subject and desire.
Žižek's discussion of Hegel as hysteric will be discussed more fully
below; and see also Glossary, HYSTERIA).

Žižek shows a far closer engagement with Hegel's writings than
does Lacan. But the main lines of his reflections on Hegel are set by
these words from *Seminar* XVII and by two passages from Hegel on
whose implications he ruminates at length (and at every opportunity[13]). The first is the justly famous meditation on negativity in the
'Preface' to the *Phenomenology*:

> Death . . . is of all things the most dreadful, and to hold fast to what
> is dead requires the greatest strength. . . . But the life of the Spirit is
> not the life that shrinks from death and keeps itself untouched by
> devastation, but rather the life that endures it and maintains itself in
> it. It wins its truth only when, in utter dismemberment, it finds itself.
> . . . Spirit is this power only by looking the negative in the face and
> tarrying with it. This tarrying with the negative is the magical power
> that converts it into being. This power is identical with what we
> earlier called the Subject. (§32)

The austere and tragic tones of the *Phenomenology* give way to melodrama in Žižek's other favourite Hegelian quotation, this time from
the slightly earlier *Jenaer Systementwürfe*, written in 1805–6:

> The human being is this night, this empty nothing, that contains
> everything in its simplicity – an unending wealth of many presenta-
> tions, images, of which none happens to occur to him – or which are
> not present. This night, the interior of nature, that exists here – pure
> self – in phantasmagorical representations, is night all around it, here
> shoots a bloody head – there another white ghastly apparition,
> suddenly here before it, and just so disappears. One catches sight of
> this night when one looks human beings in the eye – into a night
> that becomes awful, it suspends the night of the world here in an
> opposition.
> In this night, being has returned.[14]

Taken in conjunction, these two excerpts represent two ways of
approaching the conundrum of the real: as a lack in the logic of our
being ('tarrying with the negative') and as the traumatic horror of

the drive (the 'night of the world'). So when Žižek asks himself what Hegel and Lacan have in common, the short answer is as follows: 'For both of them, the "free" subject, integrated into the symbolic network of mutual recognition, is the result of a process in which traumatic cuts, "repressions", and the power struggle intervene, not something primordially given' (*Ticklish Subject*, 274). That is, both envisage the subject as an effect of lack and/or as the resistant kernel of the real, around which symbolization turns. What unites them is the 'coincidence of the real', expressed as a 'coincidence of lack' and a 'coincidence of trauma'.

Lacan's Reservations Countered

To flesh out this account, I shall look next at Žižek's position on the criticisms levelled at Hegel by Lacan in his 'Subversion' essay. Not that Žižek systematically sets out to refute Lacan – in fact, he is rarely even critical of him. Rather, the arguments presented here are dispersed through his writings and I have gathered them together for the purposes of exposition. This section follows the outline of the section on 'Lacan on Hegel' above.

1   The dialectic is imaginary and its contradictions are only apparent

Žižek's strategy here, as often elsewhere, is to turn a criticism on its head and claim it as an advantage. Yes, there is a sense in which the outcome of the Hegelian dialectic is 'always already' known. This is because it is an instance of *après-coup* and confirms that Hegel's thought is not, as it is usually held to be, teleological – that is, driven by an inevitable progression towards resolution ('the Absolute').[15]

Žižek develops this argument at length and in different ways in many of his books. In the earliest ones he maintains that the whole point of the dialectical movement is not to cancel out ('sublate') its negative phase, but to shift perspective with respect to it. '*The "synthesis" is exactly the same as the anti-thesis*; the only difference lies in a certain change of perspective' (*Sublime Object*, 176, emphasis original[16]). This is what is understood by 'the logic of the negation of the negation' – the discovery that negation can be experienced positively. 'It is to be conceived more like a paradoxical twist whereby *the question itself begins to function as its own answer*: what we mistook for a question was already an answer' (*Sublime Object*, 177, and see Glossary, NEGATION, etc.). Thus, 'one "tarries with the negative" not by abstractly opposing it to the positive but by conceiving positive being itself as materialization of Negativity – as "metonymy of Nothing", to use the Lacanian expression' (*For They Know Not*, 144).

Subsequently Žižek develops a different criticism of the standard view of Hegel as 'caught in the closed loop of teleology' (*Indivisible Remainder*, 113). Emphasizing that there is a double negation at the heart of the dialectical process, Žižek insists that far from sustaining identity in imaginary wholeness, it radically undoes it. The Spirit that returns after 'tarrying with the negative' is not the same as that which left: '*The Spirit to whom we return, the Spirit that returns to itself, is not the same as the Spirit that was previously lost in alienation*' (*Indivisible Remainder*, 123). To accomplish its return, it has to sacrifice its very substance, and it is only by losing this substance that it can become a subject (*Indivisible Remainder*, 128). This argument is not at odds with the earlier one, though it does refine it. The point of the last phase of the dialectic, says Žižek, is to acknowledge *après-coup* the loss which has taken place: 'The idea that the concluding moment of a dialectical process ("synthesis") consists of the advent of an Identity which encompasses the difference, reducing it to a passing moment, is thus totally misleading: *it is only with "synthesis" that the difference is acknowledged as such*' (*Tarrying*, 124).

Another crucial aspect of Žižek's argument is his insistence that Hegel is a philosopher of contingency, not teleology. It is only in retrospect that the outcome of the dialectic *appears* to have been necessary. But, when looked at prospectively, it is always open to chance.

Žižek's exposition of these views draws heavily on Lacanian concepts. In *The Sublime Object* the *après-coup* nature of dialectic is compared with the transference; in *For They Know Not* Hegel's logic is read through the concepts of the signifying chain and the formulae of sexuation; and in *Tarrying with the Negative* and *The Indivisible Remainder* the Lacanian reference is the split subject $. The crucial implication of these comparisons with Lacanian theory is that they stress the *symbolic* character of the dialectic, in contrast to Lacan's critique of it as *imaginary*. The converse implication, for psychoanalysis, is that it merits being read on a par with Hegel's logic.

The basic homology which Žižek perceives between Lacan's thought and that of Hegel is thus that the symbolic (or dialectic) is shot through with the real (or negativity), a homology which I will develop further. It follows that Žižek's assessment of Hegel's so-called idealism is very different from Lacan's; I shall return to this under point 5 below.

2 Hegel promotes a self-identical subject of self-consciousness

We have seen that, for Žižek, the Hegelian triad involves the internalization of nothingness or difference. Consequently, Žižek's account of identity in Hegel rebuts Lacan's objection that Hegel promotes a self-identical subject of self-consciousness. Žižek is much taken with the unceasing, restless movement of Hegel's dialectic and the implications this has for identity. No sooner does something approach identity with itself than it reverses into its opposite, a process Žižek repeatedly illustrates with the paradox that tautology is actually a form of contradiction. For example, the assertion 'Law is Law' as good as concedes that the only reason to obey the law is that it is imposed on us, and thus that there is something inherently violent, arbitrary and ultimately lawless about it (e.g. *For They Know Not*, 34). Žižek is equally fascinated by the converse formulation, whereby a thing becomes identified with its opposite, as in the Hegelian equation 'the Spirit is a bone': in its very inertia, the skull provides us with a representation of the Spirit that once animated it (*Sublime Object*, 208).[17]

The only conceivable identity, then, is one that, at the same time, includes an element of non-identity. Žižek offers nationality as an example. The English are initially defined in relation to their external borders as being separate from the Scots, the French and so on; but when we come to examine the group that we have demarcated in this way, we begin to ask who, among the English, are really properly English – is it any particular group more than others? Gradually it emerges that there is something problematic about every individual's claim to Englishness: 'The final answer is of course that *nobody* is fully English, that every empirical Englishman contains something "non-English" – Englishness thus becomes an "internal limit", an unattainable point which prevents empirical Englishmen from achieving full identity-with-themselves' (*For They Know Not*, 110).[18] Another example is that of the political propagandist who claims that all other parties act out of factional interest, while his alone does not. This claim is a clear case of promoting a factional interest: what the propagandist puts on one side of a category boundary (in the other parties) in fact returns to lodge on the other (in his own) (*Tarrying*, 133). Identity results from 'determinate reflection', in that it deposits back on the thing to be identified, in the form of an inner contradiction, the differences by virtue of which it distinguishes itself from others (*Tarrying*, 130).

Žižek uses this account of identity as fissured to argue against the prevailing view of self-consciousness in Hegel. It is not the case, says Žižek, that consciousness relates to an external object as to another subject and that self-consciousness then internalizes that relation. Self-consciousness is not my capacity to internalize another subject, but my failure to internalize a resistant object. It is precisely because the object retains its difference that self-consciousness can track the movement of reflection from subject to object and back (*Tarrying*, 128).[19] Hegel is thus brought into line with what Žižek had earlier said about Lacan: 'self-consciousness is the very opposite of self-transparency: I am aware of myself only insofar as outside of me a place exists where the truth about me is articulated' (*Tarrying*, 67). Once more, by arguing against Lacan's critique of Hegel, Žižek brings the two thinkers into alignment. Hegel becomes a philosopher of the symbolic, in the Lacanian sense of one for whom 'the truth is out there' (as the *X-Files* motto, beloved of Žižek, has it). The truth about me lies not in some knowledge I might have about myself, but in the (failed) exchanges between myself and the world. By the same token, Lacan's meditations on identity and identification are dignified as coextensive with those of Hegel.

3 Hegel's dialectic suffers from 'immanentism'

I think that what Lacan means by this criticism is that, in his understanding of Hegel, everything that is, is accounted for, produced by, and actualized within the system of his thought. Lacan contrasts this with his own thinking, which is sustained by what exceeds it.

Žižek does not deny that Hegel's thought relies on immanence, but he insists that this immanence results from the dialectical reversal into it of transcendence in the form of negativity. The passage from Kant's transcendental philosophy (which holds that the true nature of a thing forever eludes us) to Hegel's immanentism is effected not by '*filling out* the empty place of the Thing . . . but *by affirming this void as such*, in its priority to any positive entity that strives to fill it out' (*Tarrying*, 39). That is, absence or negativity are integrated into the fabric of Hegel's thinking in such a way as to leave it flimsy, not wholly consistent, unable to wrap things up. Such thought is what Žižek, following Lacan, calls 'non all'.

The effect of this 'non all' is pervasive. For example, the first section of Hegel's *Encyclopaedia Logic* explores the emergence of being as a correlate of nothing. Being cannot be conceived, says Hegel, except in relation to nothing, and thus nothing is the truth of being. But what does this mean? The very argument which Hegel advances about being attests to the way it is hobbled by the difficulty of accounting for this nothing (*Tarrying*, 119). Hegelian reasoning is not a systematic advance towards the capturing of some truth; rather, it is the recording of a series of failures: 'Let us take a moment X: all attempts to grasp its concealed essence, to determine it more concretely, end in failure, and the subsequent moment only positivizes this failure; in it, failure as such assumes positive existence. In short, one fails to determine the truth of X and this failure *is* the truth of X' (*Tarrying*, 119–20). Thus Hegel does not aspire to totality except 'in the negative experience of falsity and breakdown' (*Contingency*, 228). What is complete is so by virtue of being, at the same time, never more than partial.

By describing Hegelian logic as 'non all', Žižek is reading it through a psychoanalytical lens. In particular, he aligns Hegel's thought with Lacan's account of sexual difference, in which 'woman' is 'non all' (see my discussion of universality below, and in chapter 4). Conversely, Žižek raises Lacan's speculations about the real to the level of Hegel's logic. If Lacan is a 'transcendental philosopher' (*Tarrying*, 3), it is because all his fundamental concepts are geared to explaining the enigma of desire, and theorizing it as a defence against the irreparable negativity at the heart of language. This brings us, then, to the problematic of desire.

4 Hegel fails to integrate the dimension of sexuality into philosophy

Hegel's discussions of human sexuality are, Žižek allows, reductive. Although his philosophy is a metaphysics which seeks to integrate all aspects of human history and experience through reason, his account of sexuality remains crudely biological (*Ticklish Subject*, 83). Nevertheless, Žižek contends, Hegel speaks for desire, and for the desire to desire. This is because, as Lacan recognized, he should be read as a hysteric. As already stated, this is not to brand Hegel as sick, but to read him as disclosing to the analyst the structure of desire and subjectivity. Unable to accept that the world is as she is told it is, unsure of who she is, the hysteric is incapable of desiring *as* herself. Instead, she tries to identify with someone else's desire, blocks her own, and converts it into physical symptoms. Hysteria results in a theatrical performance in which the hysteric's identity is assumed as a role, and her psychical blockage is converted into a physical one. This performance, thanks to its dramatic disclosure of the problem of assuming subjectivity and desire, illumines their nature for us all.

Žižek thinks this is true of Hegel's use of exemplification in general: the dramatic cameos that stud the *Phenomenology* act as symptoms, because they mean more than Hegel can allow himself to say. (Cf. my discussion of exemplification in the Introduction.) More importantly, Žižek contends that 'hysterical conversion' characterizes Hegelian dialectic in general. For example, his argument that Hegel's thought is 'non all' is couched in these terms:

> Now we can perhaps understand why, for Lacan, Hegel is 'the most sublime of all hysterics': the elementary dialectical inversion consists precisely in such a reversal of transcendence into immanence that characterizes hysterical theatre – the mystery of an enigmatic apparition is to be sought not *beyond* its appearance but in the very *appearance of mystery*. (*For They Know Not*, 107)

But his favourite example of a dialectical conversion comes not from Hegel, but from Lacan. How has Lacan's understanding of hysteria progressed beyond Freud's? In the fact that he has grasped that what Freud saw as the hysteric's *repression of desire* is actually a *desire for repression* (see *Seminar* XI, session i). Žižek coins a variant of this formulation when he says of the hysteric that 'the unsatisfied desire converts into a *desire for unsatisfaction*' (*For They Know Not*, 144). By refusing to own her desire, and so allow that it might be satisfied, what the hysteric achieves is its preservation in its purest (albeit unconscious) form. The hysteric reveals how, in Lacan's words, 'desire is always also *a desire for desire itself*' (cited ibid.).

Hegel's thought, then, is psychoanalytical. Precisely because the dialectic conforms to the structure of *après-coup*, it reveals the structure of the desire that drives it, enabling the impasse to be reread not as an impediment to the truth but as the truth itself in all its inherent negativity. Thus it is that 'impasse' is transformed into 'pass', Žižek's pun on the Lacanian 'pass' which designates the analysand's promotion, at the conclusion of the therapy, to the status of analyst (e.g. *Tarrying*, 119).[20] And so, for Žižek, Hegel does not just stage desire: ultimately he understands it. Hegel thereby achieves, like the analyst, 'knowledge in the real'; by implication, the analyst's knowledge is dignified as Hegelian in its intellectual scope and complexity. The nature of this knowledge is what I shall now address.

5   Hegel assumes the unity of truth and knowledge, sundered by Freud

Assuming that the *Phenomenology* charts the ascent of Spirit to the Absolute, Lacan thinks that, for Hegel, truth would be the knowledge of what is true. Lacan's objection is that he sees 'truth' as an effect of the symbolic order, and thus as a form of fiction, whereas the knowledge which the analyst values is 'knowledge in the real' – that is, knowledge of what necessarily exceeds this fiction. Truth and knowledge for Lacan are thus radically different: truth can be articulated, knowledge can't.

The hystericization of Hegel, however, throws a spanner in the working of this objection. It means that Hegel *does* convey a knowledge that is distinct from truth. To coin a conversion of the kind Žižek favours, the form of Hegelian dialectic transforms the *desire for knowledge* into the *knowledge of desire*. Žižek's discussion of the status of knowledge and truth in Hegel brings us back to the question of the nature of knowledge, and the opposition between materialism and idealism.

Enjoy Your Symptom! provides a helpful starting point. Here Žižek argues that psychoanalysis and Hegelian philosophy are both idealist in the sense that each accepts that what we see as 'reality' in fact reflects the workings of the mind. In Freud's thought, for instance, the opposition between the 'pleasure principle' and the 'reality principle' does not mean that an inner impetus towards pleasure is tested against and constrained by external reality. On the contrary, since the purpose of the pleasure principle is to act as a kind of mental thermostat preserving us against too much stimulation ('unpleasure'), anything that we perceive as 'reality' has already been filtered through its protective mechanism. For Freud, then, ' "reality" is not something given in advance but something the ontological status of which is in a way secondary, in other words: *constituted* in the precise meaning this term acquired in German idealism' (*Enjoy!*, 49). Similarly, Hegelian idealism consists in maintaining – in his famous tag – that 'what is rational is actual and what is actual is rational': actuality does not exist independently of our rational apprehension of it.[21] Not only is our conceptual apparatus the reflection of the world, the world is also the reflection of our conceptual apparatus. Thus, for Hegel, 'Truth does not consist in the correspondence of our thought (proposition, notion) with an object but in the correspondence of the object itself to its notion' (*For They Know Not*, 164). For both German idealism and psychoanalysis, then, 'reality' is a symbolic fiction.

Žižek's comparison between Hegel and psychoanalysis does not end here. We have seen that Žižek stresses the extent to which Hegelian thought processes are fissured by negativity. Since, for Hegel, reality is the correlate of thought, the world too is caught up in these same fissures: 'The limitation of our knowledge . . . is simultaneously the limitation of the very object of our knowledge, that is, the gaps and voids in our knowledge of reality are simultaneously the gaps and voids in the "real" ontological edifice itself' (*Ticklish Subject*, 55). In psychoanalysis, the pleasure principle is likewise internally riven. The death drive – that which, in the words of Freud's famous title, lies 'beyond the pleasure principle' – installs a hitch in its workings, forcing it repeatedly round the same tracks, unable to engage with the real except at a distance. The way we construe external reality is at the mercy of this hitch and the rift which it installs between perception and our consciousness.

It follows, then, that what (from the perspective of psychoanalytical idealism) we relate to as 'reality' is actually produced as a counter-effect of this internal hitch: the resistant kernel of inner psychical reality is projected outwards as the hard world of external reality. Another way of putting this is that the term 'real', in Lacan, encompasses both what we think of as 'objective reality' *and* our pathological inner drives. Analogously, it is the very element of failure in Hegel's idealism that produces 'reality' in its resistant form: 'Hegelian "extreme idealism" consists in seeing "reality" as something which exists only in so far as Idea is not fully actualized, fulfilled; the very existence of (the "hard", "external") reality bears witness to the fact that Idea remains caught in a deadlock' (*Indivisible Remainder*, 110). Reality, then, does not just correspond to our mental apprehension of it; it is specifically correlated with the deficiencies of our apprehension: 'Our human universe is nothing but an embodiment of the radically inhuman "abstract negativity", of the abyss we experience when we face the "night of the world"' (*Enjoy!*, 53).

This conclusion leads Žižek to reconsider the term 'idealism' as applied to both Hegel and psychoanalysis. If each sees the ideal order of symbolic fiction as correlative to a hard, resistant reality which it cannot account for except negatively, then are they 'idealist', or are they in fact 'materialist'? This question is most fully developed in *The Indivisible Remainder*. Which comes first, the materialist chicken of the real or the idealist egg of the symbolic fiction (*Indivisible Remainder*, 107–8)? Žižek rehearses and then rebuts a philosophical reading of Lacan centred on the 'lack' of castration in relation to which *jouissance* emerges as the impossible limit. The target of this rebuttal may appear to be Derrida (*The Post Card* and *Resistances of Psychoanalysis*), but the irritation which Žižek betrays seems also to be aimed at his own earlier writings (much as, in *Metastases*, 173, he draws attention to the way Lacan's polemics are typically means by which Lacan distances himself from his own previous opinions[22]). To the 'false poetry of "castration"', Žižek now opposes its obverse: 'The trouble with *jouissance* is not that it is unattainable, that it always eludes our grasp, but, rather, that *one can never get rid of it*, that its stain drags along for ever' (*Indivisible Remainder*, 93).

In the pages that follow this stain is found adhering to every particular. It gives meaning to our utterances and responsibility to our acts; it inflects our voice and detaches objects from their ideological matrix. As a result, we are forced to ask whether the big Other is truly an idealist framework, 'a kind of insurmountable horizon'? Isn't it rather made up of a non-totalizable ('non all') set of real singulars, of 'contingent material singularities' (*Indivisible Remainder*, 107–8)? Žižek will find confirmation of the latter view in Hegel's concept of the concrete universal, considered below.

At the end of this discussion in *The Indivisible Remainder*, Žižek resolves this opposition between idealism and materialism with a resourcefully Hegelian gesture, by asserting the identity of its two terms: the priority of the real to the symbolic is, at the same time, an expression of '*idealism carried to extremes*' (*Indivisible Remainder*, 109). Thus driven to the limits of its identity, he contends, idealism converts into dialectical materialism: the position (associated with Marx) according to which 'actuality' is effected by human creativity operating within strict, material conditions. Of course Marx was referring to economic conditions, not to some absent void/kernel. But, Žižek argues, the fact that the 'real' is known only as an absence within the symbolic order does not prevent it from also surging in upon it 'in its very material density' (ibid.). This solution, taking us beyond the idealist fiction, leads to knowledge in the real. In this way, the separation between truth and knowledge which characterizes psychoanalysis has actually been accounted for through recourse to Hegel.

The crucial point to emerge from this discussion in *The Indivisible Remainder* is that Hegel is a philosopher not only of 'castration' (i.e. of the symbolic) but also of the insurgence of the real. Lacan had explained that 'castration means that *jouissance* must be refused, so that it can be reached on the inverted ladder (*l'échelle renversée*) of the Law of desire' ('Subversion', 324). Detailed comparison between Lacan's thought and Hegel's helps Žižek to clarify this process as resulting from a double cut. In Lacan, the first subjection to language is so traumatic that not only is it repressed ('primary repression'), but the fact of its repression is *itself* then repressed. The primary repression turns our animal instincts into drives; we resort to the fundamental fantasy as a protective mechanism in a vain attempt to palliate the shock; and the second wave of repression then represses this fantasy and locks it into place. Žižek's contention is that, in Hegel, the negation of the negation follows exactly this pattern. The first negation, in which destruction and fragmentation are unleashed, gives rise to the second negation in which, by 'tarrying with the negative', division and deficiency are incorporated into identity. But this does not make them innocuous; rather, the 'night of the world' continues to assail us in all its ghostly horror. Thus the homology between Lacan's thought and Hegel's is not just of a symbolic order punctured by negativity. In both cases, the relation of the real to the symbolic results from a double cut whereby the real is rendered *both* inaccessible *and*, because it saturates every fragment of experience, ubiquitous and unavoidable.

To sum up this discussion, then, we see how, for Žižek, both Hegel and Lacan are *formal* thinkers. The form which unites them is that of reflection and the double negation. Whereas Lacan saw Hegel as condemned to the imaginary, Žižek embraces him as the foremost philosopher of a flawed symbolic, and as a guide to the real. Hegel, more than Freud, can help us grasp what lies 'beyond the pleasure principle'. In short, by reading Hegel and Lacan together, Žižek both connects Lacan to Enlightenment traditions of rationality, *and* discovers in Hegel a proto-analytical account of the psyche. From this dialectic, Hegel, rather than Freud, emerges as the privileged guide to Lacan's thought.

Two Hegelian-Lacanian Themes

Thus far this chapter has been shaped by Lacan's reservations about the relevance of Hegel to psychoanalysis and the remarkable alignment which Žižek forges between them. I want now to look at the creative purpose to which Žižek himself puts this conjunction, by examining two Hegelian-Lacanian themes which keep recurring in his writings (indeed, I've already alluded to them on and off in the preceding discussion): subject and substance, and the universal and the particular.

While both these topics belong in part to the discipline of logic, both also have a political dimension in Hegel's thought. That is, while 'substance' can denote the world of predicates, or objects, in their relation to the subject, it can also be understood as social substance: as the domain of the collective *vis-à-vis* the individual. Similarly, in addition to its purely conceptual meaning, the term 'universal' develops historically (Hegel thinks that Christian Europe understands universality better than pagan Greece[23]), and takes on political value when invoked to define the bases of society (as in 'universal human rights', for example). The two themes are, in fact, interrelated and combined in Žižek's writings, because the deficit in subject and substance which leads to their coincidence is the same deficit as prevents access to the universal (*For They Know Not*, chapter 3; *Ticklish Subject*, chapter 2). Together, then, these themes show how reading Lacan in relation to Hegel rather than Freud enables Žižek to enlarge the focus of psychoanalysis to include historical and political analysis.

Subject and substance

The passage which provides the spur to Žižek's elaboration of this theme comes from the Preface to the *Phenomenology* (§17), where Hegel states that his philosophical system 'turns on grasping and expressing the True, not only as *Substance*, but equally as *Subject*'. Substance becomes subject when it alienates itself from itself, and then repositions itself in such a way as to take account of that alienation. That is, first it negates itself by becoming other; then it negates that otherness and returns to itself, and this double negation 'sublates' it into subject (§18). This Hegelian passage of substance into subject, via a process of double negation, is understood by Žižek as forming a parallel to Lacan's account of the mutual recognition of lack in the subject and the Other. For Lacan, the split or barred subject, $, is the correlate of the barred Other, Ⱥ (as in the claim 'the Other does not exist' because it is nothing but an impostor), since both are subject to the same lack (their mutual incapacity to take account of the real). Žižek's contention is that what we take for substantive entities – such as self and society – are hollow and deficient; that *neither* is substance. The only substance is the real of *jouissance*, which is excluded from both, but which subtends the sense of everyday 'reality' orchestrated by ideology. The Hegelian dialectical progression of substance to subject thus corresponds to the progression, in Lacan, from the mutual recognition of $ and Ⱥ as deficient to the admission of their common dependence on the delusory *objet a*; the dialectic of substance and subject is sometimes identified, then, with the Lacanian formula $ ◊ *a*. I shall trace this progression as it is described in the final chapter of the *Sublime Object of Ideology*. The argument is typically Žižekian, in that it relies on exposing the content – our relation to the real – which results from the coincidence of two forms: the Hegelian dialectic of reflection (positing, external and determinate) and the process of the transference in Lacan.[24]

Žižek's *entrée en matière* is a good example of the indirection I spoke of in my Introduction. By choosing to illustrate Hegel's ideas with an example about interpreting texts from the past, he surreptitiously promotes his own claim creatively to reinterpret Hegel (*Sublime Object*, 213–14). Positing reflection, he says, is equivalent to the belief that one has unmediated access to a text's significance ('*Antigone* is in fact a drama about . . .'). External reflection admits that this original meaning is unattainable, and that we must make do with the play of interpretations that drift at the whim of historical circumstances ('there is no single meaning of *Antigone*, we can only know what *Antigone* meant for such and such an audience . . .'). But determinate reflection negates the negativity of this position by claiming that this capacity for retrospective significance is precisely what is valuable in a text ('The "true" meaning of *Antigone* . . . is constituted *afterwards*, through a certain structurally necessary delay', *Sublime Object*, 214). This third stage of reflection is reduplicative, because it absorbs, or redoubles, the earlier negative reflection.

We achieve the 'determinate reflection' when we become aware of the fact that this delay is immanent, internal to the 'Thing-in-itself': *the Thing-in-itself is found in its truth through the loss of its immediacy.*

In other words, what appears, to 'external reflection', as an *impediment* is in fact a *positive condition* of our access to Truth: the Truth of a thing emerges because the thing is not accessible to us in its immediate self-identity. (Ibid.)

Clearly this example is as much about interpretation *après-coup*, and the potential liberation of Hegel from his immediate historical context, as it is about the structure of dialectic.

Žižek then proceeds to a virtuoso reading of Hegel's account of the subject as resulting from the redoubling of reflection which makes up determinate reflection. His argument is complex, and I summarize it in simplified form. He starts with the subject, assuming that its identity is determined by the social 'substance' of external circumstances (external reflection). Thus, for example, a complaining spouse rails at the inadequacies of his or her partner, unable to see that these are not an *impediment* to their relationship, they are its *condition*. Although the husband sees himself as the victim of his partner's faults, in fact he is getting his own message back in inverted form, since the message he is sending to his spouse is, 'Be unreasonable, demanding, incapable, etc., it's my way of reassuring myself that I myself am thoroughly reasonable, mature, competent, etc.' Determinate reflection comes with the doubling back into the subject of what he had taken to be external circumstances: he assumes responsibility for representing the world in this way, and this makes it possible for him to intervene in it and change things. In this way, he converts his representation of the world as alien to himself into one of the world as containing opportunities for him to act. This is the process whereby substance (the world) becomes subject (his capacity for intervention).

Such an assumption of responsibility for the way the world is could be seen as taking subjectivism to extremes. But, Žižek contends, we would be wrong to interpret Hegel's account in voluntarist terms. The transformation of substance into subject should instead be read in conjunction with the Lacanian concept of the 'forced choice', a concept which Lacan illustrates with the highwayman's terrifying challenge, 'Your money or your life'. Although this looks like a choice, it isn't one, because if you choose money, you lose your life, and without your life you lose your money anyway. The only way to get anything at all is to 'choose' life. This is the route the Lacanian subject must follow if it is to be a subject: it can enter language and suffer the traumatic consequences ('castration'); but it cannot choose *not* to undergo the limitation which language brings in its wake, for if it did, it would not be a subject at all. Analogously, says Žižek, in accepting responsibility for the external world the Hegelian subject performs, as though it were a free act, something he could not avoid. Thus the subject is constituted in the same way for both Lacan and Hegel, from this ' "empty gesture" which changes nothing at the level of positive content' (*Sublime Object*, 221), but simply transforms the subject's relationship to circumstances that are inevitable.

Now the argument gets more involved, as Žižek asks at what point reflection should properly be described as external. Traditionally, Hegel is read as holding that when I posit something as an appearance (or an object, etc.), then I am presupposing an already existing external world of appearances (or objects, etc.), so this is the point at which external reflection begins (cf. the opening of this chapter). Žižek, however, contends that the boundary between 'positing' and 'external' reflection falls, not between appearance and essence, but within essence itself. What happens is that the essence figures itself in two contradictory ways. On the one hand, it is something abstracted from (mediated by) appearance – we don't know what something *really* is, but we are sure it's not what it *appears* to be. On the other hand, it is held to be something that *really* exists in some immediate, uncontested way, something that is always already given prior to its appearance. When put like this, one can see that, unless the essence is split in this way, it has no means of separating out 'what it *really* is' from its appearance. As a result of this split, the essence becomes both subject and substance. It is substance in so far as it can be located in relation to appearance, and it is also substance in its specification as an already existing thing. What makes it a subject, though, is the split between these two manifestations of substance. Like the Lacanian subject, the Hegelian subject is a *gap*, a fissure, in the world of its predicates (*Sublime Object*, 226).

The final stage in the argument, then, is to pass from 'external' to 'determinate' reflection. What is involved here is seeing how these two versions of the substance are reflections of each other. The truth of substance is that supposing its real existence means ascribing positive value to what we assume to be its negative relation to its appearance. In seeing that the substance is in some sense 'manufactured' out of nothing – from the negative relation the essence is assumed to hold to its appearances – one realizes that the whole dialectical construction can just unravel, that it is nothing but the disguises of its own negativity. Tracing this course, the subject, which had been given definition by what it took to be presences on either side of it (appearance, independent essence) assumes its reality as gap or fissure in this nebulous structure, and so '*no longer presupposes himself as subject*' (*Sublime Object*, 230). In this way, the dialectic has followed the same course as analytic therapy – the subject has come to recognize the insubstantiality of what it took to be the substance (the big Other, now reduced to the barred Other); and it has undergone 'subjective destitution' (to become the barred subject). By taking cognizance of this process, the patient is free (or in Hegelian terms 'absolute') to reconsider his relation to symbolization, and to redefine his position towards what ideology had previously presented him with as 'sublime objects' (anti-Semitism, consumerism, etc.). With this reading of Lacan and Hegel together, it becomes possible to reconfigure our *political* subjection.

Universal and particular

It isn't easy to piece together Žižek's thoughts on universality. One reason for this is that he is trying to make sense of what is generally admitted to be confused in Hegel.[25] Another is that Lacan treats universality only tangentially, mainly in relation to his account of sexual difference in *Seminar* XX; Žižek's interpretation has been extensively influenced and supplemented by the teaching of Jacques-Alain Miller. Žižek first treats the topic of universality at length in *For They Know Not*, and continues unabated in recent writings, with particularly extended discussions in *The Ticklish Subject* (chapter 3) and *Contingency, Hegemony, Universality* ('Da Capo Senza Fine'). Universality is central to Žižek's thinking about sexual difference, history and politics, and I shall be returning to it in chapters 4 and 6.

On the psychoanalytical side, Žižek's first account of universality runs like this (based on *For They Know Not*, especially 21–7). The universal order is the symbolic order, or big Other, which provides the conceptual grid with which we construe the world. However, our conceptual mapping is impaired by the fact that the planes of signifier and signified are out of kilter with one another. The reason why this comes about is that one of the signifiers has no corresponding signified; it does not introduce a content into the linguistic system, but merely insinuates difference. The perpetually moving place to which it points is that of the 'lack' in the symbolic order, the primordial lack of 'castration'. This signifier is represented as S1 because, having no signified, it is singular, whereas all the other signifiers are double, hence S2. S1 is also singular in the sense that it is unique among the signifiers; hence it can also be referred to as the 'unary feature' (Lacan's *trait unaire*; see Glossary, SIGNIFYING CHAIN).

The unary feature acts as the prop of individual identification at the symbolic level. How I position myself as an individual depends on how I attach myself to this signifier of pure difference. However, as the empty space in the set, S1 also both determines and effectively takes on the value of all the other signifiers (S2). The result is that, as well as being a pure (qualitative) singular, it assumes the role of the (quantitative) particular. That is, instead of being utterly unique, it appears as just one of a set, and hence as correlated with the universal. Thus inflated with the meaning of the other signifiers, it gives the impression of totalizing the whole field of signification. This is why it is also called the master signifier, or 'quilting point' (Lacan's *point de capiton*), the signifier that 'quilts' the field of meaning. For example, the claim that we are a 'free society' acts as a political quilting point that is, in itself, meaningless – a flag to wave at cultures we wish to disparage, and that has nothing to do with the extent to which we actually are or are not free (for instance, one way we regularly show we are a 'free society' is by locking up people who threaten our 'freedom'). But in everyday thinking, the empty term 'free society' becomes 'filled out' with all the aspects of our society which we treasure (family life, nice cars, TV, etc.).

Via a process of double reflection, then, S1 appears first as negating the rest of the set, S2 – that is, as unique relative to its fullness – and next, via a negation of this negation, when the rest of the set is reflected into it, as typifying the universal in the form of the particular. For instance, when I identify myself relative to the unary feature, I don't normally think of myself as absolutely unique, as a point of pure difference. Instead, I embrace some ideologically totalizing view of myself: say, as a successful academic and mother of three. In this way, I make the transition from the singular to the particular which in turn evokes the universals 'academic success' and 'motherhood'.

A Hegelian terminology has already crept into this exposition, and clearly Žižek's development of Lacan owes much to Hegel. Hegel too is interested in the triadic constitution of the concept as comprising three 'moments', singular, particular and universal, which are dialectically related to one another.[26] Thus, for instance, the particular can pass into the universal and back, says Žižek, like the passage round a Moebius band, where what we thought were two distinct sides are in fact one continuous one (*For They Know Not*, 46). The capacity for each 'moment' to pass into another also means, paradoxically, that the universal can be located in the particular. In this way, the universal is 'always-already *part of itself*, comprised within its own elements' (ibid.); this capacity to appear among its own particulars is illustrated by Lacan's often repeated quip, 'I have three brothers, Paul, Ernest and myself'.

Another way in which the universal is located in one of its particulars is via the exception. Žižek endorses as authentically Hegelian the claim that 'the exception proves the rule', since it is precisely from our awareness of an exception to it that the existence of a rule can be inferred. A more concrete instance of the correlation between the exception and the universal is furnished by Marx's account of the commodity (*For They Know Not*, 124). All commodities are defined as being goods which can be exchanged for money, except for money itself. What universalizes the notion 'commodity' is the fact that there exists one commodity, money, which is the exception to the set.

Returning now to Lacan, this account of the universal as correlative with its exception corresponds exactly with how he defines masculinity in the 'formulae of sexuation' in *Seminar* XX. The 'exception which proves the rule' of masculinity is the mythical father in Freud's *Totem and Taboo*, the father who enjoyed uncontested sexual possession of all the women in the tribe before being murdered by his sons. Through guilt for their act, the sons became subject to the law of inhibition and repression ('castration') that characterizes all men as a result of the very fact that there was one – their father – who claimed exemption from it. As Žižek puts it,

> Lacan's basic premiss is that the leap from the *general* set of 'all men' into the *universal* 'man' is possible only through an exception: the universal (in its difference to the empirical generality) is constituted through the exception; we do not pass from the general set to the universality of One-Notion by way of *adding* something to the set but, on the contrary, by way of *subtracting* something from it, namely the 'unary feature' [*trait unaire*] which totalizes the general set, which makes out of it a universality. (*For They Know Not*, 123)

The correspondence between Hegel and Lacan looks complete. However, a new twist (or dialectical reversal) is about to be effected.

It comes in the form of the feminine formula of sexuation, which proposes a different relationship to the universal from the masculine one: one in which the signifying order plays a greatly diminished role. Women, like men, are subject to inhibition and repression, says Lacan – indeed, they are so without exception – but they are so incompletely and inconsistently. The result of this, according to Lacan, is that 'woman' is not fully actualized as a universal. I shall be returning to this problematic claim in chapter 4; what is relevant to the present discussion is the way Žižek presents this 'not-quite-universal' of the feminine. This is the 'non all' which we encountered when reviewing the so-called immanentism of the Hegelian dialectic. It means that the symbolic fiction of the universal, instead of being tugged into shape by S1, is, on the contrary, exposed as deficient and leaky. The agent of this exposure is an absolutely contingent object, here identified as the *objet a*. This is what blocks or holds open the place of lack in the symbolic order that is commandeered, on the side of the symbolic, by S1. The complex arguments concerning S1 were not a red herring – the master signifier is indeed a clue to the way the universals of ideology and identity, not to mention masculinity, are constructed – but they need to be subordinated to this new view of universality.

So, now the *objet a* and not S1 is proposed as what impedes (and provokes) the universal.[27] *Objet a* is the fantasy object that plugs the gap of the primary repression and provides the subject's original defence against 'castration'. It is, as it were, the traumatic underside of S1. The 'lack' which it gives the illusion of filling out is, Žižek is arguing, the emptiness on which the universal founders: the conceptual world cannot 'say it all'; there is always something which escapes. Also, because of its connection with trauma, the space of *objet a* discloses the dimension of violence in the universal. In effect, the universal is not so much a *concept* as a *struggle for conceptualization*:

> Lacan's 'primordial repression'. . . is precisely what creates universality as an empty place; and the 'trace of the disavowed in the formal structure that emerges' [Žižek is here referring to Butler's criticisms] is what Lacan calls *objet petit a*, the remainder of the *jouissance* within the symbolic order. This very necessity of the primordial repression shows clearly why one should distinguish between the exclusion of the Real that opens up the empty place of the universal and the subsequent hegemonic struggles of different particular contents to occupy this place. (*Contingency*, 257)

But what does it mean to say that the psychoanalytical correlate of the universal is *objet a*? *Objet a* marks not only the lack in the

Other, but also the lack in the subject. As we have already seen, it is the place where substance turns into subject. To cast this in narrative terms, it is the point at which the absence of maternal phallus coincides with the subject's 'castration'. *Objet a* is thus the axial point between the subject's alienation in the Other (in substance) and the subject's separation into himself as an utterly singular being. By the same token, *objet a* is the remainder of the real, that which the Other cannot take account of. It is the trace of *jouissance* ('surplus enjoyment') which inheres in every singular *qua* singular, and which thus underlies what was earlier described as the 'materialism' of psychoanalysis. The paradoxes we have seen – whereby the particular and universal, and the universal and the singular, all inhabit each other – are maintained but radicalized in the light of this development.

In Žižek's early books this means emphasizing the role of contingency in Hegel's thought, which in turn betrays its connection to the real: 'Hegel . . . exposes the contingent particularity to which the Universal itself is linked as with an umbilical cord' (*For They Know Not*, 126). In his more recent writings, it means exploring the contrast which Hegel appears to draw between the 'abstract' and the 'concrete' universal. Abstract universality occurs when

> [w]e speak . . . of the 'concept' of colour, or of a plant, or of an animal, and so on; and these concepts are supposed to arise by omitting the particularities through which the various colours, plants, animals, etc., are distinguished from one another, and holding fast to what they have in common. This is the way in which the understanding apprehends the Concept, and the feeling that such concepts are hollow and empty, that they are mere schemata and shadows, is justified. (*Encyclopaedia Logic*, §163, add. 1)

It is vital, says Hegel, both for philosophical purposes and for practical ones, not to 'confuse what is merely communal with what is truly universal' (ibid.). What is 'truly universal', then, will exceed the field of understanding alone. 'Concrete' universality is both this capacity of the universal to pass over into the concrete instance and take on the full, contingent reality of the singular and, conversely, the capacity of the concrete instance to manifest a universality which exceeds the prevailing conceptual framework.

I pointed out that when Žižek expounded the relation of substance to subject in *The Sublime Object* he introduced it via the analogy of reading *Antigone* in a way that appealed to the *après-coup* structure of interpretation. It is interesting that interpretation *après-coup* is also offered as a way into understanding the concrete universal in both *The Ticklish Subject* (93) and *Contingency, Hegemony, Universality* (242–9). Thus an aberrant misperception may be a case of a concrete universal: what appears to be an utterly singular, historically misinformed distortion may in fact prove to be the spur to a whole new way of symbolizing the phenomenon in question. An amusing example is produced from Cultural Studies. The concept of *film noir* has been critiqued on the grounds that the features commonly assigned to it are actually not found in any particular group of films. *Film noir* is not a historical genre of American movie, but a retrospective construct of French film studies. The kind of post-structuralist criticism levelled at these films today is similarly 'inauthentic'. It purports to represent the French thought of the 1960s and 1970s, but in fact concocts for the American academy an after-the-fact mishmash of not particularly French ideas. What we find in this criticism, then, is 'a nonexistent theoretical position analysing a nonexistent cinematic genre' (*Contingency*, 243). Yet it is precisely such *après-coup* constructions which may hold the key to 'true' universal concepts. The concept of *film noir* has proved highly productive, not only for American cinema, but for cultural interpretation more broadly. Another telling example of the concrete universal is Freud's case studies. By analysing the idiosyncrasies of individual patients, Freud was able to frame the universal insights of psychoanalytical theory. Psychoanalysis thus jumps from the singular to the universal in a way that bypasses the particular (*Contingency*, 240; *Fright*, 25–6). It is in this way that Lacan's *objet a* – the random, accidental 'remainder of the real' represented by the singular occurrence – opens the way retrospectively to the Hegelian 'concrete universal'.

The concept of the 'concrete universal' thus comes to play an important role in Žižek's running battle with 'historicism', a historical relativism which he associates with Cultural Studies and with deconstruction, and which he contrasts with his own commitment to 'historicity'.[28] Historicity has an anchorage in the real, which stands outside the temporal sequence of the symbolic. Instead of being defined by time, the real is the 'constitutive outside' that defines it. Lacking such anchorage, historicism – despite its pretensions to being a historical discipline – lacks any true historical dimension. Again, psychoanalysis provides him with an example. Should we say that Freud's insights, arising as they did in Vienna at the turn of the twentieth-century, have only limited relevance to

44 *Dialectic and the Real*

other periods and other settings? On the contrary, it is only the particular which can become universal; the point is, rather, to ask under what historical conditions a universal could emerge (*Indivisible Remainder*, 215). Far from diminishing its universality, historical specificity is the reflective key to it (*Indivisible Remainder*, 216). While it is true that for Lacan the real is an ahistorical kernel, it is precisely this which 'again and again sets in motion the movements of history, propelling it to ever new historicizations/symbolizations' (*Indivisible Remainder*, 218). Žižek's most forceful expression of his differences with 'historicists' comes in *Contingency, Hegemony, Universality* (111–12):

> The truly radical assertion of historical contingency has to include the dialectical tension between the domain of historical change itself and its traumatic 'ahistorical' kernel *qua* its condition of (im)possibility. Here we have the difference between historicity proper and historicism: *historicism* deals with the endless play of substitutions within the same fundamental field of (im)possibility, while *historicity* proper makes thematic different structural principles of this very (im)possibility. In other words, the historicist theme of the endless open play of substitutions is the very form of ahistorical ideological closure: by focusing on the simple dyad essentialism-contingency, on the passage from one to the other, it obfuscates concrete historicity *qua* the change of the very global structuring principle of the Social.

The alleged open-endedness of 'historicism' is, he concludes, the worst form of ideological collusion with the *status quo*. Only a concept of historicity grounded in Žižek's understanding of universality has truly radical potential.

Thus, like the conjunction of substance and subject, Žižek's Hegelian-Lacanian convergence of universal and particular enables political agency. One way to effect change is to seize on the exception, or on the random, contingent factor in the current scheme of things, and force its universal implications so as to produce a new historical order (see also chapter 6).

Conclusion

We can now see why Žižek ascribes such importance to Hegel as a precursor of Lacan. By reading the two writers together, he opens up a field of operation which remains psychoanalytical, but which is also philosophical, historical and political.

The major advantage which accrues to Hegel from this encounter is his promotion to a philosopher of the flawed symbolic, a symbolic fissured by the real, rather than a philosopher of imaginary totality. In an age when Hegel is once more being widely read, Žižek makes a forceful case for Hegel's relevance to modernity.[29] Indeed, he makes Hegel sound as though he has all the whackiness he himself aspires to: 'Hegelian totality is not an organic Whole within which each element sticks to its limited place, but a "crazy" totality in which a position reverts to its Other in the very movement of its excessive exaggeration – the dialectical "link" of partial elements emerges only through their "exaggeration"' (*Plague*, 93).

This reading of Hegel has, in turn, major implications for Lacan. First, the *rapprochement* between Hegel's logic and Lacan's view of the relation of the symbolic to the real increases our appreciation of Lacan as a *formal* rationalist thinker. This enables Žižek to progress beyond the pathological content which inheres in some of Lacan's thinking – for example, in his account of sexual difference (see chapter 4).

Second, by situating Lacan within a tradition of Western metaphysics extending from Plato through Kant and Hegel, Žižek extends the philosophical understanding of what, in Lacan, still remain essentially analytical notions: the subject (as we have seen in this chapter), ethics, freedom and agency (see chapters 5 and 6), and above all the real. As the interaction between Hegel and Lacan evolves in Žižek's writings from, say, *The Sublime Object* to *The Indivisible Remainder*, the emphasis is placed less on the *formal* similarities between the two thinkers and more on their engagement with the evasive but intrusive materiality of the real. Or, to put it in different terms, the view of the real as the impossible outside of the symbolic becomes offset against a 'materialist' view of it as a virtual or spectral stain inescapably inhering in every singular thing.

Third, despite Lacan's own relative political disengagement,[30] Žižek discovers the relevance of his thought to history and politics. By combining the thought of Hegel and Lacan, as we saw in the themes of substance and subject, and universal and particular, he brings out the political implications of their conjunction in what nevertheless remains an analytical framework: one that offers the prospect of 'political therapy' as radical symbolic change. Of course there have been many attempts to combine psychoanalysis with historical and political analysis. The tradition which has most consistently lent itself to these attempts is Marxism: Marx and Freud, or Lacan and Althusser, have frequently been explored in tandem. In this optic, it is not Freud whom Hegel displaces from the customary genealogy so much as Marx. The fact that Žižek began publishing just as the Eastern bloc countries were abandoning various forms of Marxist government provides a clear strategic context for this displacement. To use a turn of phrase that Žižek himself affects, Žižek is in effect making Hegel the new Marx, much as 'brown is the new black' (see chapter 6). Perhaps after the trumpeted return to Marxism in *The Ticklish Subject* and the recent enthusiasm for Lenin, the Lacan–Hegel duo will figure less prominently on Žižek's programme than formerly. Future studies of Žižek may set less store on his relationship to Hegel than I have.

Žižek's interpretation of Hegel is heterodox. No one else reads Hegel through *The Science of Logic* as a hysteric. Laclau thinks that Hegel is a panlogicist, and that Žižek's reappropriation of him as a kind of pre-post-Lacanian is unjustifiable (*Contingency*, 61–4, 73). Žižek is similarly thought off-beam by Dews ('Tremor'). However, neither of these critics is taking into account the framework of *après-coup* which determines the Lacanian attitude to the past. As Žižek himself says, in a witty revision of Marx's well-known aphorism, 'Philosophers have hitherto only interpreted Hegel; however, the point is also to change him' (*Plague*, 96).

Speaking as a non-philosopher, I think that the perspective from which Žižek is most vulnerable is not his reading of Hegel *per se*, but the use (or abuse) he makes of the notion of *après-coup*. As a strategy, it is applied unevenly, and specifically more to Hegel than Lacan, since our view of Hegel is *transformed*, whereas that of Lacan is merely *extended*. Ironically, through roping Lacan together with the philosopher of Absolute Knowledge, Žižek exposes himself to the reservations from which he defends Hegel. Does he not aspire to be the theorist of Everything? Doesn't his unceasing genuflection before the real ensconce it as his Absolute? Isn't his own account of Lacan as the fulfilment of the Enlightenment highly teleologized, as in this, his most grandiose and programmatic formulation of Lacan's quasi-messianic role? 'Our aim is to elevate Lacan to the dignity of an author who provides the key to the *Grundoperation* of German Idealism, perhaps the acme of the entire history of philosophy' (*Indivisible Remainder*, 95).[31]

Such questions also point to the self-interest at work in Žižek's use of *après-coup*. The very eccentricity and brilliance of his reading of Hegel insinuate Žižek into the history he is purporting to rewrite. Hegel is, as it were, 'invented' to provide the starting point in a series in which we can see, retrospectively, that Žižek has to be included. If Hegel is a major prophet (John the Baptist, perhaps?) to Lacan's Messiah, then Žižek is his Saint Paul. Indeed, Žižek embraces Paul as the figure who realized the potential for universality in Jesus's singular misfortunes (see chapter 5). Is Žižek the one who spins the universal from the intransigent obscurities of Hegel and Lacan, and transmits it in a form that will shape the faith of future millennia? The alchemy of *après-coup* risks distilling the contingency of Žižek's reading into a form of necessity, and retroactively consecrating the triad Hegel–Lacan–Žižek. To be true to Žižek's own insights, we have to resist the intoxication of their seemingly Hegelian inevitability.

3

'Reality' and the Real: Culture as Anamorphosis

If a person renounces Lacan, soon psychoanalysis itself will appear to him dubious, and from here is it just a step to a disdain for Hitchcock's films and to a snobbish refusal of horror fiction. How many people have entered the way of perdition with some fleeting cynical remark on Lacan, which at the time was of no great importance to them, and ended by treating Stephen King as absolute literary trash!

If a person renounces Stephen King, soon Hitchcock himself will appear dubious, and from here it is just a step to a disdain for psychoanalysis and to a snobbish refusal of Lacan. How many people have entered the way of perdition with some fleeting remark on Stephen King, which at the time was of no great importance to them, and ended by treating Lacan as a phallocentric obscurantist!

It is for the reader to decide which of the two versions he or she would choose.

(Looking Awry, p. viii)

These amusing deformations of De Quincey typify Žižek's writings on culture.[1] Different registers are being constantly brought into collision, producing dizzying shifts of perspective: Coca-Cola and Gustave Courbet jostle for the same place (*Fragile Absolute*, 21–40); Shakespeare and Kafka are treated as 'kitsch' authors in the same breath as Stephen King (*Looking Awry*, p. vii); medieval love poetry and Neil Jordan's films share the same fantasy scenarios (*Metastases*, 89–112); and all are assimilated to the heady philosophical, strongly politicized elaboration of Lacanian theory that we saw unfold in the last chapter.[2]

As if to account for such a bizarre cocktail, Žižek at one point likens his intellectual project to a Borromean knot (*For They Know Not*, 2). This figure, which comprises three intersecting loops that overlap and are tied together at the centre, was used by Lacan to represent the complex interlocking of the three orders of the real, the symbolic and the imaginary. For Lacan, the central element that ties the knot together is the *objet a*. In Žižek's version of the knot, the three loops are Lacanian psychoanalysis, Hegelian dialectic and the critique of ideology; the *objet a* at their centre is the enjoyment of popular culture. Žižek's appropriation of Lacan's figure suggests how enjoying culture, like the *objet a*, is central to his thinking, pervades all its elements, but at the same time remains ambiguous and elusive.

What is 'culture'? At its broadest, a culture consists in the beliefs we hold and the practices we follow; 'popular' culture refers to the dispositions that obtain in non-elite groups. Culture in this broad sense, then, includes ideology and religion.[3] However, when Žižek talks about 'popular culture', he is usually referring more narrowly to mass-produced, consumer-oriented forms of entertainment such as film, television, widely diffused works of fiction or computer games. In this chapter, accordingly, I will be concentrating on what we might call 'cultural artefacts' or 'art forms', and Žižek's account of belief and ideology will be left to subsequent chapters. If such artefacts 'entertain' us, this is because, in some way, they provide us with enjoyment. So, when Žižek puts the enjoyment of popular culture at the centre of his theoretical enterprise, we also need to weigh the import, for him, of 'enjoyment'.

Following Lacan, Žižek maintains that our subjection to language throws our whole relation to the body off balance; we are 'cut off' from our instincts by 'castration'. This means that sexual enjoyment is never fully achieved or achievable in itself; instead, we get 'surplus enjoyment' (Lacan's *plus-de-jouir*), the renunciation of bodily enjoyment *in favour of* language and the concomitant infection of language *by* enjoyment. It is because of surplus enjoyment that the real, while it is by definition excluded from representation, at the same time permeates every fibre; it clings to every particular, and remains 'stuck to the sole of our shoe' as Lacan put it.[4] What we call 'entertainment' is a privileged site of surplus enjoyment: the enjoyment that derives not from the direct satisfaction of the drives (if such a thing were possible), but from the satisfaction of *not* directly satisfying them. The representations of popular culture are all around us, whether we recognize them or not; and through them this enjoyment spreads its tentacles into every aspect of our lives. That is why, as *objet a*, it is ideally suited to hold together the three fields of Žižek's Borromean knot.

Žižek repeatedly asserts that enjoyment of culture is there to serve his intersecting theories, not the other way round. Thus, while his interests are myriad, his priorities are unswerving. Pouring contempt on the 'psychoanalytic interpretation of art' (*Enjoy!*, 119), Žižek tests his understanding of abstruse theoretical concepts by looking to find them actualized in our everyday culture (*Metastases*, 175–6). His recent book on Kieślowski, which starts with a polemic against cognitive film studies and 'Post-Theory', is uncompromising on this point: 'The aim of this book is not to talk *about* [Kieślowski's] work, but to refer to his work in order to accomplish the *work* of Theory' (*Fright*, 9).[5]

So is Žižek really writing about cultural forms? Is he not, rather, writing about his theoretical concerns and merely drawing his examples from culture? Despite the priority he accords to theory, the picture is not so simple. We should recall his dictum that 'enjoyment is the only substance known to psychoanalysis' (e.g. *For They Know Not*, 19). Thus it is in the enjoyment of its culture that the (lack in the) theoretical subject encounters its substance. Moreover, one could argue that the seeming incompatibility between popular culture and high theory is precisely what provides the grounds for their encounter. This is not just because of the Hegelian principle of the unity of opposites, but because each acts as an *anamorphosis* of the other.

'Anamorphosis' is the name given in art history to the technique whereby a distorted perspective is restored to legibility when viewed through an unusual contrivance (like a cylindrical mirror) or from an unexpected angle. Lacan's favourite example is Holbein's *The Ambassadors*, in which two incompatible perspectives are juxtaposed. Most of the painting – a portrait of two men in a setting busy with meaningful artefacts – looks right when viewed from the front, but there is a strange, floating object in the foreground which remains completely meaning*less* from this position. However, if the viewer moves to the far right of the painting, this object, drawn into a 'normal' perspective, becomes recognizable as a skull, while the remainder of the picture recedes into a blur.

Žižek's title *Looking Awry* announces his fascination with anamorphosis and with the prospect that the clashing juxtapositions which he practices will enable us to see things we could never see 'straight on'. Anamorphosis is thus the visual equivalent of *après-coup*: it is the backwards glance that assigns meaning to what had previously seemed troublesome, inconsistent or resistant to analysis. Žižek's primary objective, as we have seen, is to 'look awry' at theory through the seemingly incompatible register(s) of culture; but as we move from one perspective to another, the logic of anamorphosis operates dialectically to ensure that we also see culture in a new light from the viewpoint of theory. Anamorphosis thus parallels not only the Lacanian hermeneutic *of après-coup* but also Hegel's logic of reflective determination.

This chapter could address any and all of Žižek's writings, but I shall concentrate on those that seem to privilege cultural arte-facts as their subject matter: the early studies of Hitchcock and Hollywood (*Everything You Always Wanted to Know, Looking Awry, Enjoy Your Symptom!*), the later books on Lynch (*The Art of the Ridiculous Sublime*) and Kieślowski (*The Fright of Real Tears*), and various discussions along the way of cinema, art and cyberspace. The focus I adopt is dictated by Žižek's overriding interest in how cultural products reflect back to us the way we construe reality, an interest which drives his recent analyses of cyberspace and Kieślowski as much as the early work on Hollywood. Fantasy is the fundamental mechanism whereby we manage our relation to the real, and thus our relation to enjoyment. Typically it provides us with surplus enjoyment which we are unaware of experiencing; it is by orchestrating fantasy around this hidden surplus that we are able to maintain a consistent view of 'reality'. Different cultural products, through their manipulation of fantasy, strike a different balance between 'reality' and the real – controlling the dosage between the two, as it were. But what they can also do is to make explicit the way fantasy always constructs 'reality' for us and the relation which such 'reality' bears to the real.

The Psychoanalytical Object

I will start, then, with an overview of the psychoanalytical theory of the object which underpins Žižek's writings on culture. Since in the later teaching of Lacan the object is the chief support of the subject and the mainstay of its fantasized existence (see e.g. *Plague*, 9–10), this will also introduce the question of what it means to be a subject. The scope of this theoretical account is sufficiently broad to encompass discussion of culture in the wider sense (i.e. including ideology and belief), so is relevant not just to this chapter but to subsequent ones as well.

'Objects' for psychoanalysis do not necessarily coincide with objects in the everyday sense, such as egg-cups or gloves, though they may include these. Psychoanalytic objects include areas of the body that are associated with physical drives. Above all, psycho-analytic objects are the co-ordinate and support of the subject; the 'self' we imagine ourselves as having is identified by psychoanaly-sis as an object. This is why objects are crucial to how subjects per-ceive what they take to be the 'reality' around them, and why the analysis of objects at the same time defines subjectivity.

According to Lacan, all objects are defined with reference to a primordial absence ('castration') and the horror it inspires. In them-selves, then, they are symbolic, in the sense that they stand for something other than themselves, something we could never have and need to be shielded from. This absence at the heart of the object is what can become positivized as real – for example, as we saw in the last chapter, in the 'bloody head' or 'white apparition' of Hegel's 'night of the world'. But our relationship to objects lies, above all, in the register of what Lacan calls the imaginary (*Seminar IV*, 53): we imagine the world to be made up of objects; we fail to see them as the substitutes they are; and we are always being captivated and misled by them – hence Lacan describes them as 'decoys' (*leurres*). Just as a decoy offers an imaginary resemblance to another thing, so objects generate mirror-images of themselves. Indeed, where our desires are concerned, one object is very much like another, which is why people repeatedly date similar partners or, when I go shopping, I am most likely to come home with yet another black jacket.

However, there are certain objects, known as 'partial objects',[6] which are unique (or 'non-specular'), because they don't simply proliferate down the endless chain of desire; instead, they are attached to particular bodily drives. Two objects of this kind in which Žižek is especially interested are the gaze (attached to the scopic drive, or seeing urge) and the voice (attached to the oral drive). Such objects, while they have imaginary and symbolic dimensions to them, have a privileged relation to the real. They manifest the real of the drives; they impress their singularity on us; and, albeit traumatically, they communicate enjoyment.[7]

The psychoanalytic gaze has nothing to do with what we think we see; rather, it is a disturbance in the visual field which gives us the feeling of being watched and makes us doubt whether we really *are* seeing what is 'really' there. Developed from Lacan's *Seminar* XI, this sense of gaze contrasts with the way 'gaze' is often used in feminist film theory to designate the way a (powerful) subject looks at a (disempowered) object: for example, male spectatorship of the female body (I shall return to this at the end of this chapter). The psychoanalytic gaze is a matter not of seeing, but of being looked at and disarmed.

Žižek's concept of voice goes back to observations made by Lacan in *Seminar* III, but extensively elaborated since.[8] Žižek's usage remains faithful to Lacan in associating the voice with the superego, an agency which for Lacan – unlike the better-known Freudian version – condemns us to perverse enjoyment. (In Freud, the superego exhorts us to renounce satisfaction for the sake of culture; but for Lacan, as we have seen, culture is always already saturated with surplus enjoyment, and so embracing it means shackling ourselves to the pursuit of enjoyment. See Glossary, SUPEREGO.)

Classic instances of the traumatic intrusion of gaze and voice are found in Hitchcock's films. In *Psycho*, Lilah, sister of the girl murdered in the famous shower scene, approaches the house next to the Bates motel where we suppose 'Norman's mother' lives. The house shows no sign of habitation, but there is an uncanny sense that it is gazing at her (*Looking Awry*, 118–19). The floating voice which is heard in several scenes in the film, and likewise presumed to be that of the mother, is identified by Žižek with a maternal superego promoting the incestuous tie between mother and son (*Looking Awry*, 126–7).[9]

I have said that partial objects, like the gaze and the voice, are attached to the drives. However, *any* object *may* be positioned against the real of the drives and hence, like the drive objects themselves, communicate a sense of its uniqueness. In this case it is the *position*, not the content, of the object which is all-important. The possibility of positioning an object relative to the drives arises because of what Lacan (*Seminar* VII) terms 'the Thing'. The Thing is a pressure point that lies just outside the symbolic and imaginary orders, where the weight of the real is sensed. It is a place of menace, because it is where the deadly impulses of the drives are gathered. An object aligned with this point is said to be raised 'to the dignity of the Thing' (*Seminar* VII, 112; and see Glossary, THING). Rather like an eclipse, when a heavenly body becomes positioned between us and the sun, and appears surrounded by an aura of light so intense that we could never look directly at it, an object located in this way between us and the unsymbolizable Thing becomes as though irradiated by the drive, bathed in *jouissance*, transfigured, spiritualized and resplendent. Objects positioned in this way are referred to as 'sublime'. This term was elaborated by Lacan in a way that attaches the psychoanalytical concept of sublimation (in which we renounce the immediate satisfaction of a drive in favour of some other reward) to Kant's concept of the sublime (which contrasts its awesome, uplifting splendours with the less austere charms of the merely beautiful).

This conjuncture of philosophy and psychoanalysis is meat and drink to Žižek, whose work is full of 'sublime objects'. Thus *The Sublime Object of Ideology* analyses how any object, positioned against the real, can delude us with its seemingly compelling significance and impose its ideological imperatives on us. That is why we need to 'traverse the fantasy', and so discover how contingent their positioning is, how baseless their apparent authority. Popular culture abounds in objects which, located against the death drive, become suspended in an 'undead' state. They seem to have sublime bodies that are somehow exempted from ordinary mortality, like the robots in the *Terminator* films or the ghoulish inventions of Stephen King (*Looking Awry*, 21–7). Such objects are said to be 'between the two deaths', another phrase which Žižek takes from *Seminar* VII to refer to a particularly expressive form of the 'sublime' (and see Glossary, PERVERSION AND SUBLIMATION).

Lacan's first seminar on the object is *Seminar* IV. Later, in *Seminar* XX, he returns to mapping objects against the three registers of imaginary, symbolic and real. Plotting their relationships in a triangle, he identifies three abstract objects, or signifiers, designated algebraically as S($\cancel{A}$), Φ and a (*Seminar* XX, 90). These objects represent three different ways of compromising with the deficiencies in the imaginary and symbolic orders, and of holding out against (or succumbing to) the real of enjoyment which is positioned at their centre. These objects are entirely abstract; that is, they are not to be identified with actual real-world objects, but instead serve as theoretical co-ordinates which map our relations to such objects. Žižek reverts to this figure from *Seminar* XX at least four times in his writing on culture: in relation to Hitchcock (*Everything*, 5–10; *Sublime Object*, 182–7), Patricia Highsmith (*Looking Awry*, 133–7) and the cinematic representation of sex (*Plague*, appendix i). The triangle represents the way each of the orders of symbolic and imaginary relates to one another and to the real. Each of the three objects marks one of these relationships or, rather, its failure, and I shall briefly discuss each in turn.

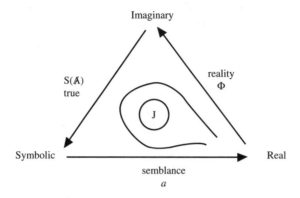

Figure 3.1   Reproduced from Lacan, *Seminar*, XX, 90.

S(Ⱥ) designates the point at which the symbolic is out of kilter with the seeming wholeness of the imaginary order. We may imagine that the world is full of naturally bestowed contents, but the symbolic is merely a tissue of differences *without* contents, and there is nothing to authorize its show of meaning. That is why 'the Other does not exist' and is said to be 'barred' and 'non all'. As we saw in the last chapter, this lack in the Other can be looked at within the dimension of the symbolic (from an idealist perspective) or it can be viewed (from a materialist one) as the failure of material singularities to add up to a consistent world of meaning. The object S(Ⱥ) is the signifier of this deficiency from either perspective; that is, S(Ⱥ) can coincide with the lack in the symbolic order, either disguising its inconsistency or else drawing attention to it. It is when it enforces itself on our attention in this way that it lives up to its name, which is 'the signifier of the barred Other'. In such cases, it may assume concrete form in what Žižek calls 'a little piece of the real': some resistant, excessive-seeming thing which both troubles the symbolic fabric that surrounds it and also appears to bind it together. An example from Hitchcock's films is the ring in *Shadow of a Doubt* which passes between the protagonists, Uncle Charlie and his niece Charlie, becoming ever more fascinating as the plot progresses. This ring is 'the piece of the real' that casts the 'shadow of doubt' over the film's narrative, provoking the development of the two characters' relationship and then destroying it.[10] (In chapter 4, we will see how this object is also associated with woman and with what Lacan calls 'feminine enjoyment'.)

Next, Φ is the point of failure of the imaginary to capture the real. The Greek letter, a capital phi, stands for the phallus which the child – in a supposition that has no basis in reality – ascribes to the mother. This imaginary maternal phallus has a privileged position in psychoanalytic theory, since it plays a starring role in the drama of 'castration'. Φ is the signifier of this non-existent signified. Because it results from the boy child's foolish overprivileging of his penis, Φ is also an object associated with masculine, idiotic, masturbatory enjoyment and, in Lacan's later thinking, with the *sinthome* that blocks the development of the sexual relationship. Strongly anchored in the imaginary and therefore, unlike S(Ⱥ), incapable of moving freely around in the symbolic system, it persists as an oppressive presence, 'a mute embodiment of an impossible *jouissance*' (*Everything*, 7). The example which Žižek gives of this object-apparition in Hitchcock's films is the birds in the film of that name which exercise a paralyzing effect on the protagonists. At times in Žižek's writing, Φ is the object whose position leads us to identify something as sublime. Any indifferent object can take on the arresting, captivating, fulfilling charm of the imaginary phallic object, which endows the symbolic with transcendental significance and purpose.

Finally, *a* – the *objet a* about which so much psychoanalytical writing turns – is the point at which the symbolic fails to represent the real, and is, as such, a mere gap or absence which nevertheless assumes significance for the subject. An example of an object which comes to occupy the place of the *objet a* is the formula of the aircraft engines which sets the plot of Hitchcock's *Thirty-Nine Steps* in motion: 'It is a pure semblance: in itself it is totally indifferent and, by structural necessity, absent; its signification . . . consists in the fact that it has some signification for others, for the principal characters of the story, that it is of vital importance to them.' (*Everything*, 6). The *objet a* is, of all psychoanalytical objects, the hardest to grasp. It is a pure deficit in the symbolic order that does not have any imaginary protrusion to fill it out (unlike Φ); nor (unlike S(Ⱥ)) does it betray an imaginary wholeness. Hence it is nothing but the rendering positive of a negative, of making an object out of what does not exist. As such, it acts like a vacuum, sucking other objects into its place. This has the effect of making any actual, real-world object on which our desire lights appear *après-coup* to be the goal of our desire. In fact, however, it is the gap held open by the *objet a* (the gap contingently occupied by the object in question) which creates the movement of desire in the first place. Hence the *objet a* is said to be the 'object-cause of desire'; and it is this, in itself meaningless, position that is adopted when an object becomes desirable. As the remainder, in the form of a nothing, of the *jouissance* that the symbolic order can achieve only in the form of a mysterious surplus, the *objet a* is also identified by Lacan with surplus enjoyment.

Of all the objects about which Žižek writes, the *objet a* is the one which preoccupies him most; and it features in numerous figures and mathemes which he takes from Lacan. Most notable of these is the formula of fantasy $ \$ \lozenge a $, which denotes that the *objet a* serves as a fantasmatic plug masking the split in the subject ($\$$). The *objet a* lies at the core of the fundamental fantasy, the earliest layer of fantasy which is laid down to cover over the trauma of the primordial repression provoked by 'castration'. Here its 'nothingness' is positivized as something infinitely precious, the invaluable treasure 'that is in me more than myself'; we have already seen it deployed in this way in the 'discourse of the hysteric'. The fact that it is nothing disguised as something matches exactly the trauma of castration, which, since it turns on the non-existent maternal phallus, is indeed a drama of nothing. A pervert, however, is one who gains so much satisfaction from surplus enjoyment, and indeed from 'castration', that he places all his sympathies on the side of the object (see *Plague, passim*, but esp. 35); Lacan's matheme of perversion is thus the opposite way round from his formula of fantasy, $ a \lozenge \$ $ in place of $ \$ \lozenge a $ (see Glossary, PERVERSION AND SUBLIMATION).

Objet a is the form of the object *par excellence*, and there are times in Žižek's writings when it serves for all the objects in Lacan's triangular figure. Thus, for example, in *Looking Awry* the opening chapters develop from a section entitled 'The Paradoxes of *Objet Petit a'* to describe phenomena perceived as 'a little piece of the real' or an 'answer of the real' (*Looking Awry*, 29–34), phenomena which will later be attributed to S($\cancel{A}$) (the button in the Highsmith story, *Looking Awry*, 134–6). Similarly, the *objet a* can be generalized to include the sublime (*Looking Awry*, 133).

All three objects – S($\cancel{A}$), Φ and a – communicate something of the *jouissance* at their centre and, at the same time, hold it at bay. By providing the co-ordinates for actual, real-world objects, they all serve to support our sense of 'reality', but they also trouble it with the uncanny menace of the real. It is Žižek's analysis of their role in the cinematic representation of sex, in his essay 'From the Sublime to the Ridiculous: The Sexual Act in Cinema' (*Plague*, 171ff), which perhaps brings out most clearly their implications for the subject. S($\cancel{A}$), he suggests, is the position to which the comic representation of sex approximates: it shows up the humorous gap between the experience we imagine sex to be and the way it is usually realized. Φ is identified by him as the position occupied by an image designed to fascinate and convey the pathetic aspect of the sexual experience; it evokes pathos or nostalgia for a lost wholeness. And *a* is the position of perverse representation: one which induces us to identify with a partial object within the scene, such as the gaze, as though the scene as a whole were being played for some subject other than ourselves. In the course of the essay, Žižek describes how pornographic films constantly slide between these three positions. As S($\cancel{A}$), pornography is split between maintaining narrative (usually comic or absurd) and graphically portraying sexual activity, always losing sight of one or the other; in its desperate attempt to 'show it all', pornography reveals its incapacity to do so. As Φ, pornography aspires to recapture a lost idyll, the total absence of inhibition in sexual experience before the Fall. But as *a*, finally, pornography commands the gaze; the presence of the camera, far from disturbing our enjoyment, enables it, since it includes us within the shameless picture, and provokes us to answering shamelessness. Via these three objects, then, we as subjects laugh, are stirred, or succumb to perverse enjoyment.

This overview of Žižek's account of the object shows, then, how the object correlates with the subject. The object acts as a necessary screen between the subject and the real. Through the positioning of objects, a sense of 'reality' is maintained. The imbalance between the symbolic, the imaginary and the real means that there is always an element of the real obtruding into this 'reality', on which 'reality' relies. If the imbalance becomes too precarious, however, then the real may irrupt into 'reality' and upset it. The pathological subjective structures corresponding to these three objects are obsessional neurosis (S($\cancel{A}$)), hysteria (Φ) and perversion (*a*) (*Sublime Object*, 185–7); when the protective screen offered by the objects is too weak, the real floods in, and the subject becomes psychotic.

Ultimately, the work of cultural artefacts – as Žižek sees it – is to explore the precariousness of this imbalance but, in the end, to save us from its worst consequences. That is, their role is to preserve for us a sense of how we arrived at what we understand by 'reality' and expose its construction without undermining it.

Cultural Analysis: Art, Film, Cyberspace

The following three examples of cultural objects show how the account I have just given of Žižek's psychoanalytical theory of the object is 'anamorphosed' and elaborated in his analysis of cultural artefacts.

The Hershey bar, Coca-Cola, and modernist art

In *The Metastases of Enjoyment* (179), Žižek borrows from an essay by Stephen Jay Gould to illustrate how the *objet a* is simultaneously vacuous and valuable. Sometimes the size of a Hershey chocolate bar goes up and sometimes it goes down, but overall it tends to get smaller. The price fluctuates too, but here the overall tendency is for it to go up. It should therefore be possible to calculate when 'that ultimate wonder of wonders, the weightless bar, will be introduced. . . . It will cost forty seven and a half cents' ('Phyletic Size Decrease', 317). Consumers will then pay to purchase a carefully wrapped void: a perfect metaphor for *objet a*. *The Fragile Absolute* (§3) fields a similar example. Coca-Cola is the ideal consumer good because it does nothing for you: it is neither nutritious nor thirst-quenching. Caffeine-free Diet Coke is the pitch of perfection, since it has managed to rid itself of every identifiable worthwhile ingredient. That is the reason why the more Coke you have, the more you want: it is the alluring form assumed by nothing, and thus the very incarnation of *objet a*. The advertising slogan, 'Coca-Cola is it', admits as much. This 'it' (as in the dreaded question 'Was that *it*?') gestures to an 'it' beyond representation to which our deepest desires are pinned.[11] The 'it' that is Coca-Cola is thus a nothing-remainder in 'reality' of an impossible real enjoyment. As such, Coke is a model of *objet a* in its role of surplus enjoyment: the *jouissance*-in-language which is all the change we get once we have 'paid' for subjectivity with 'castration'.

Seeing Coke as an *objet a* in this way offers Žižek a number of pathways into other areas: the Marxist notion of surplus value (on which surplus enjoyment is modelled) and the Lacanian notion of the superego (which is what drives us on to surplus enjoyment): 'The more Coke you drink, the thirstier you are; the more profit you make, the more you want; the more you obey the superego command, the guiltier you are – in all three cases, the logic of balanced exchange is disturbed in favour of an excessive logic "the more you give . . . the more you owe" ' (*Fragile Absolute*, 23–4). These parallels enable Žižek to consider the similarities between superego activity (the production of works of culture) and capitalist activity (the production of commodities). The commodification of culture – that is, the subordination of cultural production to the market – has long been identified as a trend of modern society, but just as evident is the converse process, 'the growing *"culturalization" of the market economy itself'* (*Fragile Absolute*, 25). Thus, says Žižek, while we buy more and more beautiful things for ourselves, our art galleries are filled with trash: exhibitions of used nappies, dead animals, etc. This mysterious exchange between what is excremental or trashy and what is beautiful and revered lies at the heart of what Lacan understands by the *objet a*. Indeed, such art enables us to revise our account of capitalism: what is essential to its economy is less the production of commodities than 'the permanent production of piles of discarded waste' (*Fragile Absolute*, 40).

The capitalistic fetishization of art objects – many of them literally body parts, like Damian Hurst's famous half-cow – could be an index of generalized perversion. (In *Seminar* IV Lacan called fetishism 'the perversion of perversions' (194), because it maximizes the subject's identification with a partial object, the maternal phallus.) Žižek goes on to argue that modernist art can nevertheless be seen as combating perversion rather than subscribing to it, since by displaying the abject as though it were sublime it calls attention to the whole problematic of sublimation.

In pre-modernist art, the sublime object was an object raised 'to the dignity of the Thing' (*Seminar* VII, 112). Such 'dignity' relies, however, on maintaining a certain distance between the symbolic order of representation and the forbidden, incestuous real beyond. What Lacan calls 'the Thing', the place where the real pressures the symbolic, has lost definition in the contemporary world as a result of the precariousness of our objects and the consequently greater invasion of 'reality' by the real. (Žižek implausibly ascribes to Courbet responsibility for single-handedly bringing down the classical sublime with his graphically obscene portrayal of the nude.[12]) Since then, the problem faced by modernist and postmodern art is that of maintaining some sense that there *is* a place to which art relates. The question which modernist art proverbially provokes – 'But is it art?' – is designed to address not the art object itself, but its suitability to the place in which it is found. Whereas the ambition of pre-modernist art was 'how to fill in the Void of the Thing (the pure Place) with an adequately beautiful object', the task assumed by artists today is that of *'creating* the Void in the first place' (*Fragile Absolute*, 26–7). It takes something which appears *out of place* (trash) to create the sense that *there is a place* for it to be at odds with.

The great achievement of modernist art is thus to maintain a minimal structure of sublimation, that is, 'the minimal gap between the Place and the element that fills it in' (*Fragile Absolute*, 31). What is defining of modernist art is not that its content is trashy, but that, through its form, it reflects on the problematic status of the sublime. This is why much abstract art (Žižek cites Kasimir Malevich) minimally evokes a sense of framing: a painted square within a square, for example, effects 'the pure formal marking of the gap which separates the Object from its Place' (*Fragile Absolute*, 32). Other avant-garde art displays an *objet trouvé*, such as Duchamp's famous urinal, *as though* it were a work of art, to underline the fact that 'anything, even shit, can "be" a work of art if it finds itself in the right Place' (*Fragile Absolute*, 33). In a sideways sally, Žižek suggests a correspondence between these developments in art and the Soviet construction of the leader: not admirable in himself, he becomes sublime as a result of the elaborate contrivances that make him so. Surprisingly, given Žižek's earlier championing of popular culture, *The Fragile Absolute* concludes with the claim that 'great art' offers us 'the magic moment when *the Absolute appears* in all its fragility' (159): that is, true art opens up the dimension of the sublime.

Hitchcock, Lynch, Kieślowski

Žižek has written a lot about these three directors; my comments concentrate on the way he sees each as manipulating the relation between reality and the real through their use of objects.

Hitchcock's films are uncanny, according to Žižek, because the menace they convey is not represented as external to everyday life, but is fed back into it 'as its "repressed" underside' (*Looking Awry*, 89). As a result, the whole surface of a Hitchcock film, although seemingly continuing to portray an untroubled world, becomes laden with unspoken danger, desire or guilt. But although this surface effectively disguises the repressed content most of the time, occasionally the hidden menace 'sticks out' in the form of an object which mesmerizes and disempowers the character confronted by it, and which acts as a kind of phallic blot (Φ) in the field of representation (*Looking Awry*, 91).

An example is provided by *Rear Window* (*Looking Awry*, 91–2), where the central character (James Stewart) fails to develop a relationship with Grace Kelly, but instead devotes all his energy to watching his neighbours' goings-on from his window. The 'blots' on this film are the stare turned on him by the wife-murderer (a gaze provoking the recognition that Stewart secretly envies him – he wishes *he* could kill Kelly) and the free-floating voice of the female singer, who alone of all the neighbours Stewart watches is never seen (and is associated by Žižek with the voice of an inhibiting maternal superego, as in *Psycho*). If, instead of disregarding these discordant intrusions or 'blots', we read the film through them, the seeming 'reality' of Stewart's neighbourhood dissolves. The various people he is observing become so many imaginings of the future that he and Kelly might have – as a humdrum married couple, or the newly-weds, or Kelly as Miss Lonely Hearts, and so on. These are the fantasized alternatives to Stewart's murdering Kelly, or being prevented from ever uniting with her by the incestuous maternal voice.

This reading illustrates the device of anamorphosis, whereby if we see 'reality', the real object is reduced to a blot or stain; but if we focus instead on the uncanny, what recedes is our sense of 'reality'. The price of seeing everyday reality is that we don't see the blot, even though this is in fact what frames and gives definition to reality. Žižek sees Hitchcock's tracking shots as drawing attention to this anamorphosis: 'the tracking movement can be described as a moving from an overall view of reality to its point of anamorphosis' (*Looking Awry*, 95). By thus emphasizing the distinction between the two perspectives, Hitchcock's films preserve the dimension of the sublime. The 'reality' they portray may be threatened by psychotic elements (the infantilizing mother) and perverse practices (such as voyeurism), but the blot serves to guarantee the perspective of the rest of the picture. Similarly, Hitchcock's use of montage manipulates the gaze (as in *Psycho*, where the house 'looks' back at Lilah) in such a way as to 'elevate an everyday, trivial object into a sublime Thing'. Without this, 'we . . . would have to endure a radical desublimation'; that is, we would have to face the abject real which remains when the sublime collapses (*Looking Awry*, 117). Hitchcock's films thus show how subjects maintains themselves, however precariously, in reality: namely, at the cost of *not seeing* something, the objects of fundamental fantasy by which that reality is defined.

David Lynch's films are altogether more brutal. Unlike Hitch-cock, Lynch does not offer a 'vertical' view of reality with its repressed, fantasmatic support; instead, the fantasy is placed 'hor-izontally' beside 'reality' (*Art*, 21), and is unflinchingly portrayed in all its horror, violently disrupting 'reality' and threatening to 'derealize' it. The tenor of Lynch's films, consequently, borders on the psychotic: 'Lynch's entire "ontology" is based upon the discordance between reality, observed from a safe distance, and the absolute proximity of the Real' (*Metastases*, 114; cf. *Enjoy!*, 129).

In his first essay on Lynch (*Metastases*, 113–36), Žižek sees the gestures towards orderliness in Lynch's narratives as symbolic and masculine, by contrast with the horrors of the real, gendered femi-nine; he suggests that *Blue Velvet*, for instance, is about the birth of subjectivity in Dorothy (Isabella Rosselini) from a kind of psychotic trance. The object which corresponds to this psychotic dimension is voice, 'a word . . . whose status is that of the *Real*' (*Metastases*, 116). Thus Lynch's sound-tracks are dominated by nonsensical noise that poses an unspecified threat to the characters; and Dorothy, of course, is a night-club singer. The Lynchian gaze, by contrast, is seen as participating in the perverse, rule-bound world of the symbolic. This is what guides Žižek's interpretation of the disturbing scene in *Blue Velvet* where Frank (Dennis Hopper) performs sadistic rituals with Dorothy while Jeffrey (Kyle MacLachlan) observes them from a closet. Is this Jeffrey's fantasy of the primal scene? Is he asuming the position of an impossible gaze witnessing his own begetting?[13] Or is it an act of exhibitionism by Frank? Žižek concludes that it should best be read as a provocation of Dorothy, aimed to shake her out of her depression (*Metastases*, 120–1).

Such sequences confirm the absence of Hitchcockian 'blot' from Lynch's films. Rather, Lynch practises what Žižek calls 'extraneation': the decomposition of 'reality' in such a way as to expose the fantasy and real elements that constitute it. However, it is precisely in this way, Žižek argues, that Lynch achieves what he calls the 'ridiculous sublime'. On the one hand we have the flimsy, absurd symbolic; and next to it we find the real, abominable Thing. In a way quite different from Hitchcock, yet with a certain kinship with him, Lynch has exposed the mechanism of sublimation without altogether dispensing with it.

Kieślowski is Žižek's most recent enthusiasm and the object of extended study in *The Fright of Real Tears*. Kieślowski began his career making documentary films, but found the intrusion it involved into the lives of other people unethical – his reluctance to film their 'real tears' is the source of Žižek's title (see *Fright*, 178) – and turned instead to fiction. Following this change of direction, his films, Žižek argues, are calculated to expose the way reality is itself a fiction (*Fright*, 66–8). Kieślowski achieves this effect via a 'horizontal' presentation in which competing 'realities' are placed side by side, in a way that resembles Lynch and contrasts with Hitchcock's 'vertical' repression. But, unlike Lynch, Kieślowski does not oppose order and horror, 'reality' and 'fantasy'; instead, in Kieślowski, 'reality' is 'spectralized' or 'de-realized' by its convergence with 'fantasy'. A good example is the Judge in *Three Colours: Red*, who appears *both* to be a real person in the film's diegetic reality *and* a 'spectral apparition, . . . someone who exists as [the central character's] fantasy creation' (*Fright*, 67). Similarly, Kieślowski devises plots in which the same character lives several alternative lives, as most obviously in *The Double Life of Veronica*. (This can be contrasted with *Rear Window* in Žižek's analysis, where Stewart's possible fantasy lives are clearly *not* part of the film's diegetic reality.) Kieślowski's fictionalization of reality is so complete, says Žižek, that his films deprive the term 'illusion' of its meaning. For there to be illusion, a reality is needed to contrast it with; but the spectralized flatness of Kieślowski's world dispenses with even the illusion of illusion (*Fright*, 68).

The equivalent of the Hitchcockian blot in Kieślowski's films is an obtrusion of the real 'which *remains (returns as) the same in all possible (symbolic) universes*' (*Fright*, 98), like the bottles of milk that recur throughout the *Decalogue*. But whereas in Hitchcock the blot acts as an anamorphosis, generating a perspective from which the rest of the film can be re-viewed, in Kieślowski, in Žižek's view, this return of the real is more akin to a Lacanian *sinthome*: a knot of enjoyment so resistant to the symbolic as to frustrate absolutely the attempt to interpret it.

Kieslowski's manipulation of the gaze, as analysed by Žižek, is also profoundly disquieting. Hitchcock's montage, whereby a subject approaches an object and the object 'gazes back', is uncanny. But Kieślowksi favours what Žižek calls 'interface': what we initially take to be a subjective shot reveals itself to be objective; the person we thought was viewing the scene on our behalf turns up in the frame. Žižek offers as an example of this the long close-up of Julie's eye at the beginning of *Blue*. Badly injured in a car accident in which her husband and daughter are killed, Julie is approached by a doctor, but we see him only as a reflection. Then we realize that the reflecting surface is Julie's own eye, which occupies almost the entire screen. By these means 'it is reality *itself* which is reduced to a spectre appearing *within* the eye's frame' (*Fright*, 52).

Thus Kieślowski is profoundly ambiguous about the nature of the sublime. He does not so much practise sublimation as analyse how it is produced. His exposure of the mechanisms whereby we construct reality emphasizes the contingency and inconsistency of the symbolic order. Thus, like the analyst, he knows that the symbolic order is inconsistent, 'non all', and he is not taken in by the radiant 'plug' of sublimation. On the other hand, again like the analyst, he is aware of the ethical value of the encounter with the real which is the consequence of this incompleteness in symbolic reality. His characters – like Veronica, unsure whether to look after her health or to pursue her career as a singer – are offered an ethical choice between life as mere continuation and mission as a response to the real. Another analysand-character, Julie in *Blue*, has a near-death experience which plunges her into subjective destitution and '*confront[s her] with the raw Real*' (*Fright*, 176). Later we see her rebuild the fantasy frame and so reconstitute a sense of reality. It seems, then, that Kieślowski leaves himself the choice of whether or not to close the non all fiction of the symbolic order by recourse to a sublime object. His priority is to point to the gap that may or may not be filled out by the sublime (*Fright*, 181).

Žižek's writings on film in general, and on these directors in particular, display a combination of theoretical brio and technical attentiveness. The psychoanalytic objects of voice and gaze serve to explore montage and sound-track, as well as vice versa. Psychoanalytic metaphors such as the 'framing' of reality by the real, or the use of fantasy objects as a 'screen', are literalized and explored in the analysis of film. *The Fright of Real Tears* offers his most painstaking analysis of cinematic technique and narrative construction to date. The theoretical consistency of approach, far from generating sameness in Žižek's analyses, finely differentiates one director from another, while his panoramic interests constantly draw their films into relation with other cultural, philosophical and political concerns.[14]

On several occasions Žižek compares the juxtaposition of narrative worlds by Lynch and Kieślowski with the opportunities for alternative experience offered by computers, whether in surfing the net or in computerized, 'virtual reality' games. These phenomena, grouped together in his writings in the term 'cyberspace', may,

Žižek suggests, have influenced their films. Since cyberspace has preoccupied Žižek since 1996 (*Indivisible Remainder*, 193–7; the earliest full essay is *Plague*, chapter 4), I include it as my final example of his cultural analysis.

Cyberspace and Oedipus

The sublime relies on a relationship to symbolic law that is neither perverse nor psychotic. This is because perversion takes the side of the object instead of 'raising it to the dignity of the Thing', whilst psychosis loses the distinction, essential to sublimation, between symbolic reality and the real. The pervert identifies with the surplus enjoyment in symbolic law (and so is, in a sense, too close to the law), while the psychotic is not subjectivized within the law at all.

Since, in a psychoanalytic reading, parental figures inscribe the subject's relationship with symbolic law, all Žižek's analyses of film are attentive to family relationships. Hitchcock, Lynch and Kieślowski, he contends (as we have seen), contrive somehow to maintain a toehold in the sublime, even if they see it in a state of collapse ('desublimation'), threatened by perverse and psychotic elements. Hitchcock's stifling mothers, the comic-horrific fathers of enjoyment in Lynch (*Art*, 35) and Kieślowski's passive, dreamy fathers (*Fright*, 128, 163), all contribute to the precariousness of sublimation in the films made by their respective directors. What relation do we have to symbolic law in cyberspace?[15] Žižek's answers to this question ring the changes on different psychoanalytical structures from the 'best' (the hysteric's quest for the sublime object) to the worst (psychosis).

In some respects, he suggests, cyberspace epitomizes the symbolic order. 'Virtual reality' does not so much exist in contrast with 'reality' as reveal that 'reality' is already a construct of fantasy. After all, the prop of the symbolic law is 'castration', which, as the non-existent loss of a non-existent member, is about as virtual as it gets (hence 'castration' is 'the supreme example of symbolic virtuality': *Plague*, 150). Cyberspace might be said to draw attention to this gap on which symbolization depends, and show us that '(symbolic) reality always-already was 'virtual', that is to say: *every access to (social) reality has to be supported by an implicit phantasmatic hypertext*' (*Plague*, 143; cf. *Indivisible Remainder*, 195). From this perspective, cyberspace would be thoroughly on the side of the Oedipal law. A likely subjective position with respect to it, therefore, would be that of the hysteric: overawed by the symbolic mandate, uncertain what place to assume in the symbolic network, treating the whole structure as a fiction, the hysteric is nevertheless persuaded that somewhere within it there exists a sublime treasure ('Is it Possible to Traverse the Fantasy in Cyberspace?', 113–16). Cyberspace, then, might be capable of maintaining us, along with Hegel and other theorists, in the role of Žižek's hysterical heroes.

There is a drawback to this analysis, however. As we have seen, the coherence of 'reality' depends on its being disturbed by some intrusion on the part of the real. This is what preserves the sense of distance between ourselves and our world, and a sense of perspective on it. We have seen how the sublimity of films by Hitchcock and Kieślowski depends on the presence in them of some kind of 'blot'. Where would the 'blot' be on the screen of cyberspace? The computer screen does not operate around a blind spot. But without something distorting the field of vision, reality is no longer held at a distance from the real; it risks becoming indistinguishable from (psychotic) hallucination (*Plague*, 133). Another way of putting this is that, in cyberspace, appearance gives way to simulacrum: instead of the symbolic depth offered by appearance, which reassures us that there is a 'beyond' to what appears, we have the imaginary flatness of mere simulacrum.[16] In other words, the 'gap' of virtual castration risks being closed with excessive, imaginary fullness.

One index of what Žižek calls this 'unbearable closure of being' is the apparently limitless choices that cyberspace offers. Without the phenomenon of 'forced choice' and the renunciation it imposes, the symbolic order is no longer in place (*Plague*, 153). From this standpoint, cyberspace threatens a collapse of symbolic efficacy that is psychotic and anti-Oedipal in the sense of 'no longer relying on the paternal symbolic authority' (*Indivisible Remainder*, 196).

There is a third possibility, however, though not one which is necessarily more alluring. With the decline of the symbolic master/father, we risk a shift from the symbolic law to rule by the father of perversion (Lacan's *père-vers*), the superego. If the subject follows the superego command to enjoy himself at all costs, he may use cyberspace to explore all kinds of experimental self-fashioning ('Is it Possible?', 112–13). In terms of psychic structures, the perverse subject objectifies *himself*, making himself the object-instrument of the Other, rather. He identifies with the hidden point of enjoyment in the workings of the law, rather than positioning himself as subject to the law (*Plague*, 159). The way this could be realized in cyber-

space is through the (perverse) treatment of it as a 'universe of pure
symbolic order, of the signifier's running its course, unencumbered
by the Real of human finitude' ('Is it Possible?', 117). For example,
internet chat-rooms offer the possibility of assuming any and every
kind of fantasy identity, however at odds with a person's social and
biological make-up; once in cyberspace, we need never be old or
limited as to our gender and sexuality.

In his most recent writing on cyberspace (from 'Is it Possible?'
onwards), Žižek proposes a fourth, more optimistic possibility.
Perhaps we can profit from this play with fantasy offered to
the subject by cyberspace by using it as a means to 'traverse the
fantasy'. That is, cyberspace might enable us to confront the 'fundamental fantasy' and recognize it for what it is: a contingent imposition of fixity and consistency on the otherwise empty place of the
subject. Whereas other cultural artefacts can reflect on the problematics of subject formation in relation to the object, cyberspace,
as an interactive medium, offers the subject an opportunity to *act*.
The centrality of this notion to Žižek's ethical and political thinking
will be explored in chapters 5 and 6.

Conclusions

Žižek's studies of cyberspace epitomize his thinking about culture
in general. Culture consists in the organization of objects and the
way these frame subjectivity. In this way, it stages the complex
relationship between reality and the real. At its most sophisticated,
culture also reflects on how this staging works. Paintings and films
can show how certain key objects act as obtrusions of the real that
enable us to maintain the screen of fantasy. In this way, cultural
artefacts both warn of, and ward off, psychosis, in which reality
collapses into hallucination because our psychic 'real' and the outer
'reality' are no longer differentiated. Cultural artefacts instruct
us, too, in the alternative paths offered by sublimation and perversion, which depend on the position of the subject relative
to the object. As a result, cultural production revolves especially
around the *objet a*. Through it we may come to recognize the
structure of our own enabling fantasy and begin again from zero.
In sum, the work of culture presents, via anamorphosis, the work
of analysis.

The examples considered here provide a sense of Žižek's cultural
range without, however, doing justice to it. I have said nothing

about music, for instance, although he writes compellingly about Wagner (e.g. *Tarrying*, chapter 5, and most recently at length in *Opera's Second Death*), Schumann (*Plague*, appendix II), Shostakovich (*Did Somebody Say?* 123–7) and much else. Nor have I done more than allude to his extensive knowledge of literature.

In another respect these examples are far from representative. By including modernist art and cyberspace alongside cinema, I have masked Žižek's overwhelming preference for narrative, whether in film, prose fiction or opera. It is striking how Žižek concentrates on this mode, given that, from an analytical point of view, he condemns it. Like Lacan, he thinks that narrative dissimulates the radical contingency and flimsiness of the symbolic order; it embodies, naturalizes and fixes fantasy in a way that can only block analytical progress (see e.g. *Plague*, 10–13; *Indivisible Remainder*, 93–5). Thus Žižek embraces in culture a mode that, in theory, cries out to be dismantled.

One reason for this predilection, perhaps, is that narrative is the mode which prevails in mass culture, for which Žižek's early books show a refreshing enthusiasm. Both *Looking Awry* and *Enjoy Your Symptom!* display encyclopaedic knowledge of, and liking for, popular American cinema; and Žižek's taste in fiction is just as appealingly catholic. It is in this spirit, for instance, that Shakespeare is treated as a 'kitsch' author: the more accessible the work, the better it lends itself to the anamorphosis of Žižek's theoretical interests and the 'staging' of theoretical problems (*Looking Awry*, 3). This warmth towards the popular marks a major divergence from Adorno, with whose interests Žižek otherwise has much in common, but who was uncompromisingly contemptuous of mass culture.[17]

However, by *The Plague of Fantasies*, Žižek's position has changed. He concedes that 'popular melodrama and kitsch are much closer to fantasy than "true art"' (*Plague*, 20), which gives them the edge when analysing ideology. But 'true art' has the advantage of exposing the fantasy for the fiction that it is. Thus, for instance, popular art might display a relationship as prohibited, whereas 'true art' would reveal it as impossible. The scare quotes around 'true art' betray Žižek's unease with the expression, and indeed the example immediately following opposes *M.A.S.H.* as a popular film to nothing more elevated than Kubrick's *Full Metal Jacket*. But later again, in *The Fragile Absolute*, 'true art' mutates into 'great art': this is now the gateway to the sublime, 'the magic moment when *the Absolute appears* in all its fragility' (*Fragile Absolute*, 159).

Interesting light is thrown on Žižek's conception of 'popular culture' by his discussion of opera. Chapter 5 of *Tarrying with the Negative* is an oasis of readability in this generally dense and difficult book. Žižek's argument rests on the fact that the development of the modern subject, from Descartes to Freud, is contemporary with the rise of opera; it focuses on how opera stages the subject's relation to the Other. Analyses of individual operas, especially Wagner's *Parsifal*, are entertainingly interlaced with discussion of modern films. It is striking, however, that twentieth-century opera is entirely overlooked: as soon as cinema becomes available, opera is forgotten. Clearly, in this book which lays claim to historical analysis, opera is needed to fly the flag of 'popular culture' in the period before cinema. If opera can plug this gap, if it is the 'cinema before cinema', this implies that 'cinema is the new opera'.[18] However, opera's credentials as 'popular culture', at least today, are pretty dubious. In their recent *Opera's Second Death*, Žižek and Dolar start out by admitting that 'from its very beginning, opera was dead . . . perceived as something outdated . . . in its very concept' (pp. viii–ix). All this prompts the question, how 'popular' is Žižek's 'culture' really?

Although Žižek loves to flirt with American culture, his tastes, I believe, are fundamentally those of a European intellectual. Hitchcock and Chaplin were fashionable in Paris in the 1980s, where they were adopted as Leftist cultural icons. Žižek's transition from Hitchcock to Kieślowski seems less abrupt once the mediation of Paris is taken account of, and his French collaborator, the film theorist Michel Chion, wrote a book on Lynch as long ago as 1992. If France contributes a certain slant on cinema, it also furnishes Žižek's main theoretical reference points: primarily Lacan, of course, and his own analyst and supervisor Miller, but also Althusser, Badiou, Deleuze, Derrida and Foucault, as well as leading film theorists like Chion and Christian Metz. Germany, in turn, is represented by Mozart and Wagner and by the great procession of philosophers: Kant, Schelling, Hegel, Fichte, Marx, the Frankfurt School and Heidegger. Aside from these cardinal references, Žižek's interests, whether in modernist American art or pulp fiction, are all consonant with those of a highbrow European. Latterly his taste in cinema is unambiguously arthouse.

Žižek's Continental European stance helps to explain his uneasy relationship with Anglo-American Cultural Studies, even though this is, in some sense at least, the field to which he has contributed most extensively. As early as 1991, in an interview in *Radical*

Philosophy, Žižek offered 'comradely criticisms' of the use made in British film theory of the Lacanian terms 'suture' and 'gaze'.

> The way the idea of suture operates here is incredible. It is precisely the reverse of Lacan. It is used to mean the bad thing, the representation, the closure. Lacan's point is much more dialectically refined. For him the suture is not just the moment of closure but also that which sustains openness. . . .
>
> The problem of the gaze is, I think, an even bigger one. The way the Lacanian problematic of the gaze works here in England is mediated through Foucault's work on the panopticon: for the male gaze the woman is reduced to an object, etc. Whereas for Lacan it is the opposite: the gaze is the object, it is not on the side of the subject . . .
> If there is something totally alien to Lacan it is the idea that the male position is that of the gaze that objectifies woman. ('Lacan in Slovenia', 27)

Such strictures have become noticeably more uncomradely, and targeted at a broader (notably US) audience as time goes on.[19] From having been the darling of Cultural Studies, Žižek is now described as their *bête noire*.[20] And a backlash against a Žižekian approach to culture is also manifest in the recent *Post-Theory* volume, which is decidedly anti-European, and evinces particular hostility to psychoanalytic film theory.[21]

To return to the starting point of this argument, then, invoking popular culture does not explain Žižek's predilection for narrative; he is not really 'in' Cultural Studies, and his interests are not noticeably 'popular' any longer. We must accept, I think, that he is susceptible to the seductions of the narrative mode, even though, on theoretical grounds, he is committed to disparaging it. Perhaps this is an instance where culture as anamorphosis does not just continue in a contrasting register the theory with which he is concerned, but also exposes a degree of antagonism between them (cf. *Enjoy!*, 113).

Another aspect of Žižek's treatment of culture that is at odds with his Lacanian convictions is his zeal to interpret. Lacan is wary of interpretation, repeatedly warning his seminar against precipitate understanding. He affects symbols and formulae because they eschew semantic content, reducing thought to compass point and outline. It is thus a very Lacanian note that Žižek strikes when he declares, of commentaries on Balkan politics, 'One should . . . put in parenthesis the multitude of meanings, the wealth of the spectres of the past which allow us to "understand" the situation. . . . It is only such a suspension of "comprehension" that renders possible the analysis of what is at stake ... in the post-Yugoslav crisis' (*Plague*, 62). But this is not at all how he himself proceeds when faced with a cultural artefact. On the contrary, he greets it with wave upon wave of interpretation, each unfurling in such a way as to overtake the one before and overwhelm the reader with the brilliance of its 'comprehension', thereby generating a perplexing 'multitude of meanings' Again, then, we find antagonism between the theory and its cultural anamorphosis.

A third inconsistency between theory and practice in Žižek's writing about culture concerns his use of history. Although in principle committed to a historical analysis, the historical framework which he brings to the analysis of culture is often crude. In theory, Žižek dismisses both the reflective view of culture ('art is a reflection of its historical context') and the *Zeitgeist* account ('art, like other aspects of its period, is a product of the spirit of the age'; see *Enjoy!*, 113); but in practice he looks for precisely this kind of conjunction between cultural phenomena and historical conditions. Thus interpretation is often led by assumptions about periodization ('pre-modern', 'modern', 'postmodern'). Žižek's 'pre-modern' is particularly vaguely sketched (for instance, it is readily conflated with the 'traditional'); but his use of history in general is always very broad brush, and he seems as willing to flout as to invoke it when it suits his argument.

Where Žižek's analyses are at their best is, however, thoroughly Lacanian: namely, when he shows how cultural products expose their own mechanisms, and thus perform the work of analysis. In this way, cultural artefacts make visible, in anamorphosis, the relation of our symbolic and imaginary reality to the real. Žižek extends this approach beyond Lacan when he uses culture in the critique of ideology and the exploration of philosophical issues. He thereby produces a psychoanalytical account of what we would call 'representation' which completely dismantles a conventional understanding of it. Any perception of reality, Žižek argues, relies on its point of inherent failure. Unless there is a remainder of the real to spoil the picture, we cannot see it; if the lack of fit between reality and the real is eliminated, we lose all sense of reality; this applies equally to works of culture and our everyday perceptions. Hence, to take the enjoyment of culture as our substance deepens our understanding of theory, our troubled subjectivity, and our relation to the world around us.

4

The Real of Sexual Difference: Imagining, Thinking, Being

The last chapter began with Žižek's description of his project as a Borromean knot (*For They Know Not*, 2). The image is misleading in one respect: Žižek's writing certainly doesn't have the clean lines of a knot. It is more of a Sadean montage: theatrical, knowing, sexy, transgressive, troubling. Sexual situations are sometimes described in overtly Sadean terms. This account of pornography from *The Plague of Fantasies*, for instance, performs the very provocation and dehumanization it describes:

> This change of the body into a desubjectivized multitude of partial objects is accomplished when, for example, a woman is in bed with two men and does fellatio on one of them . . . [her] face is turned upside-down, and the effect is one of an uncanny change of the human face, the seat of subjectivity, into a kind of impersonal sucking machine being pumped by the man's penis. The other man is meanwhile working on her vagina, which is also elevated above her head and thus asserted as an autonomous centre of *jouissance* not subordinated to the head. The woman's body is thus transformed into a multitude of 'organs without a body', machines of *jouissance*, while the men working on it are also desubjectivized, instrumentalized, reduced to workers serving these different partial objects. (*Plague*, 180)

No specific film is cited; so is this pornographic tableau actually Žižek's own creation? Such writing can seem provocative, not to say crass; and *The Plague of Fantasies* is especially prone to it. Starting from observations about lavatory design, working in homophobic reminiscences from Žižek's Yugoslav army days (24–5), reflecting uncomfortably on rape (184–9), and playing a strip-tease with fantasy whose seven veils are progressively removed in chapter 1, the book constantly reverts to the anal, heterosexist, misogynist swagger that many readers of Žižek understandably object to.

Most outspoken in this respect has been Judith Butler, whose initial critique of Žižek appeared in *Bodies that Matter* (187–222). Since then, Žižek seems to have gone out of his way to script himself as Butler's obscene, macho counterpart. She attacks hate speech, and he rails against political correctness; she is sympathetic to identity politics, he denounces it as a capitalist trap; she critiques Lacan's account of sexual difference, whereas he elevates it to a central principle of philosophy; she calls for 'a critical rethinking of the "feminine"' (*Bodies that Matter*, 189), while he inveighs against 'feminists'.

One strand of Žižek's writing about sexual difference, then, is pugnacious and, not infrequently, salacious. A converse feature, however, is that often when he is ostensibly writing about women, they disappear from view. His essay 'Why Is *Woman* a Symptom of Man?' (*Enjoy!*, 31–67) can easily leave you none the wiser; there isn't much in it that is obviously about women at all. Similarly, although *The Metastases of Enjoyment* is subtitled *Six Essays on Woman and Causality*, the theme of causality is initially much more explicit, and its connection with 'Woman' (or women) remains opaque. Žižek's writing about sexual difference tends likewise to be more obviously about difference than sexuality; chapters 2–4 of *Tarrying with the Negative* contain his lengthiest consideration of Lacan's formulae of sexuation, but are mostly about philosophy.

To understand Žižek's discussions of sexuality and gender, we need to know more about the account of sexual difference on which they turn. His main source is Lacan's *Seminar XX*, where 'masculinity' and 'femininity' are presented as two conflicting and internally contradictory attempts on the part of human beings to symbolize their relation to 'castration'. 'There is no such thing as a sexual relationship', according to Lacan (*Seminar XX*, 34), because these two attempts are neither the same as each other, nor yet complementary, but heterogeneous and incompatible. It is as though two people set about decorating the room they have to share but, instead of working in concert, one wallpapers some of the room, while the other paints other parts of it in a clashing colour. Their combined efforts both overlap and miss bits out, and each is inher-

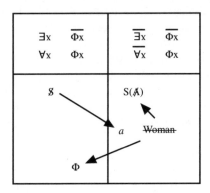

Figure 4.1 Reproduced from Lacan, *Seminar* XX, 78. The translators note that 'the top four formulas in the table had already been presented by Lacan in *Seminars* XVIII and XIX'.

ently botched, with at least one length of wallpaper being pasted on upside down, while the paint is all smeary – such is the domestic tragi-comedy of human sexuation as Lacan sees it. This absence of co-ordination between 'masculine' and 'feminine' positions is what gives rise to 'the real of sexual difference' – the primary way of theorizing the real in Žižek's writings, despite his recent turn towards the 'real of capital' or a 'Christian real'.

In the figure Lacan uses to summarize this sorry state of affairs, the analysis is presented on two levels. The top level, containing the formulae proper, uses symbolic logic to differentiate a 'masculine' (left) and a 'feminine' position (right) within the symbolic order. I shall return to these later; essentially, the masculine one is represented in my example by the wallpaper (with at least one aberrant length), and feminine one by the paintwork (which is 'non all' and doesn't cover the wall properly). The bottom level disposes, on the two sides of the table, a set of relations between the barred subject $, and the series of objects – S($\bar{A}$), Φ and a – which we have already encountered in figure 3.1.

As discussed in chapter 3 (pp. 54–8), these objects provide the co-ordinates for the way we perceive what we call 'reality'. Φ objects are associated with phallic enjoyment and the blocking effects of the symptom or *sinthome*; S($\bar{A}$) objects can be 'little pieces of the real' and relate to feminine enjoyment; and a is the marker of elusive fantasy objects, objects of desire, and objects of the drive. The triangular arrangement of these objects in figure 3.1 emphasizes how the effect of 'reality' is generated through a series of approximations between the symbolic, imaginary and real orders against the background of our *jouissance*. Their disposition in two columns in figure 4.1, on the other hand, makes explicit that this 'reality' is filtered through a sexual lens, and that these objects are also what determine subject positions. In essence, it shows how subjectivity is riven by sexual difference and bound up with fantasies, symptoms and our problematic relation to enjoyment.

Žižek's talk of sexual difference has been accused of crassness, but the obscurities of figure 4.1 seem, by contrast, to expose it to the objection of being abstruse! To anticipate the direction my argument in this chapter will take, I think that this very contradiction encapsulates the difficulty of theorizing sexual difference. Such theorizing always gives offence to someone; it is always, in some respect, too much or too little, and it is this nagging dissatisfaction, this uneasy irritant, that is 'the real of sexual difference' which Žižek's writing conveys. Ultimately, that is, his writing performs what it claims: there can be no way of wholly accounting for sexual difference, because it is what prevents language itself from being a whole to which we can all accede. This is the stumbling block of 'the real', and as I try to trace the outlines of Žižek's thought, I cannot expect to avoid it either.[1]

To go back, then, to figure 4.1: to do justice to Žižek's arguments, we must try to understand the theoretical distinctions which it maps. This chapter will look at the way its various objects define our fantasies, symptoms and subjectivity, before proceeding to the analysis enshrined in the formulae proper. That is, it will begin from the objects in the lower part of figure 4.1 which ascribe content to sexual difference before looking at the formulae which analyse that difference. Only then will it be helpful to move on to Žižek's debate with Butler, and form a judgement on the hostile response he often provokes even from readers who don't identify themselves among his target groups of 'feminists' and the politically correct. I hope to show that his interests lie less with the content of sexual difference (that is, the identification of individuals as 'men' or 'women' in the real world) than with the conflict and struggle to which sexuation gives rise. He is concerned with subjection in its philosophical and political, if not its more obviously social, sense. On this terrain, while feminists are unlikely to be able to claim him, they may none the less be able to use him.

Fantasy

Fantasy is what shapes our desire. Žižek's best illustration of how sexual difference works in fantasy is a television advertisement for beer. A girl finds a frog, picks it up, and kisses it, whereupon it turns into a beautiful young man. The young man turns to her and kisses her, whereupon she turns into a bottle of beer. The woman's desire makes the frog into the phallic object Φ, which is her fantasy of what man is; but the man reduces the woman to the fantasy *objet a*, the instrument of his satisfaction and object-cause of his desire. Žižek comments as follows: 'On account of this asymmetry, "there is no sexual relationship": we have either a woman with a frog or a man with a bottle of beer – what we can never obtain is the "natural couple" of the beautiful woman and the beautiful man' (*Indivisible Remainder*, 163; cf. *Plague*, 74). Despite the piquancy of this example, Žižek concentrates overwhelmingly on masculine fantasies of women. These are represented in figure 4.1 by the relation $ – a$, which recalls the matheme of fantasy $ ◊ a (and like it, is capable of reversing into the perverse relation $a ◊ $). I will concentrate here on two fantasies that recur again and again in his writings: the lady in courtly love and the *femme fatale* of *noir* cinema.

Žižek gets his ideas on courtly love partly from Lacan's *Seminars* (principally VII and XX) and partly from rather vague received ideas about the Middle Ages; he gives no impression of ever having read a medieval poem. However, Lacan *had* read some of the troubadours, and his ideas have proved fruitful, both in their original presentation and as reconfigured by Žižek.[2]

In 'Courtly Love or Woman as Thing' (*Metastases*, 89–112), Žižek both expounds and reverses Lacan's account. Lacan described courtly love as an anamorphosis because it makes visible the normally invisible mechanism of sublimation. To identify woman as Thing means to make of her a sublime object, aligning her fantasy image with the limit of the symbolic (the point at which the symbolic undergoes the pressure of the real) that Lacan calls the Thing. As a result of this sublime configuration of the symbolic and the imaginary with the deathly drives behind them, the lady appears radiant, all-powerful and quasi-divine, but also, at the same time, implacable, inhuman and lethal. In short, she is both idealized and horrifying. The real is unattainable not because of some hindrance or obstacle, it is so absolutely and by definition; likewise, the troubadour's depiction of the lady reveals her as not unavailable

accidentally but as *impossible* to attain. Lacan considers that, by sub-
mitting to such a figure, the troubadour makes visible the way
which desire situates its object against the vacuole of the Thing. This
in turn reveals that the object *in itself* is not the cause of desire so
much as *where* it is located. The poem Lacan studies manifests particularly graphically the misfit between the object and its place, and
the consequent failure of the lady adequately to mask the horror of
the Thing. An anti-feminist satire by the troubadour Arnaut Daniel,
it debates whether one should lick one's lady's behind if she com-
mands; hence Lacan's sardonic rejoinder, 'blow in that for a while
and see if your sublimation holds up' (*Seminar* VII, 215). The point
of Lacan's reading is to show that the medieval poem, like the
works of culture discussed in the last chapter, shares the same
perception of psychic mechanisms as psychoanalysis.

Žižek takes over Lacan's account in so far as he accepts that
courtly love is a way of combining 'sublime' closure in the symbolic
with the real of enjoyment. By elevating his lady 'to the dignity of
the Thing', the courtly lover discovers a way of making sense of
everything (service of his beloved imparts a moral and social
purpose to his universe), and this, at the same time, gives him a
thrill. But Žižek also turns Lacan's analysis on its head by asserting
that the lover's relation to the lady is not sublime but perverse. By
elaborately codifying his submission to the erotic object, the courtly
lover – like the masochist – objectifies himself in the service of love,
and gets his kicks from observing its rituals. By these means, he
foreshadows our modern proclivity to perversion as he releases
upon himself the full charge of surplus enjoyment (the enjoyment
borne *within* the symbolic law).[3] The courtly lady, then, is a perverse
fantasy, and as such as vital a part of our imaginary today as she
was in the Middle Ages.

The *femme fatale* of *noir* cinema is, for Žižek, a modern version of
the courtly lady, 'the traumatic Woman-Thing who, through her
greedy and capricious demands, brings ruin to the *hard-boiled* hero'
(*Metastases*, 102). She is 'fatal' not just in the sense that she is bad
news but also in the sense that she represents fatality: she is his
fantasy of the deathly implacability of the drive (*Looking Awry*, 66).
The courtly lady is an object of *desire*, both prohibited and made
desirable by the symbolic father of Oedipal law; the courtly lover
decorously manipulates this law to milk it of its surplus enjoyment.
The *femme fatale*, however, is more evidently an object of the *drive*,
which courses obscenely under the cover of the symbolic law and
is related in Lacan's thought to a quite different father. This

'obscene, uncanny, shadowy double of the Name of the Father' (*Enjoy!*, 158), elsewhere known as the superego, the perverse father (Lacan's *père-vers*), or the father of *Totem and Taboo*, wields power not through absence and the word like the symbolic father, but through his overbearing presence and overt power.[4]

In the *noir* universe, Žižek observes, the 'fatal' dimension of the *femme fatale* depends on this figure of the obscene father, typically represented by the domineering, cruel, gangland boss whose moll she is. When he is present, he is the 'fatal' one with the power to dispose of her (and others) as he wishes; she becomes 'fatal' only when separated from him. Žižek infers from this that the male protagonist of the *noir* fantasy identifies with the obscene father; the 'Woman-Thing' is simply one of the forms which this figure adopts, and 'nothing but a lure whose fascinating presence masks the true traumatic axis of the *noir* universe, the relationship to the obscene father' (*Enjoy!*, 160, 168).

The obscene father's importance in the *noir* world shows how the fantasy of the *femme fatale*, like that of the courtly lady, reveals the continuum between sublimation and perversion. The father-enjoyment is the fantasized exception to the general law of 'castration'. To identify with him, or with the *femme fatale* as his avatar, is to disavow 'castration' and cling instead to the delusion that man can resist the subjection and death that are the consequences of the symbolic law (*Art*, 35–6). Sometimes a *noir* narrative ends with the protagonist uniting with the *femme fatale*, and in such cases the deathliness of the drive she embodies will overtake them both (as in the film *Double Indemnity*). But if he can bring himself to reject her, as Sam Spade does Brigid O'Shaughnessy at the end of *The Maltese Falcon*, then her fascination is shattered, and the symbolic law restored. Thus, Žižek argues, the *femme fatale* does not incarnate a threat to patriarchy; she is not, as has been argued, a mythic expression of female sexual aggression rising up to challenge male dominance. On the contrary, she is patriarchy's fantasmatic support, because she is conjured into existence *in order that* the 'normal' Oedipal rule can be reasserted over and against the obscene father (*Art*, 9–10; *Enjoy!*, 169).

Both the courtly lady and the *femme fatale* are figures of masculine fantasy, and as such they tell us more about men than they do about women (cf. *Indivisible Remainder*, 155–6). Both fantasies slide from the sublime into the perverse, and in their perverse guise involve relationships of overt power and domination. Žižek's early interest in such fantasies foreshadows his later argument that the 'fundamental fantasy' relates not to sexual difference but to something prior even to that: existence as subjection (see below).

Symptom

Žižek's interpretation of the *femme fatale* changes more than does that of the medieval courtly lady, probably because he knows more about her. In *Enjoy Your Symptom!* the *femme fatale* is first considered as a symptom; then this reading (his own earlier one from *Looking Awry*) is rejected, and the case for fantasy is advanced instead. The identification of the *femme fatale* as a symptom involves Žižek exploring one of Lacan's more enigmatic *obiter dicta* according to which 'Woman is a symptom of man'.[5] What does he mean by this?

A psychoanalytic symptom is not just like a medical one, a sign that betrays the existence of some underlying disturbance, though it is that too. It is also a way in which the subject denies and fends off enjoyment by delegating it to, for example, a limb or a repeated pattern of behaviour. In this way, unlike a fantasy, which seals over the split in the subject and conceals its relation to enjoyment, the symptom draws attention to the existence of this split and presents its enjoyment for the Other to see. In Lacan's later thinking, the symptom becomes the *sinthome*, the manifestation of the subject's enjoyment which he cannot give up but should embrace as 'what is in him more than himself'. At this point, its symbolic dimension declines, and the subject's imaginary relation with enjoyment correspondingly increases in importance. (See also Glossary, SYMPTOM, and Žižek's entry 'Symptom' in Wright, *Feminism*.)

As we saw in the last section, the masculine subject's fantasy relation with 'woman' is represented in the lower part of figure 4.1 by the line joining $\$$ and a. The idea that 'woman' is man's symptom is expressed by the link between the feminine and the phallic object Φ, and by the implicit pairing, on the masculine side of the figure, of $\$$ with Φ. For 'woman' to be man's symptom, rather than his fantasy, is thus for her to be both his message to the Other and his imaginary relation to enjoyment. This means that man can communicate his symbolic existence, and relate to the real of his being, only through woman, whereas the converse is not true: woman exists independently of man. ' "Woman is a symptom of man" means that *man himself exists only through woman qua his symptom*;

all his ontological consistency hangs on, is suspended from his symptom, is "externalized" in his symptom' (*Enjoy!*, 155).

Such an explanation, however, may well seem as enigmatic as what it purports to explain. It might suggest, but certainly does not mean, that any individual man can exist only as a result of having a relationship with an individual woman. I think Žižek's meaning is rather that, among speaking beings, the possibility of an 'I' assuming the masculine position presupposes that there are others who have taken up the feminine position. That is, in order for there to be what we call 'men', there need to be beings ('women') whose relationship to enjoyment is organized sufficiently differently for them to embody it on behalf of the 'men'. (These distinctions need not correspond with biological 'men' or 'women', a point to which I shall return later.) 'Men's' inability to do this themselves produces *après-coup* the perception that 'women' are the symptom of their failure. The very fact that there is a symbolic order in which we can speak of 'men' and 'women' arises as an after-effect of the occluded relation to enjoyment on which it relies (cf. *Tarrying*, 58).

Žižek's brilliant essay on detective fiction (*Looking Awry*, 60–6) offers a symptomatic reading of the *femme fatale*. She stands for the implacability of the real and an 'unreserved acceptance of the death drive'; she is an external embodiment (or 'symptom') of the detective's own relation to the real of the drive. If the hero rejects her, then instead of reinstating symbolic law (the reading advanced when the *femme fatale* was read in the context of fantasy), he loses this crucial relation to the real (*Looking Awry*, 63).

Žižek also reads Freud's contemporary Otto Weininger as supporting the perception that 'woman is the symptom of man'. Weininger was an extreme anti-feminist, who thought that man's essential spirituality is compromised by woman. The essence of woman, for Weininger, is to embody sex. She is nothing but the materialization of man's temptation to succumb to sexual sin and so betray his spiritual nature. According to Weininger, if man can turn away from woman, she will vanish back into nothing. Take away Weininger's moralistic attitude and, says Žižek, you have a position which is very close to Lacan's (*Enjoy!*, 154; *Metastases*, chapter 6). Weininger was unable to face up to his own insight, however, and committed suicide at the young age of twenty-four. Since suicide is the feminine act *par excellence* (see below), this shows how 'woman' was more truly his symptom than he knew.

What about the woman in all this? Is being 'a symptom of man' a satisfying career for an ambitious girl? The crucial, but surprising, point in Žižek's understanding of Lacan is that this capacity on the part of the feminine to be the symptom of man is precisely what makes *her* the true subject, the distinguishing feature of which is its openness to the real of the drive (*Looking Awry*, 64). He thus values the feminine subject more than its masculine counterpart. In short, the formula 'Woman is a symptom of man' means something like 'Man is the sidekick of woman'. Žižek's conception of the feminine subject is therefore what we need to look at next.

The Feminine Subject

In figure 4.1 Lacan represents the feminine position as split in a way that echoes the split subject $, it is divided between S(A̶) and Φ. The pivot between the two is a crossed-out ~~Woman~~ (in the original French it is the feminine definite article, ~~La~~). The erasure of ~~Woman~~ means that 'woman does not exist' in the sense that 'language cannot define a determinate category of woman', or, as Žižek puts it, *'woman cannot be constructed'* (*Indivisible Remainder*, 165; the challenge that 'woman' thereby poses to language as a system of universals will be developed in the next section). If in texts like 'Why Is Woman a Symptom of Man?' or *The Metastases of Enjoyment* the role which Žižek ascribes to woman is far from evident, this may be partly because Žižek theorizes the feminine subject as inherently elusive.

Figure 4.1 suggests that the inability of 'woman' to be rendered adequately in the symbolic order produces two object-remainders. The first of these, as we have seen, is the phallic signifier Φ: her capacity to represent to masculine subjects the reversal of 'castration' and to conjure up imaginary phallic fulfilment. The second is its converse, S(A̶), the signifier of the lack which arises in the symbolic order because the imaginary phallus is just that – imaginary. What Žižek understands by Lacan's mathemes, in which the crossed-out ~~Woman~~ is linked to these two objects, is that the feminine subject is not duped by the phallic signifier. Unlike men, who are slaves to the fantasies they weave around their penis, she is not convinced by the myth of 'castration' nor persuaded that some 'phallus' can fill the lack in the symbolic order (*Indivisible Remainder*, 157–8). It is this capacity to conjure a relation to the real of the drive that would not have to pass through the detour of 'castration' and

could thus achieve enjoyment 'beyond the phallus' which constitutes *jouissance féminine* and which is represented by S(Å). S(Å) designates a *feminine* relation to the real that, while unavoidably subject
to the Oedipal order, is nevertheless aware of that order's deficiencies and its after-the-fact, fabricated character. Another way of
putting this is that, as S(Å), 'woman' provides the 'answer of the real'
to the deficiency of the symbolic order. 'Woman' thereby joins the
hysteric, the theorist and Hegel, those other heroes of Žižekian
thought, as a challenge to the hegemony of the symbolic law.

Despite this happy (?) outcome, this discussion will cause eye-
brows, and indeed hackles, to be raised. What does it mean to talk
about 'woman' or the 'feminine'? Does this have anything to do
with actual women? What's all this about 'castration'? Is this whole
account not irredeemably phallocratic and heterosexist? Isn't it
unacceptable to appropriate women's symbolic exclusion as a point
of theoretical heroism? To begin to answer these questions, we need
to review some of Žižek's many discussions of Lacan's formulae of
sexual difference. These will press home the realization that Žižek's
thinking takes us a long way from our everyday conceptions of
actual social beings. He is not a sociologist, still less an agony aunt,
but a psychoanalytical philosopher. Women or 'woman' do not
concern him so much as the complex relations between subjectivity, division and domination.

Lacan's Formulae of Sexuation

As we have seen, the masculine subject cannot form a relationship
directly with the feminine, or vice versa. Instead, each connects only
with objects that are merely indirectly related to the other subject,
in the form of fantasies or symptoms; that is why 'there is no sexual
relation'.

The formulae of sexuation at the top of figure 4.1 – which I earlier
compared with the uncoordinated efforts of two home decorators –
schematize this impasse; they are a clash of incompatible assertions
that collectively provide its rationale. These formulae rank with
'substance and subject' and 'universal and particular' as among the
topics to which Žižek reverts most frequently.[6] The 'x' found in all
these formulae stands for 'a speaking being', and the symbols
accompanying it use symbolic logic to denote the contradictory
processes whereby that being assumes a gendered position within
language.[7]

Since the formulae are concerned with the difficulty of constructing the universal categories of 'man' and 'woman', it might be helpful at this point to look back at the discussion of universality in chapter 2 (pp. 38–44). Žižek glosses the masculine formulae (on the left) as meaning: 'all x are submitted to the function Φ' (the phallic function) and yet, at the same time, 'there is at least one x which is exempted from the function Φ' (*For They Know Not*, 122–3; *Tarrying*, 56). Lacan is seen here by Žižek as furnishing possibly the most important content of Hegel's logical claim that 'the exception proves the rule'. Not only is it the existence of exceptions that defines a law, but the whole fabric of the symbolic law is defined by this crucial exception. The exceptional male is usually identified as the primordial father who defies 'castration' with his obscene ostentation and unbridled enjoyment, but who, by the same token, brings down its inhibiting effects on all of his sons. What we call 'men' are identified as those who conform to the rule which the father-enjoyment establishes by infringing it. In this way 'man' is established as a universal category.

Žižek's gloss on the feminine formulae is that 'non-all x are submitted to the function Φ' and yet, at the same time, 'there is no x which could be excepted from the function Φ' (*For They Know Not*, 123; *Tarrying*, 56); again, x stands for a speaking being entering the gendered universe of language. The formulation 'non all' is where the difficulty lies. All our knowledge is transmitted through language, so the symbolic order is in one sense 'all' that there is. Yet, at the same time, that 'all' is profoundly unsatisfying; it persistently imposes on us the sense that it is *'not* all' – as if language, like the smeary paint in my example, lacks the consistency to cover the whole of reality. It is this conjunction of 'all' with 'not all' that makes up Lacan's 'non all'. The effect of language being non all, as outlined in chapter 2, is that the symbolic fiction of the universal, instead of being tugged into coherent shape by the exception, is, on the contrary, exposed as deficient and leaky. 'Woman', unlike 'man', falls short of being a universal concept; all attempts to generalize woman into existence seem doomed to fail.

Similarly, to say that woman exposes the phallic function as non all is not to assert that she actually experiences *jouissance féminine*, as a positive, phallus-free form of enjoyment. Phallic enjoyment is 'all' there is – it is just that, at the same time, it invites the suspicion that this 'all' is not all it's cracked up to be. Thus *jouissance féminine* is not 'a mystical beatitude beyond speech, exempted from the symbolic order – quite on the contrary, it is the woman who is immersed in the order of speech *without exception*' (*Fragile Absolute*, 145). Speech is all there is: the fascinating phallic object Φ is simply not there. But what is fascinating about it is precisely its capacity to impose itself as a presence out of the very fact of its absence; and this process is what is exposed by the feminine non all.

This non all is what makes the feminine subject so exemplary. We should recall that Lacan, followed by Žižek, sees the subject as a gap in the signifying chain, a bit like an airlock in a pipe. If one imagines the airlock moving one way while the current of liquid flows the other, then the space that 'was' the bubble is constantly in the position of just having been filled out; analogously, the subject is a void which is only invested with meaning retroactively as the signifying chain passes through it (the process known as 'subjec-tivization'). This is because language as non all literally cannot take account of the (real of the) subject; it merely appears to have done so once the subject has been enmeshed in the socio-symbolic world of language.

The inability of the symbolic to account for woman confirms, then, that she is the subject *par excellence* (*Indivisible Remainder*, 160). Consequently, in the feminine subject the process whereby the void is retroactively subjectivized by the symbolic order is more visible than it is in the masculine subject. The way woman 'puts on' a series of symbolic masks is not a threat to her subjectivity, but the guar-antee that 'she is more subject than man' (ibid.). The phenomenon of feminine masquerade merely makes visible the way *any* subject acquires a succession of quite contingent attributes from the big Other: 'Woman *qua* Enigma is a spectre generated by the inconsis-tent surface of multiple masks. . . . And the Lacanian name for this inconsistency of the surface . . . is simply *the subject*' (*Metastases*, 151–2).

This, then, is the basis of the link between 'woman' and 'causal-ity' in *The Metastases of Enjoyment*. 'Woman' is a better guide to the structure of causality than man, for three reasons. Since the impact of the real is more evident in the feminine subject position than the masculine, we find causality writ larger there. Since she exposes the enjoyment mediated by the phallus as non all, we see that non all of her enjoyment (*jouissance féminine*) is caused by man.[8] And since 'woman' escapes full definition within the symbolic order, she is herself an absent cause inflecting the discourse of man. In short, she is, as I said above, 'the answer of the real'.[9]

The feminine subject is thus more exposed than the masculine one to 'the night of the world', the moment of negation in the

Hegelian dialectic when any outcome is possible (see p. 24). The implication of this which concerns Žižek most extensively is that what he calls the 'act' is gendered feminine, whereas mere 'activity' is masculine. The Žižekian act is a paroxysm that shakes the symbolic order; activity, by contrast, consoles its users and fortifies its codes.

> What we forget when we pursue our daily life, is that our human universe is nothing but an embodiment of the radically inhuman 'abstract negativity', of the abyss we experience when we face the 'night of the world'. And what is the *act* if not the moment when the subject who is its bearer *suspends* the network of symbolic fictions which serve as a support to his daily life and confronts again the radical negativity on which they are founded? (*Enjoy!*, 53)

Using Rosselini's films as his example, Žižek stresses the key role of women in all of them. Unfortunately, as the truly feminine act turns out to be suicide, this may not be such great news for women as Žižek claims (*Enjoy!*, 156). However, the concept of 'act' is crucial to Žižek's ethical and political thinking, and I'll return to it in chapters 5 and 6.

Sexual Difference as the Form of Thought

Figure 4.1 has a lot to say about how what we think of as 'real-world' men and women are represented in psychic life; but we are still no closer to knowing whether there is any biological basis for these representations. In *The Metastases of Enjoyment* Žižek poses this crucial question: 'What constitutes the link that connects these two purely logical antinomies with the opposition of male and female, which, however symbolically mediated, remain an obvious biological fact?' (*Metastases*, 155). His answer is trenchant: *'there is no link'*.

> What we experience as 'sexuality' is precisely the contingent effect of the contingent act of 'grafting' the fundamental deadlock of symbolization onto the biological opposition between male and female. The answer to the question: isn't this link between the two logical paradoxes of universalization and sexuality illicit?, therefore, is: *that's precisely Lacan's point*. What Lacan does is simply to transpose this 'illicit' character from the epistemological level onto the ontological level. (Ibid.)

That is, the formulae of sexuation don't say that the difficulty is *knowing* what sexed persons are; they say that *being* one is the root of the problem; 'being' gets lost in the lack of a link between biology and symbolization. The result of this, of course, is that it is impossible to symbolize what you are.

So how is it that what we call 'men' typically assume the masculine side, and vice versa with women? This is a major area of unclarity in Žižek's thought. Here in the *Metastases* he deals rather summarily with the 'radically contingent' fact that it is creatures with a biological penis who are positioned on the side of the symbolic phallus (*Metastases*, 155, 201–3). So unconcerned is he with the difference between penis and phallus, however, that he quite often drifts into confusion of the two (e.g. *Sublime Object*, 223; *Ticklish Subject*, 92; *Did Somebody say?*, 83–4). Indeed, Žižek is relatively uninterested in the social *content* of gender identity, given that it varies randomly, at the mercy of ideology, from one culture to another. What we perceive – in the field of representation – as 'sexual difference' is not a natural fact worked upon by culture, but an *après-coup* effect of the process of symbolization (*Contingency*, 114; cf. *Indivisible Remainder*, 217). The way to approach what is 'real' about sexuation for Žižek, then, is not through content but through form.

Thus it is that some of Žižek's most interesting writing explores the impact of sexual difference on the form of thought. The motor driving this exploration is the potential for dialectical reversal in Lacan's formulae. For example, since 'masculine' and 'feminine' are defined by certain logical relations, then those logical relations can, in turn, be gendered 'masculine' and 'feminine'. If 'man' is posited as universal through recourse to an exception, then, conversely, that view of the universal is masculine. Likewise, if all attempts to generalize about women are doomed to be partial, then challenging the universal as non all can be gendered feminine. In Žižek's discussions of the formulae of sexual difference, logical and other philosophical issues take precedence over actual men and women. Sexuation, for Žižek, is the real around which philosophy turns and on which it inevitably falters.

I have already (here and in chapter 2) indicated how Lacan's views on sexual difference are developed by Žižek in harness with the unpacking of Hegelian universality. In exploring the 'gendering' of philosophical thought in general, Žižek's central concern is, indeed, Hegelian. How, he asks, is the universal experienced as a lived, particular reality? We do not arrive at gender through some universal idea of the human being. On the contrary, we can experience the sense of 'universal humanity' only *through* the exceptional (masculine) or exclusionary (feminine) partiality of gender. The real of sexual difference is this fundamental schism that is integral to the experience of being human. We arrive at the universal (however partial or incomplete) only through this primordial condition of difference.[10]

In *Tarrying with the Negative* Žižek extends these concerns to Kant and Descartes, in what is probably his most sustained study of how thought is fractured by sexuation. (I touched on this in the Introduction, pp. 10–11, when discussing the gender of examples relating to the *cogito*.) The launch pad of his argument is an essay by Joan Copjec, 'Sex and the Euthanasia of Reason', and it will help to start by summarizing this.

How, asks Copjec, is sexual difference manifested in Kant? Since it results from the different ways in which thought recoils from the real, sexual difference is linguistic and logical, not biological or ideological. So we shouldn't look for it, she argues, in Kant's overt discussion of gender, or in some sexual bias, but in his reflections on thought ('Sex and the Euthanasia', 213). When, in his *Critique of Pure Reason*, Kant tried to formalize the limitations of reason, he came up with two kinds of irresolvable contradiction, which correspond, Copjec suggests, to Lacan's formulae of sexuation. What Kant called the 'mathematical antinomy' results from the impossibility of knowing the world as a totality; we can assert with equal reason both that it is finite and that it is infinite. For Kant, 'There is no phenomenon that is not an object of possible experience', and yet, because our experience of phenomena remains indeterminate, 'not-all phenomena are a possible object of experience'. Copjec shows how this contradiction corresponds to Lacan's feminine formulae; it is formally identical with 'there is no x that is not subject to Φ' but, at the same time, 'non-all of x is subject to Φ' ('Sex and the Euthanasia', 220–1).

How does Kant resolve this contradiction? By denying that the world *is*. But what 'is' means here has to do with reason, not being. Kant is saying that the universe cannot be grasped as a totality, but only as a succession of phenomena that cannot be totalized; so it cannot 'be' an object of our thought. This is the same sense in which, says Copjec, for Lacan 'Woman does not exist'. Her 'non-existence' results not from her non-being, but from our inability to totalize and control our experience of that being. Like Kant's universe, she cannot be constituted as an object of knowledge.

Kant's other antinomy, termed 'dynamic', plays off contradictory assertions about necessity and freedom in a way that corresponds with Lacan's masculine formulae. On the one hand, everything that happens is subject to the laws of causation (cf. 'all x are subject to Φ'); but, on the other, we also need to invoke a notion of freedom that exceptionally overrides these laws (cf. 'there is at least one x not subject to Φ'). In this case, Kant resolves the antinomy by asserting that both its terms are true, just as Lacan asserts that the seemingly contradictory relationship of men to the Oedipal law is precisely what upholds the principle of universality ('Sex and the Euthanasia', 228–9). We thus arrive at a totalized understanding ('masculine') of how the world operates, if not of how it is constituted ('feminine'). Lacan's presentation of the contradiction makes it clearer that existence, which is denied on the feminine side, is reinstated on the masculine side. Because the masculine formulae are devised to counter the feminine ones, it is because 'woman does not exist' that 'man exists' – he exists through the non-existence of woman, which is why she is his symptom.

Copjec's argument is addressed to Butler, and its focus is on how Kant's antinomies further our understanding of gender. In *Tarrying with the Negative* Žižek turns Copjec's procedure upside down, and instead discerns the contradictory workings of gender in the broader problematics of philosophy.

First Žižek steers his course through successive Lacanian revisions of Descartes's 'I think, therefore I am'. Lacan is seen as exploring the potential for divorce between 'meaning' and 'being' in Descartes's formula, a divorce also brought out by Kant with his equivocation over existence as 'being' or 'meaning'. Because for Lacan the subject is split between the conscious and the unconscious, he represents the two halves of Descartes's formula as violently torn apart: we cannot consciously both be and think; we are always a prey to lack on one side or the other. At different stages in his teaching, this led Lacan to reformulate the *cogito* in two ways: 'I think, therefore it is', and 'I am, therefore it thinks' (this latter form was discussed in my Introduction, pp. 10–11). In both cases, 'I' stands for the subject of consciousness, and 'it' for the subject of the unconscious. The first, then, means something like: 'I possess an existence merely in thought, one which is purely symbolic and imaginary and which defines itself in opposition to what really exists, namely the real'; the second, 'In order for me to exist, I have to relegate my thinking to the real'.[11] When the *cogito* is recast as 'I think, therefore it is', 'being' is relegated to the unconscious. Žižek contends that this formulation is 'feminine', in so far as the 'I' of 'I think' is deprived of existence and is non all relative to the unknown world of the unconscious. Lacan's other reworking of the *cogito*, 'I am, therefore it thinks', is 'masculine' because it asserts the I's existence at the price of what it excludes (its substance of meaning). The 'I' is universal and masculine by virtue of what it leaves out.

These reflections provide Žižek with a philosophical framework for the psychoanalytical categories of fantasy and symptom as considered earlier in this chapter. The masculine *cogito* provides the rationale of the symptom, in that 'I am, therefore it thinks' is a way of the subject saying 'I am, therefore she means' or 'woman is my symptom'. The feminine *cogito*, conversely, proposes a substance-less position from which to view the 'reality' shaped by the fantasy object: 'I think, therefore the Thing is'. When expressed in this way, it becomes clear that the gender of the subject need have no relation to the body, and that men and women can equally assume the 'feminine' or 'masculine' positions.[12]

In the next chapter of *Tarrying with the Negative* Žižek criticizes Kant's ethical thinking relative to Lacan's. Lacan's ethics are anchored in the possibility of utter destruction (and hence creation) offered by the death drive. For him, therefore, the ethical subject is the split $ in its feminine guise: the subject that is non all and open to the untotalizable universe of the Unconscious. This is why the 'act', the radically destructive and creative intervention that permits the reshaping of the symbolic, is gendered feminine. This subject, then, approximates Kant's mathematical antinomy; but instead of taking on the consequences of his own insight, Kant in his ethics remained confined to a universal, symbolic framework.

Lastly, Žižek argues that the crack of sexual difference prevents Hegel's logic from achieving totalization (*Tarrying*, chapter 4). This is because the forms of reflection enact both the feminine and the masculine patterns without resolving the antagonism between them. The first step, 'positing reflection', is the step by means of which the subject 'posits the presuppositions' – that is, makes explicit what it thinks is going on in a given situation. This process is always contingent, and can never be relied on to be exhaustive; so it represents the feminine non all. The next step, external reflection, which stands outside and enumerates the presuppositions that have been posited, has the effect of transforming them into a closed series. What this leaves out, though, is the activity of external reflection itself, as the performative which brings this universal into being. Thus external reflection universalizes on the model of the 'masculine' combination of totality with exception. The third step in the dialectical process, determining reflection, recognizes, however, that external reflection does not furnish the objective knowledge that it purports to. Instead, it exposes the very terms in which the external reflection operates as having been generated from within the initial act of positing. Thus determinate (or absolute) reflection reintroduces contingency and undecidability; and in this way 'sexual difference is inscribed into the very core of Hegel's logic' (*Tarrying*, 156).

This dialectical translation of Lacan's formulae into the problematic of conceptualization *in general* has both strengths and weaknesses. It enables Žižek to side-step the 'contamination' of sexual difference by ideological content to which even (especially?) Lacan himself is prone. Lacan's musings in *Seminar* XX on woman, love and religion as Other, for instance, bespeak attitudes to gender that are really very traditional, and can make one reach for the sick bag. By seeing sexual difference at work in philosophy and logic, Žižek shows how the sexual real infects even the highest adventures of the mind, and conditions every aspect of our thought. On the other hand, it leaves him without any plausible account of why there should be any correlation between the masculine position and men, and between the feminine position and women.

Let me sum up this chapter so far. Žižek's account of sexual difference is drawn from Lacan. Its hallmark is its lack of reciprocity between possible sexual identities. This is what is referred to as 'the real of sexual difference', and it lends itself to being approached in a series of ways. The most 'content-rich' but, by the same token, ideological is that of fantasy. When we examine gender representations as symptoms, we simultaneously gain more abstraction and a greater purchase on the pressure of the real. If, having learnt to read the symptom, we then analyse the subject, we carry this process further; the subject emerges as an empty space, retroactively supplied with meanings and affording the possibility of access to the drive. Finally, if we situate the subject within the logical formulae of sexuation, we obtain the most abstract tool with which to think about how thought itself is wrecked on the reef of the real. The way Žižek develops the formulae as a means of reflecting on the fissures in our conceptual apparatus stems from his Hegelianizing of Lacan. But he has no explanation, except for the rather lame invocation of the penis-phallus, of why social persons ('men' and 'women') adopt one psychic position rather than another.

The differences between these levels of engagement with sexual difference are important, I think, for understanding the interaction between Žižek and Judith Butler.

Butler

Butler's disagreements with Žižek are not just about sexual difference, but this is the aspect of their debate on which I will focus here. In outline, I shall argue that her critique is often wide of the mark, because she does not allow for the distinctions just set out; she imputes to the formulae of sexuation the kind of content which is appropriate only to fantasy. Žižek's defence is robust at this, the most abstract, end of his theory; however, Butler's criticisms *do* markedly affect his reading of (the content of) fantasy, and thus lead him to give a somewhat fuller account of the social implications of sexuation.[13]

Lacan's ideas on sexual difference were first disseminated in English by feminists persuaded that his work supported their own agenda.[14] Since then, Lacan (and psychoanalysis generally) has remained controversial within feminism.[15] Butler's stance, in general, is among the more sympathetic. She concedes that 'Žižek is surely right that . . . the process of subjectivation outlined by Foucault is in need of a psychoanalytic rethinking' (*Bodies that Matter*, 189). She agrees that the founding moment of subjectivity is the violent ejection of that which cannot be accommodated to the symbolic law.[16] But she insists on ascribing prescriptive content both to the law and to what it precludes (or 'abjects', 190–1), leaving no doubt that, for her, the Lacanian concept of 'symbolic law' is a way of policing dissident sexualities. She reiterates and develops these views in *Contingency, Hegemony, Universality*, a fascinating experiment in co-authorship in which she, Žižek and Ernesto Laclau debate with one another in successive rounds of essays.[17] As the book progresses, none of the discussants wins over the others, but all three refine their own positions, formulating them with increasing distinctness. Žižek and Laclau are essentially in agreement in the way they understand the Lacanian 'real of sexual difference'; but Butler angrily demands of them: 'Who posits the original and final ineffability of sexual difference, and what aims does such a positing achieve? . . . Do we accept this description of the fundamental ground of intelligibility, or do we begin to ask what kinds of foreclosures such a positing achieves, and at what expense?'

(*Contingency*, 145). It is clear that 'at what expense?' means 'at whose expense?' Imposing two clearly demarcated sexes, male and female, and their interdependence in normative heterosexuality, Lacan (Butler thinks) relegates to the shadows of abjection the variety of sexed bodies and sexual proclivities which don't fit his scheme. That which the law abjects, its 'constitutive outside' (a term she and Žižek tussle over throughout the book), is, for Butler, the set of excluded sexualities that might under other circumstances have blossomed in fulfilment. Thus for Butler, the real is not 'sexual difference', but 'prohibited sexualities'.

It is evident from this that she understands the relation of sexual difference to language quite differently from Žižek, who stresses that the real, for Lacan, is *not* a content and could *never* be recuperated as a content: 'the Lacanian Real is strictly *internal* to the Symbolic: it is nothing but its inherent limitation, the impossibility of the Symbolic fully to "become itself" . . . precisely as real, sexual difference is *absolutely internal* to the Symbolic – it is its point of inherent failure' (*Contingency*, 120). Butler, Žižek observes, systematically reads the real as if it were the symbolic, and the symbolic as if it were the imaginary. At each stage she semanticizes Lacan's thought, substituting symbolic difference for real antagonism and then confusing symbolic difference with ideological content. As a result, says Žižek, she causes us to 'regress to an *empiricist* problematic' of how far ideological representations correspond with social realities (*Contingency*, 215–16). The Lacanian position, however, is that 'far from constraining the variety of sexual arrangements in advance, the Real of sexual difference is the traumatic cause which sets their contingent proliferation in motion' (*Contingency*, 310).

> Butler is, of course, aware how Lacan's *il n'y a pas de rapport sexuel* means that, precisely, any 'actual' sexual relationship is always tainted by failure: however, she interprets this failure as the failure of the contingent historical reality of sexual life fully to actualise the symbolic norm. . . . Far from serving as an implicit symbolic norm that reality can never reach, sexual difference as real/impossible means precisely that *there is no such norm*: sexual difference is that 'rock of impossibility' on which every 'formalization' of sexual difference founders. (*Contingency*, 309)

In this theoretical stand-off it has to be conceded, I think, that Žižek's (and Laclau's) version of Lacanian thought is more faithful to Lacan than Butler's;[18] indeed, as I argued in the last section, in its resolute abstraction it is even more faithful to Lacan than Lacan is himself. Butler's criticisms miss their target – but they find another one. For they have, I believe, struck Žižek at the point at which they assume relevance for him – that is, where the ideological or fantasmatic content of the sexual relation is concerned.

Although Žižek knows that the 'woman' of masculine fantasy is not the same as 'women', he has not always been scrupulous about distinguishing them, and his early cultural readings do tend towards a certain complicity with the fantasy. Here, for instance, is a comment written in 1991 on the disappearing woman in Hitchcock's *The Lady Vanishes*: 'It is difficult not to recognize in this phantomlike figure the apparition of Woman, of the woman who could fill out the lack in man, the ideal partner, with whom the sexual relationship could finally be possible, in short the Woman who, according to Lacanian theory, precisely does not exist' (*Looking Awry*, 80). This 'ideal partner' . . . who 'fill[s] out the lack in man' sends us back with relief to the abstract squiggles of Lacan's formulae. A gauge of how far Žižek has moved on from readings like this is provided by his successive commentaries on Neil Jordan's *The Crying Game*.

This film is about an ex-IRA member (Fergus) who falls in love with the black girl-friend (Dil) of a British soldier killed by the IRA, only to discover that 'she' is a transvestite; it then narrates the consequences of this discovery for their relationship. In *The Metastases of Enjoyment* (published in 1994 and conceived before the dialogue with Butler) Žižek reads the film through the matrix of courtly love, underlining that, however the relationship between Fergus and Dil develops, it is always governed by asymmetry in the 'radical sense of a discord between what the lover sees in the loved one and what the loved one knows himself to be' (*Metastases*, 103). Three years later, however, in *The Abyss of Freedom* Žižek rejects a 'first reading' (his own earlier one) which 'remains within the abstract opposition of the heterosexual norm and homosexuality qua its "transgressive" inversion'. Instead, he stresses how queerness is the 'secret of the norm itself': what the film shows is that the core of male sexual fantasy is that 'woman' is really no different from himself, and that 'sexual difference amounts to a mere masquerade' (*Abyss*, 55). Two further years pass, and Žižek, now in explicit debate with Butler, has shifted ground again. This time the focus of his argument is *against* ascribing a substantive content, whether heterosexual or queer, to Lacan's account of sexuation. *The Crying Game* is invoked as pointing to sexual difference as a 'central enigma', but '*not* as the already established symbolic difference (heterosexual normativity), but, precisely, as that which forever eludes the grasp of normative symbolization' (*Ticklish Subject*, 271). Thus it is not the case that we have perversions etc. *despite* the norm; on the contrary, the variety of sexual orientations and sexualities *results* from the inherent impossibility of imposing any such norm (*Ticklish Subject*, 273).

These three readings show Žižek moving from occupying a 'heterosexist normative' position condemned by Butler, via a 'queer' position that is quite Butlerian, to adroitly contending that it is, in reality, *Butler* who confers a content on sexual difference and thus normalizes it in a way Žižek would reject. The culmination of this movement in *The Ticklish Subject* accompanies Žižek's far more radical rethinking of 'the fundamental fantasy' which also comes about through his dialogue with Butler.

Redefining the Fundamental Fantasy

The 'fundamental fantasy' is different from the fantasies so far considered, such as the courtly lady or the *femme fatale*. These have a public face; the fundamental fantasy, by contrast, is deeply private, providing the subject with the illusion of a consistent core. This is because, for Lacan, it is the defensive response to the primary repression which is itself then repressed. Thus it forms a kind of buffer zone between the initial, inadmissible trauma and the carefully fabricated overlay of acceptable 'reality'. It defends against the first, but also transmits some residue of its shock to the second; so, although hidden from view, it *does* inflect our overt representations.

The traditional psychoanalytical name for the initial trauma is 'castration'. It is because the imaginary phallus of the mother is conceived by the male child by analogy with his penis, and because, when the father shows this phallus not to exist, the child fears losing his too, that the traumatic imposition of sexual difference is represented by the threat of castration.[19] This first, traumatic repression is then overlaid by the symbolic (or Oedipal) law, whose controlling filters enable the subject to live with it. We saw above how Žižek, when discussing the connection (or lack of it) between the formulae of sexuation and male and female bodies, fell back on this Oedipal scenario. The penis and its 'chance' resemblance to the phallus 'explain' the greater association of biological males with the psychoanalytical position of masculinity, and females with femininity.

Given the sexual nature of these two waves of repression, a sexual content is usually ascribed to the fundamental fantasy sandwiched in between. In *For They Know Not* (197), for instance, Žižek cites the fantasy of observing one's own conception as a form of fundamental fantasy.[20] In her powerful study *History after Lacan*, Brennan argues that Lacan's tendency to identify woman as objects of the fundamental fantasy is consistent with what she calls 'the foundational fantasy' whereby subjects imagine they can control the symbolic (and political) order because they can control objects (women, and thence other commodities) in it.

This narrative of 'castration' is a well-trodden area of feminist unease with Lacanian theory,[21] and Butler is on to it too. If, she says, castration anxiety results merely from a chance analogy, doesn't that contingency, once it is embedded in the theory, in fact assume a supreme fixity?

> If the real is understood as the unsymbolizable threat of castration, an originary trauma motivating the very symbolizations by which it is incessantly covered over, to what extent does this oedipal logic prefigure any and every 'lack' in ideological determinations as the lack/loss of the phallus instituted through the oedipal crisis? (*Bodies that Matter*, 195; see also chapter 3)

As a result, the phallus becomes the measure of ideological formations, but its own ideological status is never questioned.

Butler's solution is to hijack the notions of primordial repression and fundamental fantasy for her own ends. (I base this account on *The Psychic Life of Power*, chapter 5, since this is the text Žižek critiques.[22]) She contends that we assume our positions as gendered subjects at the price of psychosis. Our primary attachment is to the parent of the same sex as ourselves. Such passionate attachments are, however, violently 'foreclosed', because same-sex love has no place in our symbolic: the primordial interdiction is not, she claims, against incest (as Lacan had maintained) but against homosexuality (*Bodies that Matter*, 135). The gender we go on to assume in the symbolic is thus achieved through repudiation of this first, prohibited object. The normative heterosexual framework requires that, had we persisted with this original attachment, we should have been of the opposing gender; as a result, we feel insecure in the gender we have assumed. Bereft of the objects of our attachment, we grow up in a state of melancholy, because what we cannot name we cannot mourn (138). However, all of our loves are then tinged with nostalgia for this primordial loss.

In *The Ticklish Subject*, Žižek counters Butler's views, but, as she had done with Lacan, he also adapts them to help advance his own. This book consists of three pairs of chapters; the first chapter of each pair critiques a position that is then reinvented and developed in the second. In the first pair the addressee is Heidegger, in the second Alain Badiou, and in the third Butler, so Butler occupies a place of honour. The nub of Žižek's argument is that a proper understanding of the subject must be based on Descartes, supplemented – pretty radically – with a Lacanian account of the centrality of the death drive. All three of his addressees have failed to understand the death drive properly – that is, as Žižek does. His disagreements with Butler are complex, but one major strand develops this theme of the death drive in a way that leads him to combat her account of the primary repression and the fundamental fantasy.[23] This is done not through a return to 'castration' and the Oedipal/symbolic configuration, but through a more radical appeal to the real of drive. Flinching penises and imaginary phalluses are left behind as Žižek resorts instead to the myth of the lamella proposed by Lacan in *Seminar* XI.[24]

The lamella is a unicellular organism like the amoeba. Since it knows no sexual differentiation and reproduces by scission, there is a sense in which it never dies. It is, says Lacan, the very figure of the libido *'qua* pure life instinct, that is to say, immortal life, or irrepressible life' (*Seminar* XI, 198). More exactly, it figures our libido before we encounter the differential structure of language. But when we are exposed to the first signifier, S1, the bearer of difference, everything changes. We become subject to sexual reproduction, and this entails death, since parents must die and be replaced by their offspring. The lamella bears the effects of this transformation (*Seminar* XI, 199). In one of his essays Lacan explains this rather more clearly than in the *Seminar*: 'My lamella represents here the part of a living being that is lost when that being is produced through the straits of sex. . . . Represented here by a deadly being, it marks the relationship – in which the subject plays a part – between sexuality, specified in the individual, and his death' ('Position of the Unconscious', 274–5). With this cut of the signifier into the libido, our whole biological organism undergoes a massive change. What was physical instinct becomes drive, and what once was whole becomes fragmented. The body is broken up by language and drive into partial objects (breast, anus, eyes, mouth) around which life and death run their inseparable course.

The lamella provides Žižek with a way of thinking both with and against Butler. First, as I have implied, it replaces the standard account of 'symbolic castration', with its narratives about penises and family rivalries, in favour of an imposition, or cut, in the real of the organism, which in turn gives rise to the real of drive. It is only once it has been cut from within by the limit of death that the organism undergoes the internal differentiation which makes symbolization possible.

The lamella also underlines how 'same sex' in the post-Oedipal phase cannot mean anything like the sexual undifferentiation of an organism before its exposure to language. A major conceptual hurdle in the way of accounting for sexual difference is the difficulty of explaining how something (difference) comes from nothing (*in*difference). Freud's essays on childhood sexuality are powerful precisely because of the tortuous scrupulousness with which he avoids positing as *prior* to the process what in fact is to be its *outcome.*[25] And this, as Žižek points out, is a major weakness of Butler's thesis; she assumes that gender identifications exist *before* the vicissitudes which lead to their formation (*Ticklish Subject*, 270–1). This leads her to get her wires crossed over what sexual identifications are, in fact, involved. If the heterosexual man has 'foreclosed' his early homosexuality, is this because he desires in the place of the object (another man) he was compelled to give up, or because he desires what he fears becoming (a woman)? This very difficulty, Žižek argues, shows how Butler has failed to get to grips with the problem of symbolization, since she assumes that some prior *thing* – maleness or femaleness – is being symbolized. But how, prior to itself symbolizing a difference between the sexes, could a subject fix upon an object of the *same* sex?

Moreover, the persistence of the lamella after the initial imposition of language ensures that no sexual identity – even post-Oedipal – is an assured content. In the expression 'same sex', 'same' does not mean 'possessing the same attributes'. The sexually differentiated subject is not identified with reference to an acknowledged social norm; rather, it 'forever eludes the grasp of normative symbolization' (*Ticklish Subject*, 271). A sexual identity is a mode of 'coping with an inherent obstacle/loss' (*Ticklish Subject*, 272). Sexual difference does not oppose two complementary contents; it is a tripartite struggle over being, with the death drive (lamella) as its impossible, unacknowledged core.

Finally, the myth of the lamella giving rise to the fragmented body of the drives helps motivate a different version of the 'fundamental fantasy' from Butler. The fantasy arises, Žižek suggests, in response to the helplessness of the fragmented body (*corps morcelé*) which arises from the imposition of the death drive. The sense of bodily rupture and dis-attachment, 'of the loss of (the support in) being' (*Ticklish Subject*, 289), needs to be assuaged. The fantasy's remit is thus to tame the violence of the cut and secure a space for a whole existence. As an instance of the form it might take, Žižek cites Freud's essay 'A Child is being Beaten', which records the three phases of a common childhood fantasy: (1) My father is beating a child whom I hate; (2) I am being beaten by my father; (3) A child is being beaten (*Ticklish Subject*, 282). A striking fact about this fantasy is that the second stage forms a necessary intermediary between the other two, but is *never* reported by patients; its existence can only be inferred. This second phase, then, is a fantasy so private that it cannot be divulged: the very characteristic of the repressed fundamental fantasy.

The originality of Žižek's account of primary repression and the fundamental fantasy cannot be overestimated. The cut of difference which it attempts to heal is neither the prohibition of incest of the Freudian tradition nor the prohibition of homosexuality with which Butler replaces it. Both these accounts approach difference from the standpoint of symbolic law and the 'name of the father', whereas Žižek's account starts from the real of drive and inscribes subjection as violence, rupture and pain. This experience is sexualized, in the sense that the traumatic cut *is* the cut of sexuality as well as of death and symbolization. But the modality of sexuality in the fundamental fantasy, given that it is designed to transform pain into pleasure, is masochistic and auto-erotic. The fantasy 'provides the subject with a minimum of being' and rewrites Descartes's famous *cogito*, 'I think, therefore I am' with 'I suffer, therefore I am' (*Ticklish Subject*, 281).

In responding to Butler's arguments, therefore, Žižek has raised fundamental questions about sexuality and sexual difference. Male and female social agents and their bodies are no longer at issue as contents of the primordial repression. Instead, 'castration' is radically redefined as a cut in the real from which difference, sexuality, symbolization and the death drive are all born. The fundamental fantasy creates the space for the subject to seek to reach an accommodation with the pain and trauma of this cut. We are dealing here strictly with the birth of the speaking subject x from Lacan's formulae of sexuation. Žižek's early interpretation of fantasies such as those of the courtly lady and the *femme fatale* as perverse and masochistic finds a retrospective theoretical support. Subjection and pain lie at the root of sex, and the conflicts and dispersal of the symbolic codes, which produce the sexual antinomies, are strategies of containment. The core of human existence is the non-existence of our subjection to the death drive of lamella, 'the "undead" eternal life itself, . . . the horrible fate of being caught in the endless repetitive cycle of wandering around in guilt and pain' (*Ticklish Subject*, 292).

Žižek's thinking about sexual difference takes us a long way from our everyday conceptions of actual social beings. The way he has come to conceive subjection in *The Ticklish Subject* is centred on sexual differentiation, but largely evacuated of sexual content. Readers wanting support for women's struggles with immediate social and political difficulties will be disappointed. Žižek does, however, provide a way of articulating sexual difference with both the limitations of thought and the brutality of power; and the degree of abstraction of his theory disengages it as far as possible from ideology. Thus, despite the colourful nature of his exchanges with Butler, he may well prove to be an ally of feminism.

Conclusions

What are we to make, at the end of this chapter, of the brutal tone I referred to at the beginning? It's not up to me either to take offence or to resist taking it on behalf of other people, so I will answer in the first person. Žižek's writing about women can seem crustily outdated, but I personally don't find it offensive, though I do sometimes find it shocking. It seems to me to be driven by very strong convictions about what he perceives to be theoretical truths, and an understandable dislike of amateurish cherry picking in what is a densely intricate (hence highly interconnected) theoretical system. Looking again at the passage I cited from *The Plague of Fantasies* in the light of his use of the lamella in *The Ticklish Subject*, I would see it as using pornographic spectacle to evoke the 'night of the world' of the body fissured by the drive. The 'organ without body' with which it concludes may have seemed, at the time, to recast Deleuze and Guattari's *Anti-Oedipus*,[26] but it is also how Lacan refers to the lamella. The *jouissance* of this passage may involve getting off on smut, but it also provokes us to see the death drive at work in sexuality. The rupturing of the biological organism into partial objects, so graphically described, is indeed obscene, but the obscenity can be read as performing theoretical work.

Many people find psychoanalysis intrinsically offensive, and Žižek undoubtedly ups the stakes. Psychoanalysis theorizes its own unacceptability with reference to the shock of the real: it offends, sexually excites, or provokes laughter in different people in different contexts. Žižek is well aware of this. One of his more provocative pronouncements against political correctness is that we fail to get to grips with the problem of sexual harassment because *'there is no sex without an element of "harassment"'* (*Ticklish Subject*, 285). Sex, like the family, is the domain of the 'too much' or the 'not enough', and Žižek's writing certainly delivers this unease.

A major achievement, though, is the extent to which Žižek succeeds in retaining this traumatic core while detaching it from its ideological content. He is very successful at exposing the extent to which notions of 'femininity' and 'masculinity' are formal and logical safety valves that don't actually quite work to shut off the real. Of course, one could wish he were different. As for myself, I would welcome his writing about Irigaray, who, like himself, has given psychoanalytical readings of canonical philosophers, upheld the value of the universal, and downplayed literalist accounts of 'castration'. But given his willingness to change, as attested in this chapter, no doubt he will be different before long.

5

Ethics and the Real: The Ungodly Virtues of Psychoanalysis

Žižek's philosophical culture is extraordinarily wide-ranging. Apart from the *rapprochement* between Hegel and Lacan, which is fundamental to his whole enterprise, his readings of Descartes, German idealism, Marxism and the Frankfurt School, Heidegger, or French post-structuralism could all provide topics for full-length studies, while a host of other philosophers – Austin, Kierkegaard, Kripke, Malebranche, Nietzsche, and others – also act as vital reference points for his speculative elaboration of psychoanalysis.

One way of perceiving a pattern in this multiplicity is to frame it with Žižek's three major targets of polemic. Of the three, he takes 'deconstructionists' (chiefly Derrida and Butler) the most seriously, but reproaches them for what he sees as their shiftless relativism.[1] He criticizes proponents of identity politics (typically 'feminists') for their complicity with global capital and its failure of universality. And he scorns 'New Age obscurantists' (often linked with 'Jungian obscurantists') for the mystical mumbo-jumbo in which they represent the universe as an interplay of forces. His objection to the first two is that he sees them as having ditched out of the metaphysical mainstream of philosophy, and to the last that, in his view, it hasn't even got that far, but instead remains mired in pre-modern neo-paganism. So his onslaught on all three of these targets takes the form of reviving a canonical philosophical agenda, featuring such topics as human nature, freedom and agency. These are addressed with reference to 'modern' (as opposed to pre- or post-modern) philosophers – pre-eminently Kant, but also Kierkegaard and Schelling[2] – in association, of course, with Lacan.

More recently, a new frame has imposed itself in Žižek's writing. Like Freud, who in *Moses and Monotheism* read the origins of our symbolic law in the imposition of monotheistic religion, and Lacan, who observed, 'Whatever some may think in certain milieux, you would be wrong to think that the religious authors aren't a good read' (*Seminar* VII, 83), Žižek has turned increasingly to Christianity as a means of furthering psychoanalytical inquiry. With hindsight, his early reliance on overtly Christian writers like Kierkegaard, Pascal and Malebranche, and his frequent reference to Hegel on the interrelations between the Greek, Jewish and Christian religions, appear as harbingers of this development. It also becomes impossible to ignore the fact that all the philosophers on whose work he draws systematically situate themselves in relation to Christian (and overwhelmingly Protestant) thought. From *The Ticklish Subject*, they have been joined by a further, and surprising, reference point: Saint Paul, whose influence in shaping Christian doctrine is recurred to again and again. Žižek's most recent books all show this religious turn, whether directly (*The Fragile Absolute, On Belief, Did Somebody Say Totalitarianism?*) or indirectly (*The Fright of Real Tears*; Kieślowski is the only religious film director he has worked on).

Make no mistake; Žižek remains through all this a staunch materialist and atheist. There is nothing pious in his use of religion, and much to surprise the religious. His early discussion of Christianity shows only a skimpy familiarity with biblical or theological texts, and although *Did Somebody Say Totalitarianism?* shows an upturn in this respect, there is as yet nothing in his use of religious writings to compare with his painstaking trawl through the textual complexities of, say, Schelling in *The Indivisible Remainder*. But although Žižek's aims remain staunchly secular, he leans on theological investigation of freedom and law, good and evil, to such an extent that his thinking is now positioned within a theological horizon.

Hence the subtitle of this chapter: Žižek's anthropology has been gradually assuming the character of a godless theology and, read through this lens, works cumulatively through ungodly revisions of the three theological virtues famously set out by Saint Paul in 1 Corinthians: faith (and belief), hope (freedom and action) and love.[3] I say 'cumulatively', because none of these themes disappears from view; instead, they accrue more religious significance as time goes on. Thus, whereas early writings about belief use religion as a source of analogy within a secular framework, in more recent texts religion itself provides the analytical framework, and there is overt discussion of belief as religious faith. Some aspects of this change have been illuminatingly charted by Moriarty in 'Žižek, Religion and Ideology', to which I am indebted.[4]

My overall exposition follows the evolution of Žižek's ungodly virtues. In order to convey the movement of his thought, I shall proceed by highlighting a series of different moments: the early writings on belief and ideology; Lacanian ethics with Kant, Sade and Kierkegaard; Schelling on the trauma of freedom; Badiou and Saint Paul; and the more recent writings on Christianity, in which, I shall argue, Žižek opts for 'atheist fundamentalism' as a form of political radicalism. The conclusion points forward from ethics to politics and the subject matter of chapter 6.

Belief and Ideology: Althusser and Pascal

The psychoanalyst Octave Mannoni offers an interesting account of belief, according to which the subject is divided between belief and unbelief.[5] The believer, that is, starts from the same structure of 'Je sais bien, mais quand même' as the fetishist, who, for example, says, 'I know very well [that mother does not have a phallus], but all the same [I believe that I am it for her]'. There is nothing pathological about this split; fetishism proper kicks in only at the point where the belief becomes fixed on a fetish object, as for instance, 'I know very well [that mother does not have a phallus], but all the same [I am unshakeably convinced that this shoe is it]'. And even then, such a division can be commonplace and perfectly 'normal'. For instance, many adults believe in Christmas through their children, and actively foster belief in Father Christmas even though they know it to be false. In effect they are saying, 'I know very well [that there is no Father Christmas], but all the same [I want my children to believe in him for me]'. And as Žižek points out, it is also quite common for ideology to operate through the delegation of belief to things (*Sublime Object*, 34). Do we not, for instance, rely also on Christmas cards to believe in Christmas for us? Don't the pious messages they contain preserve beliefs from which we would distance ourselves, yet which we can't altogether give up? This, of course, is the flip side of the way in which believing splits the subject: relying on others to hold a belief on our behalf is, in its way, an indication of how strongly we ourselves cling to that belief (*Did Somebody Say?*, 88–9).

Žižek brings this conception of belief to his analysis of ideology and, in particular, of interpellation. A term put forward by the French structuralist Marxist Althusser, interpellation is the process whereby an individual subject is led to assume his or her place within an ideological structure. It takes place when, for instance, a policeman on the street shouts, 'Hey you', and we all turn round in guilty acknowledgement whether or not we were the ones being hailed.[6] (Lacan refers to this as our 'assuming a symbolic mandate', e.g. in *Seminar* III.) Althusser insists that this recognition is, at the same time, a misrecognition: when it makes subjects of us, state power alienates us from ourselves, and deludes us as to its true mode of operation. In this way, interpellation replicates the split nature of belief. For me to feel that I am 'a member of society', I must, to some extent, believe in it. At some level I may well know ('je sais bien') that the state has no claim on me, that it relies on force and economic exploitation, etc., and yet ('mais quand même') I behave as though I believed in its legitimacy. Law-abiding behaviour results not from the threat of punishment, but from a complex complicity with power. We don't altogether believe in the law (we expect bobbies on the beat to do that for us), but we believe in it enough to conform to it, even when we don't want to.

It is easy to understand why we should not *wholly* believe in our social mandate: there is plenty that ideology is hard put to make us swallow. What Althusser's narrative doesn't explain, however, is why this summons should command belief *at all*. The answer Žižek provides is this: we don't believe in it because it makes sense to us; on the contrary, the reason we believe is that it is sense*less*.[7] Or, to put it another way, what is crucial is not one side of the split ('Je sais bien') or the other ('mais quand même'), but that which remains unformulated even unconsciously between the two. That is, it is not the symbolic dimension of interpellation that implants belief in our hearts, but the dimension of the real. In elaborating this position (*Sublime Object*, 36–43), Žižek builds on, but extends, Althusser's account (see also *Metastases*, 59–62).

Althusser does indeed look for a way of grounding belief; against all expectation, he turns to a famous apologist for the Christian faith, Blaise Pascal (1623–62), using him to argue that if we can only condition our outward behaviour, we will find eventually that it will change our inner beliefs. He paraphrases Pascal's words thus: 'Kneel, move your lips in prayer, and you will believe' ('Ideology', 127).[8] This move on Althusser's part reflects an important shift in the meaning of ideology. Originally, as the name implies, it denoted a system of ideas, but Althusser realized that 'the ideas in which an individual believes are his or her acts, inserted into material practices regulated by material rituals' (Moriarty, 'Žižek, Religion and Ideology', 126). Thus, instead of our acts reflecting our beliefs, it is rather our beliefs that are born of our acts: repeating the act of praying will instil in us belief in the reality of prayer. That is why, for Althusser, the practices imposed by various social apparatuses are the means whereby ideology is perpetuated.

However, there remains a problem with Althusser's account, in Žižek's view: namely, that it fails to account for this *'belief before belief'* which would induce us to kneel down and pray in the first place (*Sublime Object*, 40). Quoting a different fragment of the *Pensées* from Althusser, Žižek claims that Pascal saw our inner convictions as shaped by an external, nonsensical 'machine': 'Proofs only convince the mind; habit provides the strongest proofs and those that are most believed in. It inclines the automaton, which leads the mind unconsciously along with it' (*Pensées*, 274 (fragment 821), cited in *Sublime Object*, 36). Žižek interprets Pacal's 'automaton' in the sense of 'unconscious' which Lacan gave to the word. He thence proceeds to argue that we submit to the law because law is law: that is, the symbolic law is not, in itself, lawful or legitimate – it is simply unavoidable. The reason we accept it is that, if we are to be speaking beings, we cannot escape the unreasonable, traumatic imposition of the signifier. The remainder of the real which inheres in the split structure of belief is the *plus-de-jouir* of the superego: what remains of enjoyment once it has been taken up into the signifying chain. Its traumatic dimension must remain unconscious for it to determine our behaviour; this is the enjoyment with respect to which 'we know not what we do'. The role of ideology is thus to naturalize and integrate the superego. In this way, the belief that *follows* from behaviour becomes *après-coup* the *cause* of that behaviour: 'The implicit logic of [Althusser's] argument is: kneel down and *you shall believe that you knelt down because of your belief* – that is, your following the ritual is an expression/effect of your inner belief; in short, the 'external' ritual performatively generates its own ideological foundation' (*Mapping Ideology*, 12–13). Belief – or faith – thus follows the Lacanian logic of the double cut and the Hegelian logic of the negation of the negation: that is, we are able to believe (or part of us is) because we have repressed (negated) the traumatic moment that itself represses (negates) the imposition of the signifier.

This inner space where we 'tarry with the negative' creates a footing for the next of Žižek's ungodly virtues – hope – initially theorized with reference to the moral philosophical topics of freedom and agency.

Freedom and Agency (i): Kant, Sade and the 'Ethics of the Real'

Žižek rehearses Lacan's discussions of ethics, the most significant of which are in books VII and VIII of his *Seminar* and the paper 'Kant with Sade'. The differences between him and Lacan are ones of emphasis, not substance.

Lacan parts company with classical ethical theory by distinguishing sharply between ethics and morality, with ethics as the privileged term; in this he resembles his contemporary, Levinas. Žižek, however, emphasizes instead the continuity between Lacan and Enlightenment philosophy (specifically Kant). He plays down the theme of responsibility which Lacan shares with Levinas and Derrida, and concentrates on the old-fashioned questions of good and evil, law, freedom and agency. While Lacan's accounts have much to say about the relation between ethics and desire, Žižek's emphasis is rather on the relation between ethics and the drive. Thus, while Lacan's interest in ethics is at least partially symbolic, Žižek shifts the accent to the dimension of the real. This involves his reading these ethical writings of Lacan *après-coup* through the lens of later ones, notably his *Seminar* XI.

Morality, for Lacan, is a product of the pleasure principle and the Oedipal law. As we saw at the end of the last chapter, this law is resorted to as a salve for the anguish of subjection. As the vehicle of conventional morality, it offers endless opportunity for *jouissance* at one's own cowardly conformity. The *jouissance* in question is the surplus enjoyment which arises from the dark influence of the superego within the law. Lacan's superego is no benign figure who pats us on the head when we give up ('sublimate') our libidinal satisfaction (*jouissance*) in return for moral or social gain. Unlike Freud, for whom sublimation is the corner-stone of ethical endeavour, Lacan emphasizes the link between sublimation and perversion. Since I had no choice but to enter the symbolic order, the giving up of my personal *jouissance* was inevitable, and the very

idea that 'I could have had it' is an illusion: it is only in the symbolic that 'I', 'have' and 'it' have any meaning. When the *père-vers*
of the superego punishes us for having accepted this forced choice,
he is acting perversely. Although he may appear to encourage us to
sacrifice ('sublimate') *jouissance*, in reality he is binding us ever more
closely to it in the form of its monstrous surplus of *plus-de-jouir*. The
more slavishly we obey the superego imperative, the more our
sense of guilt over our illusory sacrifice increases, and the more we
need to be punished, so the more surplus enjoyment we get. This
account is taken over by Žižek in, for example, *Metastases*, 67–8, and
Ticklish Subject, 268–9. As we have seen (in chapter 3), he expands
on Lacan by elaborating the role of the superego as an object-
remainder of enjoyment in the symbolic which he calls 'voice'.

Because Lacan sees morality as belonging in the symbolic order,
with its aspiration to universality, he points the finger at Kant for
having been the first to formulate its principles. The categorical
imperative adduced by Kant, 'So act that the maxim of your will
could always hold at the same time as a principle in a giving of universal laws' (*Critique of Practical Reason*, 28), is for Lacan the prototype of the moral law. And, as Lacan wickedly observes, the same
principle is formulated rather more informatively by Kant's contemporary, the Marquis de Sade: 'Anyone can say to me, I have the
right to enjoyment of your body, and I shall exercise that right
without any limit to put a stop to whatever capricious demands I
may feel inclined to satisfy' ('Kant with Sade').[9]

Lacan praises Kant for having perceived that the object of ethics,
'the good', is not pre-given, but results from the way we apply
the law. That is, it is not the law which defines the good, but the
other way round. Sade's formulation, however, makes it easier
to see that this object, which Lacan identifies with the *objet a*, is
bound up with the subject's *jouissance*.[10] As a result, the ethical
'good' can just as readily be identified as evil, and indeed is inseparable from it. Moreover, Lacan argues, although Kant no doubt intended to confine his ethics to the symbolic, the very inflexibility
of the Kantian law already captures the inhuman horror of the real.
Sardonically paraphrasing the categorical imperative as 'never
act except in such a way that your action may be programmed'
(*Seminar* VII, 77), Lacan forcefully brings out its monstrous, alien
dimension.

The way into the ethical for Lacan is via this opening on to the
real. We should refuse the facile path of sacrifice, which merely per-
petuates the illusion that there is such a thing as a substantive moral

law; we should take Kant at his word, and act as if to create new principles *ex nihilo*. The model of the ethical which Lacan proposes in his seminar on ethics (*Seminar* VII) is Antigone in Sophocles' tragedy. Forbidden by her uncle, King Creon, from burying her brother Polynices, Antigone prefers to be buried alive rather than obey. Since she chooses not only to die herself, but also to place herself beyond the pale of the symbolic law, and so outside the domain of the living, Antigone casts herself into what Lacan calls 'the zone between the two deaths' (*Seminar* VII, 320). She is praised for being ethical in the sense of 'not giving ground relative to her desire' (*Seminar* VII, 319). This controversial formula (in the French original (368) it reads 'ne pas céder sur son désir'), implies that, for Lacan, the subject acts ethically when she passes through the realm of desire and into that of the drive – especially the death drive.

Drawing on his reading of Sade, Lacan associates the death drive not only with the potential for utter destruction, but also with the capacity to create from scratch. The ethical, then, is the constellation of events in which the subject frees herself from the symbolic law ('freedom'), commits herself to an act ('agency'), and thereby makes it possible for the law to be rethought. Kant's categorical imperative, then, can be reconceived as wholly transgressive. By calling on us to act in such a way as to provoke the law to be rethought from the ground up, Kant points beyond the protective morality of the pleasure principle. He situates ethics in the real, where notions of good and evil become indistinguishable, giving way instead to the forces of destruction and creativity. Such ethics offer us the possibility, like God, of creating the world *ex nihilo* (*Seminar* VII, session ix).

In *Seminar* VIII, Lacan continues to condemn sacrifice for its fruitless attempts to bolster the symbolic order and paper over its deficiencies. As Žižek points out, sacrifice mobilizes the fetishistic split of belief: the sacrificer says, 'I know very well [that this act will not make sense of everything], yet all the same [I believe that it will]' (cf. *Enjoy!*, 74). Lacan contrasts sacrifice with the ethical act of renunciation, an act in which the symbolic itself is given up. His illustration is taken from Paul Claudel, whose heroine Sygne de Coûfontaine is seen as offering a modern, non-sublime parallel to Antigone. Sygne *does*, in a sense, sacrifice herself for her husband, but she refuses to acknowledge her act or allow it to be taken up into the big Other. Her death, rather than providing a sublime plug to fill the gap in the Other and sustain belief in it, points rather to its insubstantiality. An empty gesture, it resonates only with its own senselessness. In this way, the very symbolic is given up, and only the real remains.

When Žižek elaborates the concepts of freedom and agency, he constantly reworks these Lacanian reference points. The examples of Antigone and Sygne, for instance, fortify his contention that the act is inherently both feminine and suicidal (cf. my preceding chapter).[11] Thus a constant touchstone for his ethics is a Lacanian-Kantian 'ethics of the real', in which the ethical is identifiable with the drive in both its destructive and creative aspects. In particular, he stresses the difficulty of distinguishing, in Kant, between 'good' and 'radical evil'. Since the basis of human nature is to be a mutilated animal, thrown out of kilter with biological life by subjection to the symbolic, we are a prey to its evil, *jouissance*-infested rule; and beyond that lies the further 'radical' evil (or *id* evil) of the drive. Žižek views this evil as the stamp of humanity as such. The sense of the 'good' which the symbolic order brings is 'a secondary, supplementary attempt to re-establish the lost balance'; thus the act means that 'Evil is Good itself "in the mode of becoming"' (*Tarrying*, 97). Although Kant is conventionally viewed as a model of rectitude, Žižek's Lacanian purchase enables him to inscribe Kant's concepts of law, freedom and agency in the alarmingly ungodly context of the real.[12]

Freedom and Agency (ii): Kierkegaard and Repetition

In elaborating this 'ethics of the real', Žižek turns to an author who played no part in Lacan's ethical thought: Søren Kierkegaard (1813–55). Like Pascal, Kierkegaard imparts a religious-theological dimension to Žižek's inquiry in a way which only underlines its ungodly character. From as early as the essay 'Why is Every Act a *Repetition*?' in *Enjoy Your Symptom!*, Kierkegaard guides Žižek's exploration of the act.

In this essay, Žižek articulates Lacan's teaching (in *Seminar* XI) on the forced choice with Kierkegaard's study *Repetition*. When we submit to the Oedipal law, we undergo the violence of the forced choice, whereby we have to 'choose' between law and madness: if we don't 'choose' to be social beings with a place in the social order, then 'we' as such don't even exist. The 'choice', then, exists only in retrospect; it is only *après-coup* that we feel we must have given something up as the price of social inclusion. That is, the moment of the forced choice was the moment we began to 'give way as to our desire'. That is why the superego is so powerful: we feel guilty at having betrayed our desire, and this vengeful, perverse dimension of the law punishes us by making us conform even more to the law, which makes us feel even guiltier, etc.

What releases us from this enslavement, Žižek contends, is the ethical act which suspends the Oedipal law by reopening the abyss of psychosis within it. 'Therein consists the Lacanian definition of the authentic ethical act: an act which reaches the utter limit of the primordial forced choice and repeats it in the reverse sense. Such an act presents the only moment when we are effectively "free"' (*Enjoy!*, 77). The act is a *repetition*, in the words of the essay's title, because it repeats the moment of our entry into the symbolic. It is as if we managed to find the door we came in by, wrest it open, and stumble back through it. This moment of liberation rids us of all the accumulated superego guilt at having 'given ground relative to our desire', and enables us to start our relation with the law over again (provided the act isn't suicide, I assume). Another form of act which Žižek envisages here, which makes rather more sense of it as grounds for hope, is revolutionary terror.

All these ideas are to be found in Lacan, and indeed were touched on in the previous section. But the language on which Žižek draws when he speaks about the act 'suspending the moral law' comes from Kierkegaard, who distinguishes three modes of repetition: aesthetic, ethical and religious. In the aesthetic mode, the subject experiences the inability to repeat past pleasure; in the ethical mode, universal norms of conduct seem designed to provide for repetition; but in the religious mode, such repetition is experienced as an impossibility: we cannot coincide with our memory or our anticipation, so we always arrive either too early or too late. The religious repetition, as encounter with the impossible, exposes the deceits of the ethical, but it also shows how the ethical is a necessary subversion of the aesthetic. (The lack of fit between these terms and Lacan's is initially confusing. Kierkegaard's 'religious' is closest to Lacan's 'ethical', and Kierkegaard's 'ethical' to Lacan's 'moral'. My point, however, is that by overlaying Lacan's terms with Kierkegaard's, Žižek makes Lacan more 'religious', albeit in an ungodly sense, than he was before.)

The prototype of religious repetition which Žižek cites from Kierkegaard is the act of conversion to Christianity as an attempt to repeat Christ's own humiliation (*Enjoy!*, 79–80). Kierkegaard, he says, wants to recapture Christ's act which served as a challenge to the Jewish law. After Christ's death, however, Christianity solidified into a body of doctrine, and thereby fell into the same ethical

mould as Judaism. In order to re-release religion from the merely
ethical, we need to re-perform Christ's act. Kierkegaard's analysis
shows, Žižek argues, that the religious is both the condition of the
ethical (formal codes are born from the religious act) and its point
of breakdown – the inner limit at which such codes are challenged
and collapse. This means that, for Kierkegaard, the religious occupies the position of the singular in relation to the universal. Unbeknownst to Kierkegaard, his formulation is comparable to that of
the Hegelian concrete universal: it is from the singular, exceptional
moment that the universal is produced (*Enjoy!*, 84). That is why
(Žižek suggests) Kierkegaard maintains that belief in Christ is not
something one should seek to justify by evidence, any more than
Christ's teachings are sustained by anything external to themselves:
their exceptional status constitutes their own authority, just as the
singular founds the rule.

The last step in Žižek's argument is as dramatic as it is unexpected. It is in just this sense, he claims, that the analyst is author-
itative. Lacan is an 'apostle' in the Kierkegaardian sense; that is, he
is the bearer of a truth which is not necessarily available for rational testing in his writings, so that 'when somebody says "I follow
Lacan because his reading of Freud is the most intelligent and per-
suasive", he immediately exposes himself as non-Lacanian' (*Enjoy!*,
101). With this approximation of Lacan to the Apostles, and even to
Christ himself, the very capitol of psychoanalysis has been assimilated to religion. Likewise, through the comparisons between the
religious and the revolutionary act, Christianity becomes an indispensable tool for thinking about the political Left (one which will
be extensively developed in Žižek's subsequent writings; see below
and also *The Ticklish Subject*, 211–12).

In a gesture calculated to *épater le bourgeois*, Lacan had turned
to Sade to illumine Kant. No less provocatively, Žižek presses
Kierkegaard into service to illumine Lacan. If Pascal explains the
real of belief, Kierkegaard confers a redemptive value on human
agency and freedom. Žižek's next appropriation of religious
thinking – that of Schelling – is more ambitious, and just as
unexpected.

Schelling's 'Abyss of Freedom'

An approximate contemporary of Hegel, Friedrich Wilhelm Joseph
von Schelling (1775–1854) devoted a large part of his *oeuvre* to the

philosophy of nature. Between 1811 and 1815 he attempted to write a speculative interpretation of creation history, *The Ages of the World* (*Die Weltalter*), three unfinished drafts of which remained unpublished at his death. Žižek responds in kind with two different, but overlapping, commentaries on the *The Ages of the World: The Abyss of Freedom* inclines more towards aesthetics, and *The Indivisible Remainder* more towards politics, but both contain much of the same material *verbatim*. What characterizes this common core is Žižek's reading of the *The Ages of the World* 'as a *metapsychological* work in the strict Freudian sense of the term' (*Indivisible Remainder*, 9) – that is, as if Schelling's account of the emergence of the world from chaos, and of history from eternity, were an account of the emergence of the human subject (specifically of the imposition of the symbolic on the real).[13] The way Žižek does this is by reading the *The Ages of the World* alongside Schelling's *Of Human Freedom* (1809), so as to bring out the similarities which Schelling implies between God's creation and man's freedom. The germ of Žižek's whole project is Schelling's disturbing vision – applicable equally to the cosmos and to the individual – of order precariously balanced on a seething morass of disorder, and at the same time incomprehensibly penetrated by it, so that, in the midst of the order there always persists an 'indivisible remainder' of chaos. Here is the passage from Schelling's *Of Human Freedom* where this vision is encapsulated:

> Following the eternal act of self-revelation, all is rule, order, and form in the world as we now see it. But the ruleless still lies in the ground as if it could break through once again, and nowhere does it appear as though order and form were original, but rather as if something initially ruleless had been brought into order. This is the incomprehensible basis of reality in things, *the indivisible remainder*, that which with the greatest exertion cannot be resolved in the understanding, but rather remains eternally in the ground. (Quoted from *Indivisible Remainder*, 75, my emphasis)

Žižek's reflections on Schelling are intricate and difficult, and contain much that I don't understand. What follows is based mainly on *The Indivisible Remainder*, with quotations from *The Ages of the World* taken where possible from the translation of Schelling's second draft included in *The Abyss of Freedom*. The key point I want to bring out is that Žižek finds in Schelling, as he did in Kierkegaard, a conception of human freedom and agency that repeats divine freedom and agency (see *Indivisible Remainder*, 20–1,

42). But this is no longer (as for Kierkegaard) a case of the individual Christian opting to imitate Christ; rather, it is a function of how
human nature and human history are situated within the entire
order of creation. The essence of human freedom is 'the moment of
"eternity in time"', the escape from the temporal chain into the
'abyss' (*Ungrund*) of the Absolute beyond (*Indivisible Remainder*, 31).
Žižek's understanding of this 'abyss' is shaped by his willingness
to assimilate it to the Lacanian real; conversely, his understanding
of such psychoanalytical concepts as 'freedom', 'act' and 'unconscious' is developed through his engagement with Schelling.

The problematic in which the 'abyss of freedom' is situated, and
which Schelling wrestles with in *The Ages of the World* drafts, is that
of how God created time. God and eternity are primary; meaning
and time are secondary. Before time, there is the abyss of absolute
freedom which, prior to the imposition of God's word, is (in a sense)
everything there is; but it is also (in the absence of all meaning and
difference) nothing (*Ages of the World*, 133). The difficulty, then, is to
represent to ourselves 'how this Nothing of the abyss of primordial
freedom became entangled in the causal chains of Reason' (*Indivisible Remainder*, 16). Or, as Žižek later puts it, in a way that memo-
rably captures how unlikely and off balance the whole process is,
'how did our universe get caught in the cobweb of Reason in the
first place?' (*Indivisible Remainder*, 74).

The creation of time involves a paradox, since creating time
means creating the past; thus, when time was created is not when
time is conceived of as having begun; the past never was and never
could have been present. What the invention of the past does is to
overlay with the temporal order what was (and is) eternal; time is
just a qualitative transformation of eternity (*Indivisible Remainder*,
31–2). The relation between time and eternity is analogous, Žižek
suggests, to the Lacanian relation between desire (which is
symbolic) and drive (which is anchored in the real) (*Indivisible
Remainder*, 13).

The analogy doesn't seem so far-fetched when Žižek presents
how Schelling conceives of the moment of beginning as in itself
double. The undifferentiated pit of eternity has to be wrested into
difference, and this process engulfs it in a vortex of rotating
impulses, a frenetic 'orgasm of forces':[14] a crisis of decision/
differentiation (*Entscheidung*) that is utterly traumatic. Žižek praises
Schelling's attempts at envisaging this 'terrifying intermediate
stage' when 'God is submitted to the blind necessity of a constricted
rotary motion' (*Indivisible Remainder*, 37). From the bliss of eternity,

God finds himself plunged into nightmare, constraint, and the propensity for evil, 'a wild madness, tearing itself apart' (*Indivisible Remainder*, 24). Faced with this unbearable deadlock, the light, good and *logos* of the created order come as an immense relief. Thus *'eternity itself begets time in order to resolve the deadlock it became entangled in'* (*Indivisible Remainder*, 31). The release into the world of creation and order leaves behind the traumatic moment of *Entscheidung*: differentiation, once accomplished, must be forgotten in order that the world of difference can assume its reality. Schelling, in other words, presents creation following the logic of the Lacanian double repression. His moment of differentiation/decision, with its rotating forces, corresponds with the first cut of the signifier (and the birth of drive from instinct); while the repression of this traumatic horror by the orderliness of the *logos* parallels submission to the Oedipal law (and the birth of desire).

This double movement of creation inaugurates a zigzag of impulses between disorder and order by which the whole cosmos will eventually be defined, a process described by Schelling as an alternation between contraction and expansion. Through the act of contraction over expansion, differentiation/decision is enacted, and the object and identity of creation are, as it were, expelled from the expanse. Each moment of contraction-decision effaces the expansion-delirium before it; thus human history, and each individual human being, are all echoes of the first limitation of primordial freedom in God's act of creation. In the following passage, Schelling discerns such an act of self-creation in each individual:

That primordial deed which makes a man genuinely himself precedes all individual actions; but immediately after it is put into exuberant freedom, this deed sinks into the night of unconsciousness. This is not a deed that could happen once and then stop; it is a permanent deed, a never-ending deed, and consequently it can never again be brought before consciousness. For a man to know of this deed, consciousness itself would have to return into nothing, into boundless freedom, and would cease to be consciousness. This deed occurs once and then immediately sinks back into the unfathomable depths; and nature acquires permanence precisely thereby. . . . If, in making a decision, somebody retains the right to reexamine his choice, he will never make a beginning at all. (*Ages of the World*, 181–2)[15]

Like the emergence of time from eternity, this moment of free decision resembles the trauma of the forced choice when the subject is first cut by the signifier: an experience that has to be repressed, and the moment of its repression repressed as well.[16]

There is, then, for each individual a founding moment of freedom that remains unconscious, and which is an echo of the originary abyss of freedom from which the whole created order sprang. But Schelling does not want to say only that we have known freedom in a way that we can't possibly recall to mind. He also wants to explain the fact of being free as a reality of human experience. For this, we need to go back to the paradox of the creation of time.

As I said at the outset, when time is created, so is past time. The past overlays eternity with something that *seems* like time but never actually was. This created past, we can now see, acquires its content through this second repression, in which the crisis of differentiation is banished by the imposition of order. The effect of this repression is that the trauma of decision is violently ejected into the past; this is the past that never was and never could have been present. As a result, the overlay of eternity with a created past of madness ('the unconscious') inhabits us all. Human beings are always decentred, or 'out of joint', because of it; it persists in us as an 'indivisible remainder'. (Žižek assimilates this coexistence of the decentred being with the persistent remainder of the abyss to the Lacanian matheme $\$ \lozenge a$; see *Indivisible Remainder*, 27, 43–6). Human beings are free, then, because we retain contact with the originary abyss via this turmoil. Hence 'there is no actual freedom without an unbearable anxiety' (*Indivisible Remainder*, 17). In the wake of God's choices, we too have the possibility of choice between good and evil, order and disorder. Thus there is a freedom beyond 'the primordial act by means of which I choose my eternal character', and that is the act of 'submerging myself in the primordial abyss [*Ungrund*] of the Absolute, in the primordial will which wills nothing' (*Indivisible Remainder*, 69).

As in his discussion of Kierkegaard, Žižek is keen to emphasize the revolutionary potential of Schelling's thought in this period; although his subsequent writings are politically conservative, the politics of the *The Ages of the World* are 'very close to Marx' (*Indivisible Remainder*, 41). It is also through his reading of Schelling that Žižek comes to characterize Lacan as a 'dialectical materialist' (see my chapter 2).

Thus far, Žižek's religious guides to the ungodliness of psychoanalysis have all been pretty heterodox.[17] In his next major project, *The Ticklish Subject*, by contrast, Žižek turns to the unimpeachable orthodoxy of Saint Paul. Filtered through the atheistic philosophy of Alain Badiou, the Apostle becomes another guide to under-standing the relation between moral law and ethics. Freedom from the law offers an approach to agency in which faith, hope and charity combine.

Badiou's Saint Paul: Faith and the Truth-event

My last chapter outlined how, in the last part of *The Ticklish Subject*, Žižek argues both with and against Butler in order to refine – and reform – his theoretical grasp of the fundamental fantasy. In the middle part of the book he does the same with Badiou over ques-tions of universality and agency.

On the whole, Badiou is welcomed as an ally. He has not sold out to 'deconstructive fictionalism' (*Ticklish Subject*, 131); like Žižek, he is a universalist committed to the revolutionary (as opposed to the reformist) Left. Within this common ground it is the problem of *how* universality is articulated with revolutionary agency that provides the ground for disagreement. The gist of Žižek's critique is that a Lacanian-derived account of the act is better suited to Badiou's pro-gramme than Badiou's own notion of 'event', because it is better fitted to radical politics.

Žižek's argument here, as throughout *The Ticklish Subject*, revolves around what he terms the 'pre-ontological'. In *The Ticklish Subject*, 'ontology' is used in a broadly Heideggerian sense to refer to being-in-the-world – that is, to being that is intelligible within a human horizon of meaning. The term 'pre-ontological', then, is associated with the pre-symbolic.[18] Žižek first introduces the term *à propos* of Hegel's 'night of the world' (*Ticklish Subject*, 34). Hegel's horrific vision of the body in fragments is, says Žižek, an essential preliminary to symbolization, for how is the 'I' to discern the separation of external objects unless it has somehow experienced withdrawal into inner madness and division? If we cannot dash our inner imaginings to pieces, how are we to proceed to a symbolic naming of parts? Isolation and destruction lie at the heart of what it is to become human. The Lacanian name for this is the death drive that both enables and results from the symbolic order: 'The with-drawal into self, the cutting-off of the links to the environs, is fol-lowed by the construction of a symbolic universe which the subject projects on to reality as a kind of substitute formation, destined to recompense us for the loss of the immediate, pre-symbolic Real' (*Ticklish Subject*, 35). The pre-ontological is also exemplified, however, by Descartes's withdrawal into 'universal doubt and reduction to *cogito*' (*Ticklish Subject*, 34). Throughout *The Ticklish Subject*, Žižek is arguing for a Cartesian-Lacanian view of the subject as (in the words of the subtitle) 'the absent centre of political ontology' from where the pre-ontological can be accessed and (hopefully) the ontological order transformed. The function of what Žižek calls 'the act' is to blast a passage through the ontological blockage with which the subject protects itself, so to expose its emptiness and make this transformation possible. And the death drive, he argues, is the domain of the pre-ontological, which alone can power this process.

Badiou sees the world of being (ontology) as periodically punctuated by what he calls 'events', which 'belong to a wholly different dimension – that, precisely, of non-Being' (*Ticklish Subject*, 129–30). What distinguishes the event is that it carries a shock of truth; it makes legible for the first time what was repressed or rendered invisible by the current order. However, the event and its truth are never recognizable within the order of knowledge that is sanctioned by the prevailing ontology; within that order, they are genuinely undecidable. To become a subject, for Badiou, is to choose to be faithful to the potential for revelation in the truth-event. Through the subject's fidelity, a new system of knowledge and a new order of being can be instituted. The example Žižek takes from Badiou at this point is the French Revolution, which irrupted inexplicably, revealed the abuses of the *ancien régime*, and led to a new political era.[19]

There is much about Badiou's account that finds favour with Žižek. He applauds him for seeking a truth that resists ontologization and is at odds with the common way of thought (*Ticklish Subject*, 132–3). He appreciates that, for Badiou, the event and its truth are not ontological; they emerge 'out of nothing' (*Ticklish Subject*, 136). In his reformulation of Badiou's argument, Žižek nevertheless suggests that Badiou is not altogether successful in this ambition. Badiou's 'event' can be discerned only in the light of 'a previous Decision for Truth' (ibid.). Given that the event, then, is always perceived in retrospect, it is only the fact of reaching this decision that reveals the past to have been undecidable; once the decision is made regarding an event, its undecidability is at an end. The event is thus less pre-ontological than non-ontological in the sense that it genuinely does not exist prior to the decision to recognize it as such: its recognition is an act of faith. (This is clearer when Jesus's resurrection is taken as the key example of an event, since neither Badiou nor Žižek believe that it ever took place.)

Recognizing the event, however, means that the truth which it is held to contain is to some extent represented (or representable) within the system of knowledge which has come about in the wake of the decision. Indeed, the truth can impose itself on people, like a miracle (*Ticklish Subject*, 134). This partial assimilation of truth to the symbolic is suggested by the similarity between Badiou's account of the subject's call to fidelity and Althusser's concept of interpellation: 'Isn't the process Badiou is describing that of an individual interpellated into a subject by a Cause? . . . Is not the circular relationship between the Event and the subject (the subject serves the Event in his fidelity, but the Event is visible as such only to an already engaged subject) the very circle of ideology?' (*Ticklish Subject*, 145). Thus the problem, for Žižek, with Badiou's account is that the event is not ontological enough, whereas the truth risks sliding back into the very ontology it was supposed to challenge.

The major part of this argument is conducted over a reading of Saint Paul. Badiou identifies the Christian religion as 'perhaps *the* example of a Truth-Event' (*Ticklish Subject*, 130). Saint Paul not only recognized this truth-event; he also, in the three theological virtues of faith, hope and love, theorized our subjective relation to it:

> Faith is faith in the Event (the belief that the Event – Christ's rising from the dead – really took place); Hope is the hope that the final reconciliation announced by the Event (the Last Judgement) will actually occur; Love is the patient struggle for this to happen, that is, the long and arduous work to assert one's fidelity to the Event. (*Ticklish Subject*, 135)

The fact that the event in question (the resurrection) is one neither Badiou nor Žižek believes in illustrates the contention that the event is constituted retrospectively by the decision to identify it as such; it does not need to have taken place for it to be the grounds for a truth. Thus for Badiou, Žižek contends, faith is the primary virtue of the three; this confirms his assessment of Badiou as a Catholic dogmatist in the tradition of Pascal, and underlines the connection he has asserted between Badiou's notion of the event and Althusser's account of interpellation (*Ticklish Subject*, 142–5).

Badiou sees the truth which Saint Paul extracts from the resurrection-event as exemplary because it is both unique and universal (*Ticklish Subject*, 143): there is but one truth which all should acknowledge – hence 'the foundation of universalism, in Badiou's title. This truth is identified by Badiou at the level not of law, but of grace. The law may appear universal, but it is, in reality, particularist, in the sense that 'it is always a Law defining a specific community at the expense of excluding the members of other ethnic, etc. communities, while Divine Grace is truly universal, that is, non-exclusive, addressing all humans independently of their race, sex, social status, and so on' (*Ticklish Subject*, 147). This principle of grace is thus an instance of what Žižek elsewhere refers to as a 'concrete universal', in that its universal dimension is grounded in the very singularity of its occurrences. It is an insurgence of the real which dramatically inflects the whole symbolic order.

Arguments over the 'real' of grace lead to the most complex part of Žižek's disagreement with Badiou, which turns on this passage from Saint Paul's Epistle to the Romans:

> What follows? Is the Law identical with sin? Of course not. But except through the law I should never have become acquainted with sin. For example, I should never have known what it was to covet, if the law had not said, 'Thou shalt not covet.' Through that commandment sin found its opportunity, and produced in me all kinds of wrong desires. In the absence of law, sin is a dead thing. There was a time when, in the absence of law, I was fully alive; but when the commandment came, sin sprang to life and I died. The commandment that should have led to life proved in my experience to lead to death, because sin found its opportunity in the commandment, seduced me, and through the commandment killed me. (Romans 7: 7)

Saint Paul declares that law gives birth to sin ('when the commandment came, sin sprang to life') and thus that law and sin, or prohibition and transgression, are mutually dependent. But both Badiou and Žižek agree that this is not the limit of Saint Paul's account, any more than the Oedipal law and its inherent desire to transgress are the sum of Lacanian psychoanalysis. Paul's concern is whether we can escape the resulting deadlock and, if so, how. And, Lacan-like, his answer is, Yes, through grace which inspires us to Christian love (*Ticklish Subject*, 148–9). If the affirmative value of love, rather than the negative power of prohibition, becomes the motive for action, then we can hope to interrupt the vicious circle of law and sin and achieve freedom:

For a Christian believer, the fact that he does not do certain things is based not on prohibitions (which then generate the transgressive desire to indulge precisely in these things), but the positive, affirmative attitude of Love which renders meaningless the accomplishment of acts which bear witness to the fact that I am not free. (*Ticklish Subject*, 150)

Love is thus the force of the real that resists the law; and it plays, in this part of *The Ticklish Subject*, the same role as lamella in Part III (see my last chapter).

In his argument thus far, Žižek has followed Saint Paul and Badiou in defining the 'real' of human freedom and agency with reference to the theological virtue of love. Where Žižek parts company with Badiou is over how the opposition between law and grace relates to the dichotomy of life and death. For Badiou, the ontological order is deathly. The truth-event, by contrast, is on the side of life; it offers a means to transcendence and to what Badiou calls 'immortality'. Rebuking Badiou for failing to link the truth-event with the death drive, Žižek invokes Lacan's recasting of that same passage from Romans:

Is the Law the Thing? Certainly not. Yet I can only know of the Thing by means of the Law. In effect, I would not have had the idea to covet it if the Law hadn't said, 'Thou shalt not covet it.' But the Thing finds a way by producing in me all kinds of covetousness thanks to the commandment, for without the Law the Thing is dead. But even without the Law, I was once alive. But when the commandment appeared, the Thing flared up, returned once again, I met my death. And for me, the commandment that was supposed to lead to life turned out to lead to death, for the Thing found a way and thanks to the commandment seduced me; through it I came to desire death. (*Seminar* VII, 83)

This passage (Žižek quotes rather more of it) shows Lacan recognizing that the imposition of symbolic law gives rise to the death drive ('when the commandment appeared, the Thing flared up, . . . I met my death'). But Lacan taps the force of the drive in order to break out of the morbid cycle of law and transgression, and open up 'the domain of *Love beyond Law*'. Lacan, Žižek observes (*Ticklish Subject*, 153), uses Paul's very words to refer to this; the way he does so is, however, not the way of Badiou or Saint Paul: 'psychoanalysis is not "psychosynthesis"; it does not already *posit* a "new harmony", a new Truth-Event; it – as it were – merely wipes the slate clean for one' (ibid.). More fundamental for Lacan than the assertion of a new faith *à la Badiou* is the need to withdraw into the inner 'night of the world' in which any structure – such as faith – is utterly broken down ('through it I came to desire death'). Total symbolic collapse is the pre-condition of rebuilding. Hence for Lacan the pre-ontological cannot be a truth-event; it can only be the monstrous nothing of the death drive, the force within us of the undead lamella (*Ticklish Subject*, 154–5), 'the negative gesture that clears a space for creative sublimation' (*Ticklish Subject*, 159), which is activated by what Žižek calls the act.

This leads to clarification of the contrast between the respective writers' concepts of the subject. Badiou's subject, defined by decision and fidelity to the event, is defined with relation to a content; whereas the Lacanian subject is the pure negativity of the death drive (*Ticklish Subject*, 160), a void awaiting subjectivity. Whereas Badiou asserts the subject's 'immortality', Lacan insists on its contingency and finitude – for him, as we saw in chapter 4, to be human is to be mortal (*Ticklish Subject*, 163). Badiou's concept of the subject is that of the master who decides, whereas Lacan's is that of the hysteric who questions (*Ticklish Subject*, 164). In the last resort, Žižek concludes, the act is the very opposite of the truth-event which leads to a decision: 'The authentic act itself in its negative dimension, the act as the real of an 'object' preceding naming, is what is ultimately *innommable* [unnameable]' (*Ticklish Subject*, 167). Lacan is therefore more open to the possibility of revolution than Badiou; and the Lacanian concept of the act better fulfils Badiou's requirements of the event than his own event does.

Žižek has adopted a theological framework for this analysis. And ultimately, I think, his reading of Saint Paul is more Pauline than Badiou's. Among the three theological virtues, Badiou accords the greatest value to faith. But Paul had declared the greatest of the three to be love; and Žižek, seeing it as the virtue with the greatest leverage in the pre-ontological real, would agree. All through *The Ticklish Subject* he uses the examples (often linked together) of love and militant politics: both can engender acts which enable us to break the frame and start again. As an instance of the act he cites Mary Kay Letourneau, the thirty-six-year-old schoolteacher who ran off with a fourteen-year-old schoolboy. This shock to morality was, at the same time, he contends, an authentic ethical act in which 'the very core of her being' was at stake (*Ticklish Subject*, 386). The example is troubling and underlines – as with the event – the difficulty of identify-

ing what an authentic act could be; but it certainly shows the privileged ethical position that Žižek accords to love.

To sum up thus far: Žižek has drawn on religious thinkers
because he finds in them a means of purchase on what he calls the
real. The extremity of religious thought, its willingness to explore
beyond the limitations of human reason and self-satisfaction – in
short, beyond 'morality' – confers on it a radical understanding of
belief, freedom and agency that might lay the foundations for Leftist
political action. If, in his earliest writings, Žižek was most interested
in belief, he has always identified psychoanalysis as a source of
hope, and now, increasingly, he has turned to love as the way of fulfilling that hope.

Agape: The Order of Charity

In Žižek's most recent books, love continues to rule, and religion
plays a yet more significant role. All three of *The Fragile Absolute*
(subtitled *or, Why is the Christian Legacy Worth Fighting For?*), *On
Belief*, and *Did Somebody Say Totalitarianism?* take a direct interest in
Christianity and promote (Žižek's recasting of) it as a corrective
to the ills of capitalism. Christianity is never read from the standpoint of belief – Žižek is scornful of religious revivalism – but as a
way of conceptualizing the relationship of the real of freedom to
symbolic law. The major themes of these books are developments
of views advanced in *The Ticklish Subject*.

Thus an abiding preoccupation remains the nature of Christian
universalism. Christian teaching explicitly addresses outcasts, and
enjoins us to reject our insertion into the socio-symbolic order. It is
thus far from being 'universalist' in an obvious way; it certainly
does not sanction existing hegemonies; its universality is based on
exclusion and singularity which bypass the symbolic framework, so
that 'each individual has *immediate* access to universality' (*Fragile
Absolute*, 120). This is no humanist call to value the precious uniqueness of the individual, however; rather, the individual is 'reduced
to the *singular point of subjectivity*' (*Fragile Absolute*, 127). The Holy
Spirit is interpreted as a universal community to which each individual gains admittance in function of this singularity. That is what
becomes of the body of Christ after his death; Christ can be said to
be 'resurrected' solely in so far as he assumes the form of this community of believers; there is no place in authentic Christian doctrine
for the afterlife (*On Belief*, 91).

Christianity has the great advantage, in Žižek's eyes, of being monotheistic. Modern technology, in particular cyberspace and the new reproductive technologies, delude us into embracing a new form of the Gnostic (or dualist) heresy in which material and non-material worlds are governed by different forces; New Age religions, for their part, regress to pagan polytheism. The effect on us of the symbolic order is to impose a sense of the body as *simultaneously* excremental and sacred. To be human is to be a mutilated animal; our natural bodily rhythms have been thrown violently off balance by the imposition of language, so that we are no longer at home in our own bodies, or our bodies in their environment. We should recognize that the bodily functions that shame us are inseparable from what we perceive as our spiritual, or sublime, dimension (*On Belief*, 103–5). Christianity is thus paradoxically pressed into service by Žižek as an argument *against* faith in spiritual reality, and *in favour of* a dialectical materialism whereby the armature of our thought is shaped by the irreducible real of the body.

Hence another recurrent argument of these books is the continuity between Christianity and the dialectical materialist thought of Marx (*Fragile Absolute*) and Lenin (*On Belief; Did Somebody Say?*). Christianity, Žižek reiterates, should be recognized as the ultimate source of these thinkers' revolutionary zeal. Christian *agape* offers a mode of revolutionary affirmation (the act) which suspends the law. This is the 'fragile absolute' of Žižek's title: 'Christian charity is rare and fragile, something to be fought for and regained again and again' (*Fragile Absolute*, 118). The core narrative of Christianity, Christ's death, is a model of the act as feminine renunciation – a theme that is returned to in *On Belief* (68–84) and *Did Somebody Say?* (45–60). Discussions of Christ's passion provide an opportunity for Žižek to show how his concept of the act evades such symbolic concepts as payment, debt or justice, which (according to Žižek) are unjustifiably applied to the crucifixion/redemption. The most developed argument is the one in *Did Somebody Say?*. Christ's death, he contends, is not a sacrifice. The purpose of sacrifice is to plug the gap in the symbolic, and so preserve the fiction of its existence, but Christ's act is the antithesis of sacrifice, since it blows apart the fabric of law to reveal our essential freedom. *The Fragile Absolute* concludes by exhorting us to exercise this freedom as 'the community [in the Holy Ghost] of believers *qua* "uncoupled" outcasts from the social order – with, ideally, authentic psychoanalytic and revolutionary political collectives as its two main forms' (*Fragile Absolute*, 160). The Church of England would indeed be amazed to learn that the true purpose of its teaching was to enable the under-class to band together for therapy and revolution.

As a religion of singularity, separation and renunciation, Christianity is associated by Žižek with drive, not desire (e.g. *On Belief*, 92–5). This has a number of implications. The most central we have already seen: Christianity belongs in the field of what Lacan calls ethics (not morality) and of the act (not sacrifice). In line with his earlier writings on the identity of good and evil in Kant, Žižek emphasizes the ethical ambiguity of the drive as manifested in Christianity. It is not to be confused with the good, although it may result in redefining what we mean by good. It can just as well be identified with the propensity for evil (*Fragile Absolute*, 122). Christianity is against the good in favour of faith (*On Belief*, 150). Nor can it be revealed; rather, it remains an enigma *in itself*. Christ's words on the cross, 'Father, why did you forsake me?', are the equivalent of the child's in Freud's famous dream of the burning child: 'Father, can't you see I'm burning?' (*On Belief*, 145). The utter inadequacy of the response from the father in both cases marks the imperfection and abjection characteristic of Christianity, and points to our sub-jective destitution before the real of the drive.

Žižek uses the Trinity to formulate his most recent thinking about the real (*On Belief*, 82–3). God the father is the figure of the real *as real*, as what escapes symbolization absolutely, but menaces us as a 'violent primordial Thing'. The universal-categorical role of the Holy Spirit instantiates the real as it inheres in the letter, in scien-tific formulae, for instance, or in Lacan's mathemes; this is a symbolic manifestation of the real as a meaningless, inhuman imposition. Thirdly, the fascinating figure of Jesus presents us with the real in its imaginary guise, with its capacity to pose as a sublime appearance. Through him the drive is manifested to us in all its comic simplicity. In an unexpected revision of the doctrine of the incarnation, Žižek compares the Christian's worship of Jesus to a heterosexual male lover's fascination with his partner's vagina (*On Belief*, 94–5). The reason both objects are captivating is not that they are adored as being themselves 'the Thing' the subject is after, nor yet that they stand for something else (the mysterious Thing beyond), but that they make the real manifest in the gap between these two positions. In this way their very lack of sublimity displays the real. (Note that Žižek's presentation of Christianity here as a 'desublimated sublime' parallels his contemporary interest in the 'ridiculous sublime' in Lynch's films and the 'desublimation' prac-tised by Kieślowski; see chapter 3 above.)

In no sense is Žižek's Christianity the revival of some childhood faith. Slovenia, the most Western of the Balkan countries, is historically a Catholic country. Most other Balkan states were traditionally Orthodox. But the account of Christianity which we find in these recent books recalls neither Catholicism nor Orthodoxy. It has no priesthood, iconography, liturgy or sacraments (except for a brief mention of confession). These features make it more like Islam (which Žižek virtually never mentions, although it is the religion of neighbouring Bosnia) than the forms of Christianity found in the Balkans. With its emphasis on the unmediated participation of the faithful in the charitable order of the Holy Spirit, on 'equality and direct access to universality' (*Did Somebody Say?*, 54), Žižek's Christianity recalls nothing so much as Protestant fundamentalism. And in the Introduction to *On Belief* he perhaps explains why this, of all versions of Christianity, should be attractive to him. Here Žižek recalls a Larry King show in which representatives of various faiths each displayed their liberalism towards the others. The exception was a Baptist from the Southern states who insisted that to 'live in Christ' was the only way to avoid burning in hell. Žižek sympathizes with this refusal to compromise: 'The basic premise of this book is that, cruel as this position may sound, if one is to break the liberal-democratic hegemony and resuscitate an authentic radical position, one has to endorse [the] materialist version [of the Baptist's position]' (*On Belief*, 1). Radical politics, Žižek is asserting, is the materialist atheist equivalent of Protestant fundamentalism.

Žižek's writings on Christianity are undoubtedly thought-provoking. Like the terrorist who deploys his enemies' own resources against them, Žižek reverses the West's most conservative ideology against itself; to each of its most established hegemonies, Right-wing piety and Leftist liberalism, he opposes a set of ideas which neither can abide. He seems to be attempting to perform in writing an intellectual equivalent of his concept of the act. He certainly disturbs the symbolic fabric of theory around himself, but whether this disturbance will effect any lasting symbolic change remains to be seen.[20]

Conclusions

I have used this chapter to discuss Žižek's readings of a broad intellectual tradition concerning 'human nature'. Rousseau famously declared that 'man is born free but is everywhere in chains'; for

Žižek, psychoanalysis offers an elaboration of this problem and the hopes of a solution. Žižek's writings can be seen, then, as positioning Lacan's thought within the framework of Enlightenment and post-Enlightenment reflection on freedom and agency. This in turn is placed within a wider frame: that of the theological discussion of faith, law and grace. Ultimately, the framework that surrounds this is that of Christianity itself. Taking this furthest limit as my own outer frame, I have shown how Žižek presents psychoanalysis as offering secular equivalents of the theological virtues of faith, hope and, above all, love. The way he does this is to use theological writings as an anamorphosis of his psychoanalytical convictions.

I say 'psychoanalytical': but the very terms of this exposition show how psychoanalysis is, for Žižek, inseparable from moral and political philosophy. His interest in belief goes alongside his concern with ideology; hope is manifested in the possibility of freedom and the revolutionary act; and love, whilst likewise finding expression in the act, also provides the basis of political universality. A fuller exploration of these political concepts is found in my final chapter, where I will return to the possibility that Žižek envisages his writing as act.

6

Politics, or, The Art of
the Impossible

In my Introduction, I identified the driving force behind Žižek's thought as political. By this I don't mean just that his writing has political themes, but rather that its whole impulse is political. At bottom, Žižek wants to make the world a better place, and looks to Lacanian analysis and therapy to achieve this. The result is that his diagnoses are (at least in part) analytical, and the cure, if there is to be one, relies on therapeutic concepts such as 'traversing the fantasy', 'subjective destitution' and 'the act'.[1]

The political, for Žižek, is all encompassing. The Lacanian theory of the subject on which he relies is predicated on reciprocity between the Other (the symbolic fabric of the world out there) and the unconscious. It is not just that the individual unconscious is formed by the outside world; the way we shape the outside world is just as much the expression of our unconscious. That's why, in the words of one of his favourite quotations, the X-Files motto, 'The truth is out there' (e.g. Plague, 3). There has been a political undercurrent throughout this book. Chapter 2 argued how Žižek's defiant conjunction of Lacan with Hegel forges, from unlikely materials, tools both of political analysis and of political therapy. My last three chapters have illustrated the indissoluble interrelation between subjectivity and the political world. Interpretations of culture form part of the critique of ideology (chapter 3); sexual difference determines our capacity for political subjection (chapter 4); ethical notions of freedom and agency lead into political ones (chapter 5).

The inseparability of the personal from the social does not mean that the 'political', for Žižek, designates nothing more than a change of scale: a step up from the individual to the collective, as it were. The motto 'the personal is the political' can all too easily divest the political of any meaning that could not be expressed simply *as* personal, and Žižek has no truck with it. On the contrary, the recent tendency to anchor the political in the personal has led to qualifying as 'political' many movements that he outspokenly scorns, such as political correctness and the various forms of identity politics. Nor is the political for him just a continuation of ethics, as if poking one person in the eye was an ethical issue, but doing the same to thousands somehow made it 'political'. For Žižek, the political field is defined in the old-fashioned way by power: the ways power is imposed, managed or resisted; whose interests are served or disserved by it; and its effects on the production and distribution of resources. And his political engagement is not, and could never be, solely intellectual. Rather, he is concerned with how one gains power, with the exercise of government, and with the control of institutions. In chapter 4 of *The Ticklish Subject* he disparages those French Marxists who appear to have renounced all thoughts of obtaining power. Although some of his early political themes (totalitarianism, anti-Semitism) are inherited ones (for example, from the Frankfurt School), they also form part of his own life experience. He has lived through the breakup of the former Yugoslavia, seen the rise of nationalism in the former Eastern bloc, and played an active role in Slovenian politics.

To say, then, that the political, for Žižek, is all encompassing is to say that power and his response to power permeate everything. It is consequently less illuminating to envisage the political as a framework in which his thought is contained, than as an energy which moves it. One sign that it is the impulse, as much as the content, of Žižek's thought is that it is what primarily informs the last chapter or section of nearly all his books. Especially fine examples are provided by the closing chapters of *For They Know Not*, *Tarrying with the Negative*, and *The Ticklish Subject*. It is in recognition of this directionality in his writing that I have made this my final chapter too.

Another sign that the political impetus is dominant is that Žižek's political opinions are what have changed the most in the course of his English publishing career. From writing primarily against totalitarianism from a position that was, in name at least, liberal, he has come to write primarily against capitalism from a self-confessedly Marxist standpoint. In his most recent books he has begun to be highly critical of Western liberalism and to query the very category of 'totalitarian' that was so central to his earlier work.

It appears from these remarks that 'direction', for Žižek, over-whelmingly means 'direction against'. He now quite explicitly adopts a hostile stance towards prevailing orthodoxies. For example, he welcomes the publication of the *Žižek Reader* as the occasion of 'burning the last bridges that connect [him] to the hege-monic trends of today's academia and force its readers to perceive [his] work the way it stands alone' ('Preface', p. x). *Did Somebody Say Totalitarianism?* is conceived as a theoretical abattoir where the sacred cows of liberal Western academia are rounded up and slaughtered.

But I don't mean to imply that Žižek is just some *enfant terrible* sounding off against pet dislikes. Žižek adheres passionately and uncompromisingly to what he sees as the Left, even if his version of what this means is constantly evolving – indeed, such evolution is, as I've said, proof of its importance. One of the factors to undergo the greatest change is his relationship to Marx (1818–83) and Marxism. The next section of the chapter will chart the outline of this movement. I will then examine more closely successive stages of Žižek's political thought. The final section will reflect on the brinkmanship of his proposed solutions and the practical hope they offer.

Lacan, Hegel, Marx

At first Žižek's Marxism proceeds gingerly, almost covertly. In his Introduction to *The Sublime Object*, Lacan and (with amusing dis-regard for chronology) Hegel are hailed as post-Marxist thinkers because, unlike Marx who saw revolution as a solution, they acknowledge as insurmountable the 'impossible-real kernel' (4, Lacan), 'the global radical deadlock' (6, Hegel) of political life. This Lacanian–Hegelian duet, then, provides the score for the 'Marxism without much Marx' which characterizes Žižek's work up to *The Ticklish Subject*.

Žižek's conception of 'ideology', for instance, is thoroughly Marxist. For him, ideology involves the tilting of our entire per-ceptual plane in favour of the powerful and against the disem-powered, so that we misperceive where our interests lie and fail to recognize the economic and political realities that govern our lives. Žižek's constant grappling with the impossibility of seeing outside our own delusion – that is, his 'critique of ideology' – is likewise thoroughly Marxist. But he sets about it with typical indirection, often arguing *with* Lacan and Hegel *against* Marxists such as Althusser. In his Introduction to the volume *Mapping Ideology*, for instance, Lacan and Hegel enable him to veer historically to one side and the other of Marx, at once outflanking and outdoing him.

So long as Žižek's attention is focused on ideology and its critique, then the fact that Lacan and Hegel provide, in his view, the best account of the operations of the symbolic and imaginary orders keeps them in the forefront of political analysis. But as he increasingly loses interest in forms of political antagonism apart from class, so he reaches to a more traditionally Marxist concentration on the mode of production as the core of the political. As one chapter subheading has it (*Ticklish Subject*, 347), 'It's the *Political* Economy, Stupid!'. If there is a 'direction towards', as well as a 'direction against', in Žižek's political thinking, then it lies in the gradual reinvention of Marxism as a political philosophy within an overall psychoanalytical purview.

The way this is effected relies, unsurprisingly, on a combined appeal to Lacan and Hegel. Žižek's move is to envisage the constant potential for breakdown in capitalism not (as Marx did) as the limit on which it will founder but, on the contrary, as the condition of its continued existence. Thus what appears as an external obstacle to capitalism is reflected back into it as part of its internal definition (Hegelian determinate reflection). Or, to put it in Lacanian terms, we pass from impediment to impossibility:

> If we abolish the obstacle, the inherent contradiction of capitalism, we do not get the fully unleashed drive to productivity finally delivered of its impediment, but we lose precisely this productivity that seemed to be generated and simultaneously thwarted by capitalism – if we take away the obstacle, the very potential thwarted by this obstacle dissipates. (*On Belief*, 18–19)

This dialectical conversion of impediment into impossibility is, of course, the same as Lacan makes with regard to the (absence of) sexual relation. The real of sexual difference lies in the fact that what we take for an external prohibition is, in fact, an inherent impossibility. Thus, while Žižek still refuses to look to revolution and communism as solutions to capitalism – he says of communism, for instance, that it is a capitalist fantasy (*Fragile Absolute*, 18) – he nevertheless believes that describing the political economy in

Marxist terms enables us to identify capital as the political real (see e.g. *Ticklish Subject*, 276; *Contingency*, 223).[2]

The consequences of this change towards Marxism are twofold. First, as the diagnosis for which a cure is sought changes substantially, so too does the cure. In the early books dealing with the critique of ideology, the move is towards traversing the fantasy and uncovering the void at its heart, whereas the later books in which the political analysis becomes more Marxist concentrate rather on the act. Second, in these later works, the diagnosis seems to me to be less well matched by the therapeutic measures invoked. The ills of the capitalist world call for drastic, even earth-shattering treatment, but it is less clear what form this might take now that the Marxist solutions of revolution and communism have been abandoned. There is a large-scale revolutionary energy in Žižek that doesn't easily accommodate the modest, individual-based conception of cure that psychoanalysis has to offer (indeed, that it is not even confident of being able to provide). Critics of Žižek's work are often Marxists who find his programme not Marxist enough. Laclau, for instance, complains that 'Žižek's thought is not organized around a truly *political* reflection but is, rather, a *psychoanalytic* discourse which draws its examples from the politico-ideological field' (*Contingency*, 289).[3]

Furthermore, as Žižek concedes (*On Belief*, 15–33), Lacan is unpromising as a revolutionary ally. His famously unsympathetic retort to the students of May 1968 was 'As hysterics, you demand a new master. You will get it!' (*On Belief*, 30). The best hope of tracing a politics in Lacan, Žižek suggests with a nod to Miller,[4] is through the successive ways – from his Gaullist authoritarian beginnings to his recognition of capitalist dispersal – that Lacan envisaged the organization of *jouissance*. The same approach also works for Žižek himself, as I will now explore. *Enjoyment as a Political Factor* is the subtitle of *For They Know Not*, but it could have been attached to any of Žižek's political writings. The following three sections chart the successive ways in which he sees this 'political factor' operating in the critique of ideology, in anti-capitalism, and in his reservations about liberalism.

Critique of Ideology

Let me for a moment misrepresent Lacan's view of the subject: stop its ceaseless movement, take away its paradoxical twisting around impossible spaces, flatten it out like an over-large sandwich, and then spear a cocktail stick through it. The point where the stick goes into the sandwich to hold it together forms the quilting point (*point de capiton*), and the point where it goes through the filling under-neath, which you can't see but is what makes the sandwich desir-able to you, is the *objet a*. But if you think you're going to enjoy eating it, you're deluding yourself, because the rule, as with Alice in Wonderland, is 'jam yesterday and jam tomorrow but never jam today'. And anyway, the person who sold you the sandwich was planning on making money out of you, not giving you a good time. The best thing to do is to envisage the place marked by the stick as a hole, and recognize that the only reality of any significance is the hard, unyielding plate underneath, which (thanks to the sandwich) you can't see.

This is a very crude image, but it helps clarify how Žižek's writing about ideology is sometimes about the struggle over the quilting point, sometimes about the role of fantasy and its unseen, spectral presence as *objet a*, sometimes about the resistant real beyond, and sometimes about what people *think* about their own or other people's enjoyment – all distinct, but related, topics. Prop-erly Lacanian accounts of the processes involved here can be found in Žižek's exposition of the graphs of desire in *The Sublime Object* (87–129), or of fantasy in *The Plague of Fantasies* (chapter 1). Žižek's writing about ideology, which has been very influential, has also been the object of intelligent analyses by Daly ('Ideology and its Paradoxes') and Glynos ('Grip').

Hegemony, the 'quilting point', and cynicism

A striking passage at the beginning of *Tarrying with the Negative* describes the revolt which overthrew Ceauşescu in Romania. There one could see

> the rebels waving the national flag with the red star, the Communist symbol, cut out, so that instead of the symbol standing for the organizing principle of the national life there was nothing but a hole in its centre. . . . The enthusiasm which carried them was lit-erally the enthusiasm over this hole, not yet hegemonized by any positive ideological project; all ideological appropriations (from the nationalistic to the liberal-democratic) entered the stage afterwards and endeavoured to kidnap the process which originally was not their own. (1–2)

Politics is the struggle over the meaning and control of the ideological quilting point, momentarily exposed here in all its emptiness.[5]

In traditional and authoritarian societies the quilting point can be identified as S1, the position associated with the master. But what characterizes totalitarianism, according to the last chapter of *For They Know Not*, is that its ideology is instead quilted to S2, the chain of knowledge. The implication of this is that ideology is associated not with the Oedipal father, but with the superego compulsion to enjoy. Another way of putting this is to say that totalitarianism is an inherently perverse form of power. This is because totalitarianism, according to Žižek, does not rely on the arbitrary, the exceptional or the charismatic, which would all be features of S1. Instead, totalitarian power structures are supported by appeal to bureaucratic 'objectivity' and 'neutrality'. They rely, too, on 'objective', disengaged compliance on the part of their subjects. Thus, Žižek repeatedly argues, cynicism is an inseparable element of the modern totalitarian state. In this way, totalitarianism manifests the fetishistic split of 'Je sais bien mais quand-même' (see chapter 5).[6] The cynicism of, for example, Nazism towards itself is by no means a reason to take it less seriously – on the contrary, the fetishistic structure whereby 'we know very well that the Jews are not responsible for all social ills' and yet 'we believe that they really are' is exactly what led to the Holocaust (*For They Know Not*, 244–5). Soviet citizens were likewise entirely cynical towards the Communist Party and its *nomenklatura*, but this did not for a moment prevent them from complicity with the regime, or indeed from becoming Party members themselves. On the contrary, it was what powered their relationship with it.

Modern bureaucratic societies are, however, likewise perverse; the fetishistic split dominates Western ideology, and attacks on the cynicism to which it gives rise are one of the constants of Žižek's writing. The way ideology works nowadays is through promoting the delusion that we live in a 'post-ideological' world. But nothing, he maintains, could be more ideological than the belief that one could identify a place outside ideology from which to critique it. On the contrary, the cynical distance which we imagine we take towards ideology is precisely what constitutes the space of ideology. Ideology is the way we structure the whole of 'reality', and so the classic definition of ideology as 'false consciousness' is already taken on board as an element in this 'reality' (*Sublime Object*, 29). Thus the old-fashioned critique of ideology through recourse to 'demystification' has to be discarded. Cynicism is the successful appropriation, by the hegemonic group, of the subversion and sarcasm deployed against it by its detractors. It insinuates a distance between mask and reality while retaining the mask. 'Cynical distance is just one way . . . to blind ourselves to the structuring power of ideological fantasy: even if we do not take things seriously, even if we keep an ironical distance, *we are still doing them*' (*Sublime Object*, 33). This brings us to fantasy as what provides S1 or S2 with fantasmatic content.

Fantasy and spectrality

The effectiveness of hegemony stems from the fact that it is not confined to the symbolic. Ideology works because it taps into the concealed realm of fantasy that underlies and conditions the contents we ascribe to language and prevents us from challenging ideological representations. We have already seen how ideology secures 'sublime objects' by placing them against a backdrop of *jouissance* (chapter 3). The role of fantasy in underpinning ideology is the main theme of *The Plague of Fantasies*, and what follows is based on its opening chapter.

Fantasy is located in the *objet a*. The fundamental stuff of fantasy is not the transgression of the law but its installation, since it is fantasy that 'plugs' the trauma of our initial subjection, and supports the appeasing overlay of Oedipus (see chapter 4). Fantasy, as it were, provides the screen on which the film of ideology is played. Žižek cites as an example the 'saintly' activities of Mother Teresa in Calcutta. We depict her as bringing hope to the hopeless of the Third World, and this enables us to represent their sufferings in a moral and religious context, rather than a political one. Westerners could donate money to Mother Teresa in a way we found redemptive and uplifting, and which, additionally, relieved us of any sense of political responsibility for the plight of India. Instead, it licensed us to see it as 'a place so utterly desolate that no political activity, only charity and compassion, can alleviate the suffering' (*Plague*, 18). Žižek often speaks of the Balkans as a 'fantasy screen' in this sense: for instance, the recent upheavals there allow the West to witness, in fantasy, the discovery of its own treasure of democracy (e.g. *Tarrying*, 200).

In order to be effective, fantasy has to be implicit. The inner space installed by fantasy, while it has the potential to become the space of freedom (chapter 5), can only become so if it is recognized for what it is: the effect of a forced choice. We may believe that we could be free of ideology, but this is ideological delusion at its worst. One way to overcome the ideological effects of fantasy – that is, to 'go through the fantasy' – is to act as though there really is a choice; this exposes the mechanisms whereby fantasy was installed by going through them in reverse. Thus an excessive literalism in obedience to the law can reveal how ineffective it becomes once it is no longer supported by fantasy. This is the point, for instance, of working to rule. If a work-force takes its regulations literally, the institution grinds to a halt, because it in fact depends on there being unspecified supplementary demands on their labour. Working to rule exposes the fantasy structure of 'loyalty', 'commitment', etc. (i.e. exploitation) on which the 'rule' relied.

The underlay of fantasy, therefore, is in no way benign. On the contrary, fantasy is shot through with the trauma of the repressed Thing behind. For this reason, Žižek associates fantasy with spectrality: it is the point where the repressed Thing returns in all its cruel obscenity. In *The Ticklish Subject* he also refers to it as 'pre-ontological'. The essay which perhaps best explains his views on this is the Introduction to *Mapping Ideology*, to which I've already referred.

The overall argument of this essay is that, far from there being a position outside ideology from which to critique it, the 'beyond' of ideology is something that can never be recuperated as content; its limit is not something that we could ever touch, it lies by definition out of reach. It is the moment of negation, the point of primal repression, or the point of clash of an irreducible antagonism – that is, of the real. This limit is marked by what Žižek here calls a 'spectre', which is the site of the fundamental fantasy. Ideology arises from this site like a spectre from the grave; it is a delusional emanation that stalks and shapes 'reality'. Contrasting his own view with Derrida's in *Specters of Marx*,[7] Žižek argues against seeing the spectre as a symbolic call to responsibility (as belonging, that is, to the signifying order). Rather, we should seek to dispel it or lay it to rest, so as to expose the gap for what it is. It is through the spectre of ideology that we can diagnose society's pathology. Thus, in political terms, we would traverse the fantasy and undergo subjective destitution.

In *The Metastases of Enjoyment* (54–85) and elsewhere Žižek develops his account of spectrality and ideology. Power in general, and Right-wing power in particular, is supported by an obscene, superegoic underside (S2); and, as we have seen, the superego thrives on surplus enjoyment, the remainder of the real which provides the irreducible core of fantasy (*objet a*). Official institutions are shadowed by unofficial ones which appear to be transgressive but which, in reality, act as the necessary spectral support of officialdom. An example is the 'nightly terror' of the Ku-Klux-Klan which acts as the 'shadowy double' of the official, daytime law in small-town America (*Metastases*, 55). A white man can be recognized as a part of the 'community' so long as he tolerates the Klan, and even participates in its rituals.

> Yet he will be effectively excommunicated, perceived as 'not one of us', the moment he disowns the specific form of *transgression* that pertains to this community – say, the moment he refuses to partake in the ritual lynchings by the Klan, or even reports them to the Law (which, of course, does not want to hear about them, since they exemplify its own, hidden underside). (*Metastases*, 55)

Such underlying obscenity is especially characteristic of totalitarian regimes. As the analysis in *For They Know Not* explains (260–72), this perverse and obscene shadow side of the law results from the way S2 is poised over *objet a*, which provides the signifying chain with a conduit to the real of enjoyment.

In a similar manner the reasons why we identify with particular political leaders are not simply symbolic, but engage the seamy underside of fantasy. For instance, we vote for people not for their qualities, but because of unconscious identification with their faults. The majority of Americans liked Clinton *because* of his crude energies, not in spite of them; his goings-on in the Oval Office only improved his popularity ratings. We voted for Tony Blair in Britain because we think he is deceitful and a master of spin, even though we also believe he is sincere. The fetishistic split that ensured his success ran something like this: 'We believe he is upright and moral, but all the same, we know he is scheming and underhand and thus can be relied upon not to change things much, though he may make the *status quo* work a bit better.'

The theft of enjoyment

We have seen that fantasy acts as a screen, and that its role is to provide a protective layer between the primary repression and the secondary overlay of the Oedipal order. It thus separates drive (in the real) from desire (in the symbolic), and furnishes the symbolic with narratives of how the *jouissance* lost through the forced choice has been 'stolen' from us by others: 'What we conceal by imputing to the Other the theft of enjoyment is the traumatic fact that *we never possessed what was allegedly stolen from us*: the lack ("castration") is originary, enjoyment constitutes itself as "stolen"' (*Tarrying*, 203; cf. *Plague*, 32). Žižek's theme of the 'theft of enjoyment' reworks Hegel's dialectic of lord and bondsman (*Phenomenology*, §§178–96), exploring its implications for the contemporary political scene, especially racism and nationalism. A thoroughgoing instance of such analysis is the final chapter of *Tarrying with the Negative*.[8]

This examines how political identifications involve 'a shared relationship toward a Thing, toward Enjoyment incarnated' (*Tarrying*, 201). What we call 'a way of life' is the way a 'community' bases itself on the organization of enjoyment. National feeling arises from a common reference to enjoyment (such as festivals), and national tensions from fear that some other group threatens this enjoyment, or has a perverse relationship to it. Animosity towards other racial groups often concentrates on what they eat, or the smell of their food, or the way they themselves smell. The disgust which such things arouse is itself a form of enjoyment, the surplus enjoyment that arises from the conviction that these groups indulge in excessive enjoyments of a kind which we ourselves have renounced (*Tarrying*, 206). Totalitarian regimes make use of racial minorities as a kind of 'shock-absorber': if all the disgust of enjoyment can be projected on to, and borne by, another group, this helps to preserve the balance of the pleasure principle for the rest. Capitalist regimes are likewise eager to off-load their inherent imbalance and excess on to a racial Other, since this enables them to fantasize themselves as 'communities' rather than as impersonal 'societies' (*Tarrying*, 209–11). White liberal intellectuals are no more comfortable than racists with other people's enjoyment. They may be 'tolerant' of black community politics, but not of white rednecks (*Tarrying*, 213–14). Thus they merely reshuffle the cards, but keep the same deck. What is needed is not to embrace some alternative fantasy of enjoyment, but to gain a purchase on the structure which gives rise to fantasies of enjoyment in the first place. That is why, the book concludes, 'our very physical survival hinges on our ability to consummate the act of assuming fully the "nonexistence of the Other", of *tarrying with the negative*' (*Tarrying*, 237).

Conclusion

In the Marxist tradition the opposite of, and remedy for, ideology is Marxism, however defined. Althusser's critique of ideology, for instance, was predicated on a scientific, structuralist elaboration of Marx's thought. Žižek's critique, by contrast, operates through the substitution of psychoanalysis for Marxism. In his view no symbolic tool, however rigorous, is adequate to the task so long as it fails to recognize that the representations of power are supported by enjoyment. A purely symbolic approach does no more than replicate the structures of disavowal (the fetishistic split) on which ideology itself depends. A Lacanian approach discerns structures which are governed by the way fantasy mediates their occluded substance of *jouissance*, and proposes ways of altering our relationship to it.

Anti-capitalism

It is not until *The Ticklish Subject* that Žižek concentrates on capitalism as the political organization of enjoyment. Now psychoanalysis finds itself paired not so much, as hitherto, with Hegel as with Marx as a means of diagnosing political pathology.

The way we live now

Sustained analysis of late capitalist society begins in the final chapter of *The Ticklish Subject*.[9] Žižek sees it as a world in which Oedipus is under threat and faith in traditional forms of symbolic authority (S1) is at an all-time low. Monotheism is in retreat before the neo-paganism of New Agers; social cohesion has crumbled away into overlapping ethnic or identity-based interest groups; moral authority is in crisis, and decision making is remitted, as if in desperation, to proliferating committees.

Whereas previously Žižek's analyses have proposed two fathers competing over the symbolic law – the Oedipal father of symbolic authority and the superego father of enjoyment – now they are joined by a third. Identified as the father from Freud's *Moses and Monotheism*, this third father is the father of will and prohibition. He is not shadowy and obscene like the *père-vers*; he more closely resembles the Oedipal father in being ignorant of enjoyment and an enforcer of 'castration'. The difference between the father of will and the Oedipal father is that the former has power without authority. There is no legitimacy to his claims on us, just the traumatizing insistence that law is law. Žižek characterizes him as the 'inscrutable "dark God" of capricious "irrational" Predestination', 'the capricious abyss that lies beyond any global rational order of *logos*, a God who does not have to *account* for anything he does', 'this God of groundless Willing and ferocious "irrational" rage' (*Ticklish Subject*, 318–19) – in short, the Calvinistic God of the Reformation. This form of law, in which legitimacy and 'natural authority' are suspended, conditions the subject of modernity from Descartes onwards: the subject, that is, of modern science, of meaningless tragic renunciation (like Sygne de Coûfontaine), and of terror (as opposed to tyranny, always defined by its flouting of legitimate authority).

The problem with late capitalism, Žižek asserts, is that it is not just the symbolic Oedipal father – the legitimate order of premodernity – that is in decline. This traumatic 'real father' of modernity has also been unseated: 'When, today, one speaks of the decline of paternal authority, it is *this* father, the father of the uncompromising "No!", who is effectively in retreat' (*Ticklish Subject*, 322). The result of this retreat is that what Žižek calls 'symbolic efficiency' no longer obtains. The force behind prohibition having been withdrawn, there is no longer any agreed rule by which we need to live. Thus we turn to gurus, do-it-yourself books, agony aunts, professional shoppers, quangos and a plethora of other miniaturized substitutes for the big Other.

> Not only cyberspace but also domains as diverse as medicine and biogenetics on the one hand, and the rules of sexual conduct and the protection of human rights on the other, confront us with the need to invent the basic rules of proper ethical conduct, since we lack any form of big Other, any symbolic point of reference that would serve as a safe and unproblematic moral anchor. (*Ticklish Subject*, 332)

Instead of having a symbolic function that provides us with a point of identification in the symbolic (S1), an ego ideal based on the symbolic father, we proliferate symbolic authorities that are jumped-up versions of our ideal ego, and hence a sign of narcissistic regression (*Ticklish Subject*, 334).

Žižek recognizes that his description shares common ground with Anthony Giddens's account of the 'risk society'.[10] Giddens argues that we have now entered a postmodern era characterized

by information overload and a concomitant obsession with calcu-
lating outcomes, so that we are increasingly preoccupied with the
multiplicity of options before us, the risks associated with them, and
the difficulties of decision making. Specifically, Žižek acknowledges
as common ground with Giddens the sense that the modern subject
is 'reflexive' – that is, that the absence of coherent directives in the
society around us is reflected back into us as a requirement individually to assume responsibility for our own self-fashioning.[11] But
he differs from Giddens in two respects. On the one hand, Žižek
maintains, Giddens ignores the political and economic determi-
nants of our social situation (enter Marx). On the other, his analysis is restricted by not having recourse to psychoanalysis (enter
Lacan). At this point, I shall stop relying solely on *The Ticklish
Subject*, and include others of Žižek's recent writings to give a fuller
picture of how his anti-capitalist position combines the Lacanian
and then the Marxist account.

The Lacanian account

The problem with Giddens's theory, for Žižek, is that it ignores the
psychic dimension. True, contemporary society offers us what
seems like unlimited choice; in practice, however, this 'freedom'
provokes intense anxiety, which has to be explained not just in
terms of an individual's place in society, but of his or her subjection
within a symbolic order. A striking feature of this subjection is its
hysterical character. The postmodern capitalist subject, in Žižek's
view, desires nothing so much as to enter into variants of Hegel's
lord-and-bondsman relationship, which Žižek discusses using
Lacan's terminology of master and slave:[12] 'The rigidly codified
Master/Slave relationship turns up as the very form of "inherent
transgression" of subjects living in a society in which all forms of
life are experienced as a matter of the free choice of a lifestyle'
(*Ticklish Subject*, 345). The process underlying this, Žižek suggests,
is that we compensate for the master's demise in the public or symbolic sphere by reasserting his existence in the private or libidinal
one – for example, by entering sado-masochistic relationships, or by
subjecting ourselves to harsh private disciplines such as exercise
routines, dietary regimes, etc.

Such voluntary enslavement corresponds to the contemporary
form of the fundamental fantasy which, as Žižek argued earlier in
the same book (see my chapter 4), is masochistic. And it reflects the
psychoanalytical insight that the unconscious, far from being a site

of resistance to law, is the privileged locus of compliance with it – as a result, that is, of the superego compulsion to enjoy. Unbeknownst to Giddens, then, the reflexivity of the risk society extends to our libidinal make-up. The apparent claim to unlimited freedom of choice on the part of the postmodern subject is reflected back into him or her as the complicitous subservience to constraint. External authority gives way to a self-disciplining, attentive self-regard. The reign of Oedipus has given way to that of Narcissus.

Among the symptoms of this process, Žižek notes the rise in the 'culture of complaint' in which, 'far from cheerfully assuming the nonexistence of the big Other, the subject blames the Other for its failure and/or impotence' (*Ticklish Subject*, 361). Reproaching the Other for not functioning as it should is an attempt to conjure it (back) into existence, and, by insisting on its responsibility towards us, to claim 'compensation' from it. For what? For the sense of under-privilege which, Žižek suggests, arises from a hysterical demand that the Other as master should confirm the subject's narcissistic treasure, his *objet a*. In our increasingly litigious world, we resort to law to '*confirm the Other in its position in the very gesture of attacking it*' (ibid.). The 'freedom to be ourselves', then, paradoxically results in our tightening the constraints of regulation around our actions, and in demanding that the Other act on our behalf. A radical politics, by contrast, would lead us to suspend regulation and act ourselves.

If the 'culture of complaint' starts in the mode of hysteria, it is also perverse in that it seeks to bind the law to the service of our own *jouissance*. Žižek perceives the fragmentation of the symbolic by 'multiculturalism' as another case in which what is apparently an expression of political freedom becomes a form of perverse subjection: it promotes subservience to 'life-style' and role play, in which the subject's enjoyment becomes lodged in a pre-set rule (or 'style') (*Contingency*, 104). Multiculturalism relies on valuing differentiation: I identify myself in relation to a whole series of possible subcultures, and, as these become more discriminating, I also *disidentify* from them, clinging to a sacred essence of inner difference, my 'complex, unique personality' (*Contingency*, 103). Another way of putting this is that the conviction that one has an authentic existence outside ideology is especially a property of late capitalist, multiculturalist ideology. Žižek had formulated a version of this view as early as *Tarrying with the Negative* (216), where he singles out 'fear of "excessive" identification' as 'the fundamental feature of the late-capitalist ideology'; 'the Enemy is the "fanatic" who "overidentifies" instead of maintaining a proper distance towards the dispersed plurality of subject positions'. It is not just multiculturalism, then, but also its theoretical elaboration as the deconstructive/post-structuralist critique of identity, that is hand in glove with capitalism. These ostensibly Leftist positions in reality promote 'the form of subjectivity that corresponds to late capitalism'.

> Perhaps the time has come to resuscitate the Marxian insight that Capital is the ultimate power of 'deterritorialization' which undermines every fixed social identity, and to conceive of 'late capitalism' as the epoch in which the traditional fixity of ideological positions (patriarchal authority, fixed sexual roles, etc.) becomes an obstacle to the unbridled commodification of everyday life. (*Tarrying*, 216)[13]

Žižek contrasts the *activity* of identity politics with the *act* as he understands it: identity politics seeks to confirm identity, whereas the purpose of the act is fundamentally to alter the agent (*On Belief*, 85). The way forward, for Žižek, lies in combating symbolic fragmentation and reasserting universality. This needs to be done in the manner he has elucidated by reading Lacan in conjunction with Hegel: through building a 'concrete universality' on the basis of what is excluded in the current hegemony. Only in this way can the perverse subject recover a healthier relationship with symbolic law (*Contingency*, 90–135).

Thus Žižek discerns the late capitalist subject as having hysterical and perverse symptoms. The third element in his diagnosis is psychosis. One common expression of this is the proliferation of conspiracy theories, identified by Žižek as paranoid. Paranoia is most simply defined as the belief that there is an Other of the Other: that is, that the apparent gaps and deficiencies of the symbolic order are made good by some secret real Other beyond. A naive trust in religion or science as a hidden reality holding the key to an otherwise nonsensical world is paranoid, for example. Lacan's own definition of psychosis (*Seminar* III, 13, 320–2) is that it is a state in which what is foreclosed in the symbolic returns in the real. Thus the political 'work' accomplished by paranoia is the psychic reinstatement of the Other as real, in the teeth of its symbolic nonexistence. In late capitalist paranoid fantasy, the failure of law in the symbolic returns as the rule of some terrible real Thing: UFOs, invading aliens, weapons of mass destruction, terrorists. The value of a conspiracy theory is that it accounts for (indeed, foments) anxiety by fostering the delusion that there is 'something out there' pulling the strings and responsible for what is happening to us (see e.g. *Ticklish Subject*, 364). To parry these powers of horror, we need to take responsibility for ourselves by recourse to what Žižek – disturbingly – calls 'the good terror' (*Ticklish Subject*, 378): the radical political act whereby our relation to the symbolic order can be redrawn.

In *The Fragile Absolute* (§4; cf. *On Belief*, 59–62), Žižek summarizes the psychic change effected by late capitalism as one from 'the discourse of the Master' (S1) to a discourse centred on the surplus abject/object *a*. Evidence of this recentring on the *objet a* can be seen in the centrality of waste to capitalism; in a shift in mode from tragedy to mock comedy; or in the cult of the victim (§5). This role of *objet a* as nothing/surplus helps Žižek to throw a bridge between psychoanalysis and Marxism, and this is what I shall look at next.

The Marxist account

It is clear that, throughout the preceding section, Žižek's analysis has relied on capitalism in diagnosing our pathology. What does the Marxist account of capitalism contribute to this diagnosis? The Marxist solution of communist revolution may no longer be tenable, but Marxism nevertheless enables us to see that the current economic system is not politically neutral, and that we must repoliticize it.

Returning to the notion of a 'risk society', Žižek therefore points out that the cause of all its risks is, in fact, political: it is 'the uncontrolled use of science and technology in the conditions of capitalism' (*Ticklish Subject*, 350). Wouldn't an answer be, then, to place the control of such enterprises back in the hands of the public who are affected by them? Žižek also restores political visibility to class antagonism. The relationship of workers and capitalists to production is unequal, but it is disguised by globalization: the USA is the home of bankers and managers, while their labour force is in the Third World, far from view (*Did Somebody Say?*, 134).

Another strategy of politicization is to resist the commodification of diversity. Marxism exposes Leftist enthusiasm for multiculturalism as complicitous with precisely what the Left used to condemn, since it tacitly condones capitalism and class difference (*Contingency*, 96). 'Political correctness' suffers from the same fault – it merely marks 'a retreat from disturbing the real (economic, etc.) causes of racism and sexism' (*Did Somebody Say?*, 139). The dialectical method, adapted by Marx from Hegel, enables us to see that the point of exclusion in the current system (for example, the underclass) is the one from which to generate new concrete universals. Universality is our best recourse against globalization, which commodifies everything in the interests of the hegemonic capitalist class (*Fragile Absolute*, §2).

Here the continuity between Christianity and Marxism, explored in *The Fragile Absolute* and *On Belief*, comes into play. Christianity offers an account of the act as Christian love, or *agape*: that is, as a mode of affirmation that breaks out of the vicious cycle of law and transgression (see chapter 5). By the same token, it holds out the promise of universality modelled on the singular and the excluded. Within such a reformed symbolic faith the subject can hope to attain some distance from the threatening real. Marxism, it is implied, offers a means to a new community of the Holy Spirit based on a confrontation of the contemporary political world with renewed, politicized forms of charity, faith and hope.

The Fragile Absolute (23–4) also spells out the connection between the prevailing subject position as *objet a* and the Marxist theory of political economy. (I referred to this passage in the discussion of art as *objet a* in chapter 3.) Marx's account of capitalist productivity needs to be reread in the light of Lacan's adaptation of the term 'surplus value' to 'surplus enjoyment'. Just as the psyche turns around the lack/surplus at its heart, so productivity turns on the imbalances, the alternation between lack and excess inherent in capitalism. The psychic *objet a* is the site of the primordial lost object, and confers desirability on any object that comes to occupy its place; likewise, the capitalist machine is fuelled by the multiplication of commodities set to incite an essentially insatiable desire. As surplus enjoyment, the *objet a* binds the subject ever more tightly to obey the law; as surplus value, it commits the economy to the spiralling growth of the capitalist enterprise, with its ever greater expenditure and ever greater debts. The fact that the subject encircles the *objet a* which stands in the place of the drive is what makes it the 'answer of the real'. Thus, the *objet a* is the necessary point of exclusion over which the contemporary subject, and contemporary society, are defined. In capitalist production, the *objet a* points to the fact that 'the ultimate limit of capitalism . . . is Capital itself' (*Fragile Absolute*, 17; also *Ticklish Subject*, 358).

The real of capital

'Capital', then, has become the limit of our thought. That is to say, Žižek proposes, it has become impossible to challenge the pre-eminence of capital, or to conceive of living otherwise than under capitalism. Thus there is a sense in which capital is the real which determines what we understand by 'reality' (*Ticklish Subject*, 276). This controversial suggestion is elaborated in *Contingency, Hegemony, Universality*, in which Žižek, Butler and Laclau debate the way forward for today's Left. All are agreed on the need to change the prevailing ideology. But, Žižek maintains, change always takes place relative to some unchanging limit, and today that limit is capital. Capital is the invisible, obscene underside of today's institutions which is never questioned, and, in this sense, it is the real (*Contingency*, 223).

Žižek's formulation provokes an outcry from his interlocutors. Butler contends that the foreclosure of capital from signification is 'real' in *her* use of the term, not Žižek's – that is, it designates something which is unthinkable under current political conditions, but could be recuperated to thought if conditions changed (*Contingency*, 277). Laclau is openly contemptuous. 'Now, [Žižek] knows as well as I do what the Lacanian Real is; so he should also be aware that capitalism *cannot* be the Lacanian Real' (*Contingency*, 291). Capitalism, Laclau maintains with some force, can exist only because it is a symbolic system. Of course symbolic systems have holes in them, which is why capitalism is messy and contested; but it remains the system, not the hole.

In *The Fragile Absolute* (§§2, 4–7) Žižek comes to the defence of his identification of capital as the real. Capital courses on its way, indifferent to its impact on social reality. It is the spectral drive, the systematic structure concealed behind actual experience, a manifestation of the evil that lurks within the social *id* (*Fragile Absolute*, 15). To grasp the sense of 'real' that is meant here, it helps to go back to *The Indivisible Remainder*, where Žižek first begins to speak of psychoanalysis as being, like Marxism, a 'dialectical materialism' (see chapter 2, pp. 31–3). Capital is not real in the sense that the impossible deadlock of 'castration' is. It is not a real of lack; on the contrary, it is real in the sense that material singularities are real: they cannot be assumed into language, but their impact on our experience is irrefutable. This is what Žižek will later call 'the real real' (*On Belief*, 82). Likewise, the logic of capital is irrecusably real in the sense that Lacan's mathemes are real. All attempts to recast them in language are imperfect; but the formulae themselves capture the crazy structures that determine the way we speak – this is what Žižek refers to as 'real abstraction' (*Fragile Absolute*, 16; in *On Belief*, 82, he calls it the 'symbolic real'). Finally, he reminds us, the Lacanian real is not the substance of some banished content, but the violence of its repression (the primordial repression). This violence continues to haunt our fantasies, and thus there is a spectrality of capital, just as there are spectres associated with other political formations. So there is also an 'imaginary real' of capital which is never actualized but which we cannot escape (*Fragile Absolute*, §6).

Žižek's claim that capital is real remains hard to understand. A consequence of it, however, is that we should recognize differences of power and economic status as being as traumatizing as those of sexual difference, and as smeared with horror and obscenity. Indeed, this seems to be the direction indicated by Žižek's identification, in *The Ticklish Subject*, of the foundational fantasy as a masochistic scenario.

Conclusion

Žižek's account of capitalism is very similar to that which he gives of cyberspace (see chapter 3). It precipitates the collapse of symbolic authority and reduces the subject to the status of an object – the abject/object *a* of Lacanian algebra. Under its virtual, or spectral, reign, the real threatens to crash down on reality. The hysterical, perverse and paranoid tendencies to which this gives rise are at once expressions of anxiety and defensive attempts to make good the loss of external authority by reinstating it as inner enslavement. Capitalism itself, whether or not it is 'real', seems never to be open to question.

Desperate though the situation is, however, Žižek doesn't abandon hope of radical change: '[Laclau's] justified rejection of the fullness of post-revolutionary Society does *not* justify the conclusion that we have to renounce any project of a global social transformation, and limit ourselves to resolving only partial problems' (*Contingency*, 101). If change there is to be, it can come only by committing what he calls the 'act': the radical upheaval that will make it possible to forge the universal anew. Thus the closing words of *The Ticklish Subject* exhort us to take the risk of severing ourselves from existing 'reality' in the hopes of creating something better:

> The choice is between bad and worse; what Freudian ethics opposes
> to the 'bad' superego version of *You may!* is another, even more

radical *You may!* . . . no longer vouched for by any figure of the
Master. Lacan's maxim 'Do not compromise your desire!' fully
endorses the pragmatic paradox of ordering you to be free: it exhorts
you to dare. (*Ticklish Subject*, 392)

Anti-liberalism

It is this determination to dare that separates Žižek from liberalism.
Liberals, he thinks, are more or less satisfied with the *status quo* and
against the radical act (*Contingency*, 127–8). Like Hegel's 'Beautiful
Soul', they wring their hands over the current state of affairs while
in fact benefiting under it and passively promoting it.[14] In practice,
they are no different from conservatives. If anything, Žižek has
more respect for conservatives, who at least radically contest capitalism and call for new universals, even if they are the wrong ones
(e.g. *Did Somebody Say?*, 242–4).

Butler cautions that the positions Žižek now espouses would, in
the USA, indeed be associated with the Right (*Contingency*, 278).
Laclau condemns Žižek as a totalitarian, or else as confused (*Contingency*, 289). It is true that Žižek, a self-identified 'old-fashioned
dialectical materialist' (*Did Somebody Say?*, 216), often reads like a
crusty old codger. The Left isn't what it used to be, and the world
is going to the dogs, are his unceasing complaints as he sounds off
at the political apathy and moral self-righteousness of modern
Western academics. The prevailing liberal orthodoxies of queer,
post-colonial, and Holocaust studies afford him ample occasion for
irritation throughout *Did Somebody Say Totalitarianism?*.[15]

The basic thesis of this book is, nevertheless, both true and hard-
hitting: namely, that 'totalitarianism' is an ideological notion 'firmly
located within the liberal-democratic horizon' which 'actively *prevents* us from thinking' (3). 'Totalitarian' is less a political description than a slogan, a rallying call inviting us to condemn whatever
it qualifies. Liberalism underwrites freedom of thought, but only
within prescribed limits. In some respects it is itself totalitarian: for
example, in its enthusiasm for deconstructing binaries such as
sexual difference, and its refusal to recognize the crucial importance
of class antagonism (*Did Somebody Say?*, 237–43).

And what is the 'freedom' of which liberalism boasts when
distancing itself from 'totalitarianism' (*On Belief*, 112–22)? Of course,
Žižek admits, Lenin's draconian measures now have a bad name;

with hindsight we can see where he went wrong. But is liberalism better? Doesn't it deprive us of rights in the name of 'freedom of choice'? When we lose security of employment, it admonishes us to enjoy a 'portfolio career' in which we can 'choose' a succession of different jobs; when the public health service is inadequate, it entitles the poor to 'choose' across a whole range of expensive private options which they could never afford. By pretending that such choices lie within our own discretion, liberal regimes disguise the constraints to which we are effectively subject. Moreover, liberalism as such denies the repressive force of our subjection to the symbolic in the first place: 'So the paradox is that "liberal" subjects are in a way those least free: they change the very opinion/perception of themselves, accepting what was *imposed* on them as originating in their "nature" – they are no longer even aware of their subordination' (*On Belief*, 120). Lenin had the merit of underlining how any freedom is freedom for a particular group to do a particular thing; that is, that freedom is always located within the context of political struggle. Real freedom of choice comes when we don't select from a pre-given menu of options, but determine the options themselves. To do so, we need to find a way out of the forced choice with which the political *status quo* presents us. Lenin, this discussion concludes, is a better guide than liberalism to how this can be achieved, since all his efforts were geared to holding open the revolutionary choice (*On Belief*, 122).

A pro-Leninist stance is also in evidence in *Did Somebody Say Totalitarianism?*. Lenin did not believe in fitting the act to the circumstances, but in using it to change them (*Did Somebody Say?*, 114). Such an act cannot be effected without 'the terrorism that characterizes every authentic ethical stance' (*Did Somebody Say?*, 91). A return to authoritarian rule may actually be desirable, since at times, Žižek asserts, 'one *does* need a Leader in order to be able to "do the impossible". The authentic Leader is literally the One who enables me actually to *choose myself* – subordination to him is the highest act of freedom' (*Did Somebody Say?*, 247).

Provocative statements such as these are typical of the risks inherent in Žižek's political prescriptions. Is his Leftism so authoritarian as indeed to be indistinguishable from the far Right? Is his celebration of the 'act' tantamount to a psychopath's charter? Is he an advocate of terrorism and nothing more? These are the questions I address in the final section of this chapter.

Kill or Cure? Žižek's Political Brinkmanship

Žižek's political thought relies on brinkmanship. His exhortation to literalism in executing the law (good) has to be demarcated from his denunciation of perversion as conservative (not good); his attack on cynicism (as bad) is hard to distinguish from his encouragement to adopt a distance from the symbolic order as non all (good); his promotion of universality depends on the possibility of discriminating between the singular excluded (good) and the particular exception (not good) as correlates of the universal; and, most difficult of all, his notion of the political act (extremely good) relies upon a fine sense of its difference from the political atrocity (awful). The fact that the act, for him, is overwhelmingly associated with either suicide or terror (or both) is disquieting; his recent assault on liberalism does little to reassure most of us who are basically wet liberals and take a lot of persuading. I shall review these flash-points of risk before offering a brief conclusion.

Perversion and literalism

Žižek repeatedly advocates adhering to the letter of the law as a means of exposing it as 'non all'. The law as such is flimsy; what makes it effective is the hidden support of fantasy and the traumatic violence which that fantasy transmits/disguises. Yet he denounces the conservatism inherent in another form of adherence to the law: that instanced by perversion, 'the model of false subversive radicalization that fits the existing power constellation perfectly' (*Ticklish Subject*, 251). Contrary to popular belief, perversion is not a means of access to the radical freedom of the unconscious, but a form of fixation on fantasy. The unconscious is abyssal; it is formed by cuts; it is not a set of contents, but an absence; and it is fantasy that fleshes it out. The substance of fantasy is the *objet a* as surplus enjoyment. Thus, by his resolve to act out certain fantasies, the pervert maintains, and confers fixity upon, the obscene support of law. Even though he may appear transgressive, he confirms the way the law is currently constituted. An exaggerated legalism, by contrast, in its literalism, forces a gap between law and fantasy, and thereby reveals the insubstantiality of the law once it is deprived of its fantasmatic support. 'Working to rule' is, in this way, like feminine masquerade (see chapter 4): a way of showing that the law is non all. These are procedures which, however, have to be distinguished from cynicism.

Cynicism and freedom

Cynicism is one of Žižek's most consistent targets throughout his writing. The reason why he opposes it is that (like perversion) cynicism poses as subversive, whereas in fact it reinforces ideology, since its imaginary distance from it is something ideology has already taken into account. Indeed, irony and detachment, the belief in an independent, authentic position outside ideology, are examples of ideology at its most insidious. In contrast to this, Žižek exhorts us to a freedom that *does* consist in inner distance from ideology. The discovery that the symbolic order is 'non all', the possibility of 'traversing the fantasy', and committing the 'act' are all expressions of this freedom which demand that the subject distance him or her self from the law. Problem and solution thus appear to converge.

Žižek confronts this difficulty in *Did Somebody Say Totalitarianism?* (14), where the formula 'he knows very well what he is doing, but he is doing it' is admitted as allowing contradictory readings in which 'the lowest and the highest coincide'. For the cynic, the formula reflects a willingness to go along with the way the world is, despite inner ironic distance from it; for the radical political agent, however, it expresses a resolve to change the way the world is, no matter at what personal cost. The cynical split, in short, is performed within the symbolic, whereas freedom involves 'traversing the fantasy'. Thus cynicism belongs 'within the pleasure principle', freedom beyond it. Indeed, it is the space occupied by fantasy, the sense of it as an inner core, which creates the distance 'traversed' by the free subject in its momentary plunge into the real. Cynicism is only a false or pseudo freedom from ideological constraint, whereas genuine political freedom is the subject's birthright, which can be attained only through subjective destitution.

Universality

The space of political universality is one of ideological struggle. For a hegemonic group to establish itself at the expense of others, it needs to colonize this space in its own interests. The political universal is thus usually the exact opposite of what one might take it to be: not an abstraction from a set of particulars, but the manifestation of the express interests of a particular group. Even something apparently excluded from the symbolic register can be the support of a universal which is not, of itself, politically valuable – like perversion, for instance, in which 'the dimension of universality is always sustained by fixation on some particular point' (*Plague*, 104).

So how are we to recognize a 'good' universal? I am not sure Žižek has an answer, other than a priori ones, to this question. A valid universality for him is one that will unite groups of whom he approves in a struggle of which he approves. This emerges in his discussion of the 'concrete universal' in *Contingency, Hegemony, Universality* (referred to in chapter 2) in the passage where Žižek proposes *noir* cinema and 'French theory' as examples of the forging of 'concrete universals'. In neither case is the universal 'abstracted from' existing particulars, for the good reason that the particulars don't exist; we thus have, as Žižek amusingly puts it, a 'non-existent' theory addressed to a 'non-existent' corpus. But his attitudes to the two sides of his example are revealingly divergent. He supports the concept of *film noir*, and indeed uses it repeatedly; emerging from outside the field of the particular, it speaks to him of truth. Where theory is concerned, however, he despises what he sees as the Anglophone misappropriation of French thought, and strenuously advocates a 'return to Lacan' – hence his strictures on Cultural Studies. On the political front, similarly, he dismisses universals adduced in the interests of identity politics, but approves those brought forward in the name of those he recognizes as genuinely economically exploited and politically excluded.

The act

As I said when discussing Badiou's concept of the 'event' (in chapter 5), it is not self-evident what constitutes an 'event' (or an 'act'). Examples of what Žižek calls 'acts' vary widely in scope and impact. At the lowest level of *agape* there is a kind of Pollyanna-ish 'saying "Yes!" to life in its mysterious synchronic multitude' (*Fragile Absolute*, 103; also *Fright*, 172; cf. *Ticklish Subject*, 150). Then there is the *fait divers* of Mary Kay Letourneau's affair with a boy under the age of consent. Some characters in works of literature or film perform an 'act' when they sacrifice what they hold dearest, committing what Žižek calls 'a strike against the self'. An example is Kevin Spacey's shooting of his own wife and daughter, who are being held hostage by rival gangsters, in *The Usual Suspects* (*Fragile Absolute*, 149–50). Others literary characters, like Antigone and Sygne, or Sophie in *Sophie's Choice* (*Enjoy!*, 70ff), act in such a way as to kill themselves, whether physically, symbolically or both. When we move to the political dimension, and the act is no longer the affair just of an individual, there is a marked raising of the stakes. Talk is no longer about renunciation or suicide, but terror. The historical Terror of the French Revolution is a constant reference point, and we learn that 'there is something inherently terroristic in every authentic act' (*Ticklish Subject*, 377). The 'political act *par excellence*' (ibid.) would be revolution, even though that seems not to be an option today.

On the other hand, Nazism and Stalinism fail to qualify as events (or acts), because (says Žižek) they don't emerge *ex nihilo*, and nor do they institute a paradigm change; instead, they rely on appeal to some 'global order of being' (*Ticklish Subject*, 132 – the wrong kind of universal?).[16] He reaches the same conclusion *vis-à-vis* the events of September 11, 2001, which, one might have thought, have some claim to be read as an act, since they involved multiple suicide, declarations that the world would never be the same again, and the forging of a new universal movement against terrorism.[17] Yet Žižek stresses instead how the bombings were already internal to American fantasy, and how what seemed like an external irruption against the USA was in fact 'a distilled version of our own essence', the reversion upon us of centuries of Western violence. So far, in his view, the new is yet to emerge from these events. He exhorts us not to be deterred by such pseudo-acts, but to 'search even more stringently for the "good terror"' (*Ticklish Subject*, 378).

The problem is that the 'good terror' is as elusive as the 'good universal'. It is a blow for change that Žižek recognizes as coming from the Left – that is, from where he positions himself – but that is impossible to anchor in any other way. Saying 'Yes!' to life could be more of an act than bombing the World Trade Centre. As Grigg puts it, 'there is no objective criterion and there can clearly be no appeal to any subjective features to distinguish an act of absolute freedom from a gratuitous act' ('Absolute Freedom', 123).[18]

Of course, Grigg's critique doesn't say anything Žižek would not agree with. The whole point of the act, for Žižek, is that the subject surrenders all guarantees and gives up its *objet a* as a hostage to fortune. The act is perilous, but it has to be: the purgative force of the death drive is the only force adequate to cauterize the wound of civilization, whether it be individual 'castration' or political subjection. As another of Žižek's favourite quotations has it, 'the wound can only be healed by the spear that smote you':[19] it is only by momentarily suspending symbolization that its terms can be altered. Hope, freedom and agency can come only through madness. Such a concept of the act is incompatible with political calculation. This is not to say that Žižek does not believe in political *activity*. But activity does not have the capacity for radical change that is born with the act.[20] The choice, as he repeatedly says, is between bad and worse: worse is better than bad if good will follow. There is a striking combination of optimism and pessimism in this view: pessimism about the situation as it is, optimism that it could be transformed.

What is the therapeutic basis for this optimism? Žižek's theorization of the act varies in this regard. Broadly speaking, he remains within the framework of Lacan's definition according to which 'an act [*acte*], a true act, always has an element of structure, by the fact of concerning a real that is not self-evidently caught up in it' (*Seminar* XI, 50). In Lacan, the *acte* is distinct from hysterical 'acting out', and also from the *passage à l'acte*, a psychotic impulse in which the subject's relation to the symbolic order is suspended, and the subject as such therefore ceases to exist, but is instead objectified.[21] The true act – like a praxis, as he defines it at the beginning of *Seminar* XI when defining psychoanalysis itself – is a way to 'treat the real by [means of] the symbolic' (15). This phrase is echoed in *Contingency* when Žižek says:

> Precisely because of this internality of the Real to the Symbolic, it *is* possible to touch the Real through the Symbolic – that is the whole point of Lacan's notion of psychoanalytic treatment; this is what the Lacanian notion of the psychoanalytic *act* is about – the act as a gesture which, by definition, touches the dimension of some impossible Real. (*Contingency*, 121)

In *Enjoy!* Žižek nevertheless seems to inflect the term in the direction of Lacan's *passage à l'acte*. In the second chapter he uses examples of suicidal behaviour from Rosselini's films that recall Freud's case study of the young homosexual woman who tried to kill herself in an act of desperate self-abdication – the case which, for Lacan, typifies the *passage à l'acte*. For example, when the character Edmund in Rosselini's *Germany, Year Zero* commits suicide, Žižek says that 'he passes over to the act' (*Enjoy!*, 35). This bent continues at least to *The Ticklish Subject*, where, in the course of an argument with Badiou, Žižek criticizes him for opposing the 'full revolutionary *passage à l'acte*' (*Enjoy!*, 166).

More recent writings have refocused his understanding of the act. An important passage in *On Belief* (81–5) picks up but modifies a note in *Enjoy!* where Žižek plots the concept of act through the registers of symbolic, imaginary and real.[22] The act, he now says explicitly, is not the hysterical 'acting out' (of the imaginary), nor an act/edict (of the symbolic), nor yet again the psychotic *passage à l'acte* (of the real). 'The act proper is the only one which restructures the very symbolic co-ordinates of the agent's situation: it is an intervention in the course of which the agent's identity itself is radically changed' (*On Belief*, 85). This passage continues with a comparison between the act and belief. This shift towards symbolic responsibility is evident too in the roughly contemporary *Contingency, Hegemony, Universality* (121–2):

> So when we are reproached by an opponent for doing something unacceptable, an act occurs when we no longer defend ourselves by accepting the underlying premiss that we hitherto shared with the opponent; in contrast, we fully accept the reproach, changing the very terrain that made it unacceptable – an act occurs when our answer to the reproach is 'Yes, *that* is precisely what I am doing'.

It seems to me that the licence Žižek gives himself *vis-à-vis* Lacan serves two purposes. First, it enables him both to keep and to reverse Lacan's formula whereby, via the act, we can 'treat the real by means of the symbolic'. The act, as Žižek understands it, will also 'treat the symbolic by means of the real' – that is, allow us to reboot in the real so as to start up our relationship with the symbolic afresh. Second, it means that he effects a convergence between Lacan's *acte*, which belongs on the side of the analyst, and Lacan's *passage à l'acte*, which belongs on the side of the patient. In so doing, Žižek has brought together the two halves of the analytic scene in a way which I signalled in my Introduction *à propos* the anecdote of his therapy with Miller, where Žižek scripts himself as both analyst and patient.

These two moves may leave the reader uncertain as to the therapeutic value of the act. In terms of political 'treatment', the earlier work on ideology, with its prospect of traversing the political fantasy, may be the more effective. Žižek's conflation of the analyst's '*acte*' with the patient's '*passage à l'acte*' leaves me uncertain as to the balance between desperation and responsibility, madness and hope, that his concept of the act has to offer. In the therapeutic situation, the patient – even if he 'passes to the act' – is to some degree safeguarded by the presence of the analyst. But in the social or political arena, where the transference is with other social and political agents, the agent has no such protection; and once the roles of analyst and patient are confused, the structure disappears that makes that protection possible.

However, it is also possible to see Žižek's location of the act between analyst and patient in a more positive light. I should like to conclude this argument, and this book, by suggesting that Žižek positions himself both as trying to help bring about change, but also as a part of the world which needs to change. The way he writes, consequently, is a form of 'act' which participates in both the analyst's knowledge and the patient's complaint. This final section, then, links up with the one on Žižek's personal style in my Introduction where I described him as superimposing these two roles as a means of 'writing about the real'.

Conclusion: The Abject Slovene and the Political Act of Writing

For They Know Not What They Do begins with Freud's letter about a Slovene whom he judged unfit for psychoanalytical treatment because he was morally undeserving, and also because his condition (impotence) was beyond the reach of analysis. As Žižek points out, Freud's remarks perform precisely the deadlock which Lacan will make explicit as the fulcrum of his theory. Freud begins with an impediment (the Slovene's moral degeneracy and unworthiness), and surreptitiously transforms it into an impossibility (the Slovene is anyway beyond the reach of therapy). The first argument both bolsters, and conceals, the second. Thus it was, Žižek concludes, that Freud let the Slovenes down, whereas in Lacan they found a psychoanalyst who could attend to their abject plight.

This figure of the Slovene recalls Žižek's anecdote about his analysis with Miller. Like his fellow countryman, Žižek both resists analysis (doing his best to thwart and outmanoeuvre Miller) and provokes its reformulation. His frantic writing is a hysterical performance intended to prompt the reader into the position of analyst. But at the same time, his provocative posturing rouses us from psychotic indifference and prompts us to hysteria, allowing him then to assume the discourse of the analyst. Lucid, confrontational, exasperating and exuberant in its brilliance, his discourse hurtles against our reasonable expectations. It takes us on an obstacle course to impossibility, and then, back through the narrow gate of impossibility again, to freedom and boundless new horizons.

As Žižek says in the last words of his interview 'The One Measure of True Love' following the events of September 11, 2001: 'We face a challenge to rethink our co-ordinates and I hope that this will be a good result of this tragic event. That we will not just use it to do more of the same but to think about what is really changing in our world.' His recent works may not be a form of symbolic *activity* that would make the world a better place. But if they expose us to the real, provoking us to rethink our entire situation, then they are a form of political *act*.

Glossary of Žižekian Terms

For further information regarding psychoanalytical terms, refer to Evans, *Introductory Dictionary*; Laplanche and Pontalis, *Language*; and Wright, *Feminism*; and for more on Hegelian terms, to Inwood, *Hegel Dictionary*.

ACT: a concept of central importance to Žižek's ethics and politics. Initially Žižek inflects the concept in the direction of Lacan's *passage à l'acte*, a psychotic action in which the SUBJECT *objectifies* herself and the relation to the symbolic is suspended: 'And what is the *act* if not the moment when the subject who is its bearer *suspends* the network of symbolic fictions which serve as a support to his daily life and confronts again the radical negativity on which they are founded?' (*Enjoy!*, 53; for the term 'symbolic', see REGISTER). Subsequently, however, the act becomes closer to Lacan's *acte*, an action engaging the real but with symbolic significance for which the subject assumes responsibility (see *Contingency*, 121ff). Thus, in *On Belief*, 84–5, Žižek contrasts his understanding of the 'act' with both hysterical 'acting out' and Lacan's *passage à l'acte*. What remains crucial to Žižek, however, is the capacity of the act, as a moment of rupture and absolute freedom, to reposition the subject relative to the symbolic: 'the act proper is the only one which restructures the very symbolic co-ordinates of the agent's situation: it is an intervention in the course of which the agent's identity itself is radically changed' (*On Belief*, 85). Its effect, then, is to 'traverse the FANTASY'; so it may have tremendous therapeutic value. Examples of the act as conceived by Žižek are suicide, terrorism, renunciation (the surrender of one's *OBJET a*), love and militant politics; his thinking draws on Kant, Hegel, Kierkegaard and Schelling, and, most recently, on Christian theology.

APRES-COUP: The psychoanalytical view of time is that it does not progress in a linear way but in a kind of backward loop, so that the crucial tense is the future perfect: what 'will have been'. For example, a childhood experience *will* reveal itself *to have been* traumatic if it is reactivated as such – for example, in a neurotic symptom – by some subsequent turn of events. The concept of *après-coup* does not mean that the past does not determine the present – it does, but in a way that is itself overdetermined by the present. Thus significance is always grasped retrospectively. An elementary effect of *après-coup* is that it is not until the end of a sentence that the meaning of its beginning can be ascertained. A more complex instance is that the SUBJECT, which is nothing but the failure of S1 to represent it to S2, is nevertheless perceived as what *will have been filled out* by S2 (see SIGNIFYING CHAIN). For this reason, the subject is said to be an effect which retroactively posits its own cause. There is nothing teleological about *après-coup*; the point is that what may seem inevitable is a purely contingent state of affairs. The process of *après-coup* shapes Lacan's reading of Freud and Žižek's readings of both Lacan and Hegel: each reader reveals from his or her own, contingent viewpoint 'what's in the text which could not be written there' ('Lacan in Slovenia', 26).

BARRED OTHER: see BIG OTHER.

BIG OTHER: This is Žižek's translation of Lacan's *Autre* with a capital A. The big Other is where the authority of the symbolic order is assumed to lie (see REGISTER). For example, if I say, 'I declare this meeting over', then the point of this speech act is to register in the big Other that the meeting is closed (*Enjoy!*, 98). Belief in such authority equates to supposing that there is something additional to the symbolic order which props it up. But the idea that there is 'an Other of the Other' is psychotic (see PSYCHOSIS); this is why we need to discover that the big Other 'does not exist', that it is merely an impostor, that it is lacking or inconsistent as a result of its deficient relation to the REAL. The outcome of this discovery is known as 'the barred Other' (Ⱥ). Ⱥ is the correlate of $, the barred SUBJECT, which is likewise deficient in its relation to the real. It is represented by the object S(Ⱥ), known as the 'signifier of the barred

Other'. A̶ is also a way of acknowledging that the Other is 'non all'; see NEGATION, etc. Although the Other is primarily associated with the symbolic order, Žižek (like Lacan) discerns in it the horror and inhumanity of the real. For example, the irreducible otherness of other people is a form of the real which is registered in the Other.

'CASTRATION': the process whereby one becomes a (sexed) SUBJECT. Lacan's concept of castration refers less to the Oedipal drama (central to Freud's thought) and more to the imposition of language; the 'phallus' still plays a starring role for Lacan, but only by virtue of being what is lacking. Žižek continues and accentuates this linguistic bent; the scare quotes round 'castration' mark his distance from the Freudian theatre of emasculation. He is principally interested in the phallus in its symbolic dimension, as the phallic signifier Φ. In this object, the absence/negativity of the phallus is rendered as a positive presence, as a pure appearance which fascinates and seduces the observer.

Castration is often identified by Žižek with the 'forced choice'. This is the process whereby, when we enter the symbolic order, we are led to imagine that we had a choice, and that we gave up unmediated access to ENJOYMENT in exchange for inclusion within the law. But this is an illusion. In fact we had no choice at all, since if we hadn't submitted to the constraints of language, we could not have been subjects, and so there would have been no 'we' and no sense of 'having access' to anything. The sense of loss is created after the fact, and gives rise the elusive object-remainder, *OBJET a*.

In his later books Žižek distances himself from 'the false poetry of castration' as centred on lack in the symbolic order (*Indivisible Remainder*, 93). In *The Ticklish Subject* he adopts Lacan's account of the lamella, a unicellular organism, as an alternative way of talking about subject formation. This new account grounds subjectivity in the impact of the SIGNIFYING CHAIN on the DRIVE rather than on Oedipal law and DESIRE. The notion of 'castration' thereby becomes even further removed from the Oedipal drama and the phallus.

DESIRE: for Žižek, the important dimension of Lacan's teaching on desire is its opposition to DRIVE. Desire is both repressed and produced by the Oedipal law, and it therefore falls under the secure, pacifying regime of the PLEASURE PRINCIPLE. It operates like a chain, providing the subject with a series of objects to pursue, all of which are substitutes for the enigmatic *OBJET a*. Because desire comes to us from the Other, it is a mistake to think of it as subversive; on the contrary, it is banal in the extreme.

DESUBLIMATION: see PERVERSION AND SUBLIMATION.

DISCOURSE: Žižek adopts from Lacan's *Seminar* XVII an account of four discourses: those of the master, the university, the analyst and the hysteric (see *Cogito and the Unconscious*, 74–113). These discourses are each composed of four interconnected elements: S1 (the master signifier), S2 (the chain of knowledge), $ (the split subject) and *a* (the remainder of the real which is differently construed in all four discourses) (see also *OBJET a*, SIGNIFYING CHAIN, SUBJECT). Each of the discourses disposes these four elements in a different way, and a single rotation switches their disposition in one discourse to that in another. The four positions charted by the formula are: agent, addressee, production and truth, thus:

$$\frac{\text{agent}}{\text{truth}} \quad \begin{matrix} \rightarrow \\ \\ \leftarrow \end{matrix} \quad \frac{\text{addressee}}{\text{knowledge}}$$

The 'discourse of the master', where the master signifier is the agent, is represented as follows:

$$\frac{\text{S1}}{\$} \quad \begin{matrix} \rightarrow \\ \\ \leftarrow \end{matrix} \quad \frac{\text{S2}}{a}$$

That is, the master signifier is in the position of agent, upholding his authority as a subject, although the truth of the subject is that it is split. The subject as master addresses himself to all the other signifiers which between them make up the chain of knowledge (S2). However, what 'falls out' from this process, or is produced by it, is the remainder, *a*, the element of the real which eludes signification. To reach the discourse of the university, all the elements shift one place anticlockwise. Now the position of agent is occupied by S2, S1 has become the hidden truth of the university (the fact that its claim to knowledge in fact rests on arbitrary authority), the addressee is the untutored real, and the product, the outcome of university teaching, is the split or hysterical subject. The next rotation produces the discourse of the analyst. Here the object-remainder *a* is placed in the position of agent, to give:

$$\frac{a}{S2} \quad\begin{array}{c}\rightarrow\\ \\ \leftarrow\end{array}\quad \frac{\$}{S1}$$

Finally, the discourse of the hysteric is represented as follows (see also HYSTERIA):

$$\frac{\$}{a} \quad\begin{array}{c}\rightarrow\\ \\ \leftarrow\end{array}\quad \frac{S1}{S2}$$

DRIVE: what a biological instinct becomes once it is subject to the signifier. Drives are thus connected both to the SYMBOLIC order of signification and to the REAL of the foreclosed biological body (see e.g. *On Belief*, 100–4). Initially a sexually undifferentiated libido, figured as the unicellular organism lamella, the biological life force becomes drive as a result of 'CASTRATION'. This brings sexual difference, death and fragmentation. Fragmentation in turn gives rise to partial objects, such as voice (see SUPEREGO) and GAZE. The 'most radical form' of drive is the death drive (*Ticklish Subject*, 291) which Žižek defines thus: 'it precisely does *not* lie in [the] longing to die, to find peace in death: the death drive, on the contrary, is the very opposite of dying, it is a name for the "undead" eternal life itself, for the horrible fate of being caught in the endless repetitive cycle of wandering around in guilt and pain' (*Ticklish Subject*, 292). Drive turns endlessly round its object; its ENJOYMENT consists solely in keeping going. For this reason it lends itself to the two interrelated structures of PERVERSION AND SUBLIMATION, both of which are designed to keep it from attaining its object. Drive is contrasted with DESIRE, which is located in the symbolic order. Drive is not the same as the REAL, but it is the closest the psyche gets to it, and is therefore regularly associated with it.

ENJOYMENT: Žižek's translation of the Lacanian term *jouissance*. Although *jouissance* carries stronger and (because it can connote orgasm) more sexual associations than English 'enjoyment', 'enjoyment' has the benefit of gesturing towards the signified ('enjoy-meant') in a way similar to *jouissance* (*jouis-sens* = 'enjoy-meaning'), as Žižek often makes explicit (e.g. *Sublime Object*, 44). The signified in question is the REAL, of which enjoyment is the manifestation ('the Real *par excellence* is *jouissance*': *Sublime Object*, 164). Enjoyment is 'the only substance acknowledged by psychoanalysis' (*For They Know Not*, 19). It is the aim of the DRIVES, especially the death drive, which is why enjoyment is often qualified as 'deathly'. Enjoyment is also qualified as 'idiotic', because we are unaware of it; it is by definition excluded from the experience of the speaking subject.

In Žižek's usage, enjoyment is usually identifiable with what Lacan calls 'surplus enjoyment' (*plus de jouissance/plus de jouir*). Given that the real as such is inaccessible, enjoyment comes in the form of a surplus, or remainder, that permeates all of our SYMBOLIC institutions as their obscene underside, and which is represented in Lacan's algebra by the *OBJET a*. At the same time as being unknown to us, it is compulsory: 'enjoyment itself, which we experience as "transgression", is in its innermost status something imposed, ordered – when we enjoy, we never do it "spontaneously", we always follow a certain injunction' (*For They Know Not*, 9). The agency which compels us to enjoy surplus enjoyment is the SUPEREGO, and the object whereby it does so is the voice.

Feminine enjoyment, sometimes referred to as 'enjoyment beyond the phallus', is not a positive form of enjoyment, but arises from the fact that the enjoyment available within the symbolic order is 'non all', i.e. all there is, but nevertheless not enough; see NEGATION, etc.

FANTASY: the means whereby the psyche fixes its relation to ENJOYMENT. Fantasy is not opposed to 'reality': on the contrary, it is what structures what we call reality, and determines the contours of DESIRE. Likewise it is not 'escapist'; rather, it is shot through with the traumatic enjoyment which it helps to repress; thus fantasy both shields us from the REAL and transmits it. Lacan's matheme of fantasy, $ \$ \lozenge a $, denotes that the barred SUBJECT is protected from its lack, or split, of the real by the fundamental fantasy. The concept of fantasy plays an important part in Žižek's account of the functioning of works of art and of political ideologies. Fantasy is immobilizing, and one end to psychoanalytic therapy is to go through or 'traverse' the fundamental fantasy, thereby disclosing its arbitrary and unfounded character. See especially *Plague*, chapter 1.

FATHER: Žižek distinguishes between the symbolic or Oedipal father of the PLEASURE PRINCIPLE and the IMAGINARY obscene father of the SUPEREGO, also known as the *père-vers* or 'father-of-enjoyment'. In *The Ticklish Subject* he completes the triad with the father of the REAL, a figure of horrifying violence who corresponds to the Reformation God of Judgement, and whose demise in modern secular society is responsible for our psychic malaise. See also REGISTER.

FORCED CHOICE: see 'CASTRATION', PERVERSION AND SUBLIMATION.

GAZE: an object attached to the scopic drive (elaborated by Lacan, *Seminar* XI). Like all Lacanian objects it is an imaginary construct, but it has an exceptionally strong attachment to the REAL. Žižek stresses that it is object and not subject: the gaze does not involve my looking but my being looked *at*. See most recently *Enjoy!*, 2nd edn, 202–3.

HYSTERIA: one of the two forms of neurosis (the other being obsession), in which the subject resists integration to the symbolic order. We assume a subject position by responding to the Other via the play of reciprocal recognition: the Other calls upon us to assume what Lacan calls a 'symbolic mandate', and we recognize that mandate because we already recognize the Other as entitled to issue it. Lacan's 'symbolic mandate' has affinities with Althusser's notion of 'interpellation', whereby state authorities transform people into political subjects; hence Žižek equates hysteria with 'failed interpellation' (*For They Know Not*, 101). The hysteric is uncertain in the face of interpellation: I may recognize the mandate, but is it really meant for *me*? (cf. *For They Know Not*, 156). This uncertainty results in a deadlocked relationship to desire, since the hysteric is reluctant to assume desire as his or her own, and seeks instead to desire from the position of someone else. This in turn generates the SYMPTOMS typical of hysteria, as the blocked desire is metamorphosed into a physical impediment such as lameness or a speech defect. Symptoms like these appeal – usually unsuccessfully – to the Other to make sense of them. A *dialogue de sourds* is thus established by means of which the hysteric refuses the Other's mandate and defies the Other's comprehension. That is the reason why 'hystericization' is valuable in therapy. It points to the discovery that the Other is an impostor – that there is not really any authority legitimated to summons us, or qualified to give account of our condition. Žižek builds on Lacan's characterization of Hegel as 'the most sublime of hysterics' (*Seminar* XVII, 38) to confer on theory and philosophy the positive values associated by psychoanalysis with hysteria. Hysterics, women and theorists are the heroes of Žižek's texts.

IMAGINARY: see REGISTER.

JOUISSANCE: see ENJOYMENT.

LAW: Žižek uses this term very freely to refer to anything pertaining to the symbolic, or the BIG OTHER – language, social institutions, the regimes of the various FATHERS. The law is not solely symbolic, since it is also infiltrated by ENJOYMENT in the form of the SUPEREGO.

NEGATION, NEGATIVE, NEGATIVITY: Hegel's famous expression, that we must 'tarry with the negative' (*Phenomenology*, §32), is frequently quoted by Žižek in his Lacanian reading of Hegel's logic (see also REFLECTION). Hegel treats negation differently from earlier philosophers, in that he thinks that a double negative (or negation of negation) does not simply return one to one's original starting point; rather, the layers of negation are integrated into, and included within, the resulting affirmation. Hegelian negation also comprises forms of opposition which we might not think of as 'negation'; e.g. 'other than' is a type of negation for Hegel. Žižek assimilates Hegelian negation to the REAL since it permeates and shapes thought without being realized in it. The 'negation of negation' is read in tandem with the Lacanian concept of 'CASTRATION', which is also double: first there is the traumatic imposition of the signifier, and second the repression of this trauma (see also SIGNIFYING CHAIN). Another form of negativity which is important to Žižek is that of 'non all'. When language is said to be 'non all', this is because it is at once 'all' (that there is) and 'not all' (in the sense of not consistent, not convincing, not satisfying). That is, an element of negativity persists in it (see BIG OTHER); the same is true of feminine ENJOYMENT.

'NIGHT OF THE WORLD': a quotation from Hegel's *Systementwürfe* which Žižek cites repeatedly as capturing the trauma of inner division following 'CASTRATION' when the unity of the biological organism is sundered and the DRIVES are formed.

OBJET a: a paradoxical object which is the remainder of the REAL in the SUBJECT and the Other; its name derives from the 'little' or imaginary other of Lacan's early teaching, but in his mature thought it is equipoised between the three REGISTERS. *Objet a* acts as the pivot of many analytical structures, where it functions in contradictory ways as presence/absence, treasure/shit, sublime/abject. It is associated with the real as ENJOYMENT in the form of the remainder of the enjoyment which we gave up in 'CASTRATION', and can only accede to in the form of the mysterious surplus, or *plus-de-jouir*, of the law. Because the *objet a* is the object around which the DRIVES revolve, but which they never attain, the mathemes of both PERVERSION AND SUBLIMATION plot the relation between the barred SUBJECT and *objet a* as, respectively, $a \lozenge \$$ and $\$ \lozenge a$. As remainder of the real, *objet a* also features in a series of different positions in the theory of DISCOURSE which Žižek adopts from Lacan. It is also the mysterious object which appears to cause DESIRE but which is in fact created by it. Because it is both the object and the cause of the subject's desire, and determines what form this desire will take, *a* is the object associated with FANTASY, the matheme of which is also $\$ \lozenge a$ (i.e. the same as the matheme of sublimation).

OTHER: see BIG OTHER.

PERVERSION AND SUBLIMATION: Žižek accepts Lacan's tenet that we do not actually want to satisfy the DRIVE; or rather, that its satisfaction lies in keeping it going on an endless cycle at a safe distance from its object, rather than in allowing it to attain this object – this safety feature is what constitutes the PLEASURE PRINCIPLE. What Freud called the 'vicissitudes' of the drive are therefore their normal functioning. The two 'vicissitudes' which Žižek regularly discusses are perversion and sublimation.

In perversion, the drive is inhibited from attaining its ultimate object, ENJOYMENT, by the fact that the subject sides with the law prohibiting it. Indeed, following the forced choice (see 'CASTRATION'), the subject could never have had access to enjoyment anyway. By siding with the law, the subject takes up instead the position of the object-remainder of enjoyment within the law (i.e. surplus enjoyment; see also *OBJET a*). Perversion is allied with conservatism because the pervert is committed to the enjoyment that can only be found within the law; see *Ticklish Subject*, 247–51. This makes the pervert the servant of the SUPEREGO. The matheme of perversion, then, is $a \lozenge \$$: it puts the pervert in the place of *a*, and reveals his fantasy as that of serving some other subject. The form of perversion which Žižek discusses most is fetishism, because of the link (via Marx) with commodities and ideology; see e.g. *Sublime Object*, chapter 1; *Plague*, chapter 2.

In sublimation, the subject does not objectify *itself*; instead, it positions its objects against the real of the drive, so that they both block out and transmit its deadly impulse in a way which makes them seem somehow to have transcended death. This is what makes such objects appear 'sublime'. Žižek often refers to sublimation using the expression which he takes from Lacan of 'between two deaths'. The 'two deaths' in question vary from case to case. Sometimes the sublime object appears to have crossed the limit separating physical life from death, yet without that death being recorded symbolically in the BIG OTHER (as is the case of a cartoon animal which undergoes drastic violence but nevertheless seems to spring back into shape), and sometimes the sublime object has been cast out of the symbolic order without being yet physically dead (as is the case with Antigone); see *Sublime Object*, 131–6, and *Looking Awry*, 83–7. Another way of describing sublimation is that it raises an object 'to the dignity of the THING'. Desublimation occurs when this effect of the sublime collapses and we glimpse the real in the object in its everyday mundanity (*On Belief*, 89–90).

PLEASURE: crucially differentiated from ENJOYMENT. Enjoyment is not 'pleasurable'; on the contrary, it is associated with what Freud calls 'unpleasure'. See PLEASURE PRINCIPLE.

PLEASURE PRINCIPLE: a psychic mechanism consisting in the repression exercised by the Oedipal LAW (the secondary repression). Its function is to protect the subject from ENJOYMENT; this is why the Oedipal father is said to be ignorant of enjoyment. The pleasure principle is thus associated with DESIRE, not DRIVE, and with the symbolic order (and the Other) rather than the REAL. See also REGISTER, PERVERSION AND SUBLIMATION.

PSYCHOSIS: a state in which the distinction between reality and the REAL has been lost and which, since it leaves the subject unable to distinguish between hallucination and the perception of real objects, is tantamount to madness. Cyberspace is said to threaten subjects with psychosis because the world of the internet and computer games presents an undifferentiated world of virtuality, which Žižek equates with the real. In *The Ticklish Subject* Žižek describes the subjectivity typical of late capitalist society as psychotic, because it has lost the structure of Oedipal LAW that distances (via 'CASTRATION') the subject from the real of enjoyment. This connects with Lacan's account of psychosis (in *Seminar* III), according to which it results from the signifier of the 'father' being foreclosed in the symbolic, only to return in the real. The form of psychosis which Žižek discusses most frequently is paranoia, in which the subject believes that 'there is an Other of the Other', i.e. that the BIG OTHER really exists.

REAL: the problematic nub around which all Žižek's writing turns. In Lacan, the real is one of three REGISTERS, the others being the symbolic and the imaginary. Although in his early writings Žižek sometimes represents the real as a monstrous entity, this is a device of exposition aimed at conveying the horror or trauma with which the real is associated. The real exists only in contradistinction to reality, and it corresponds to the limits, and limitations, of language. Hence it can be approached from the standpoint of the lack in language which results from 'CASTRATION' and shows up in the imbalance within the SIGNIFYING CHAIN. But it can also be theorized from the perspective of what resists language, as the insatiable wheel of the DRIVE, for example, or the obscenity of ENJOYMENT. Ways of thinking about the real cannot engage with it directly, but only as 'a cause which in itself does not exist – which is present only in a series of effects, but always in a distorted, displaced way' (*Sublime Object*, 163). This distorted, displaced pressure of the real is sensed in a series of objects, pre-eminently the *OBJET a* (see also PERVERSION AND SUBLIMATION). Žižek's quest for the real has led him a long way from its Lacanian association with the split instituted in language by sexual difference. As what constitutes the unrepresentable singularity of individuals, the real is an element in the development of what, following Hegel, Žižek calls 'concrete universality'. In the political sphere, he sees ideology as way of organizing the real and, from *The Ticklish Subject*, he has controversially hailed capital as real. More recently again, he has read the Pauline theology of grace as offering a means of escape from law into the liberating real of radical change. In his most recent writings, Žižek reflects the real into the triad of registers, distinguish the 'real real' of the THING, the 'symbolic real' of mathematical or scientific reality, and the 'imaginary real' of singular difference (*On Belief*, 82).

REFLECTION: Žižek takes this term from Hegel's 'Logic of Essence' in his *Science of Logic*. The successive moments which constitute the dialectical process are a series of three different forms of reflection. Each one negates the previous one, which is why the process as a whole involves a double NEGATION, or 'negation of the negation'. Reflection retains some of the sense of 'mirroring' as well as 'thought'. The process of successive reflections is what constitutes objects, then subjects, and finally the subject-as-object (i.e. self-consciousness). Žižek's most extensive discussion of reflection is in *The Sublime Object*, 224–30, but its pattern of reversal and return characterizes all of his writing.

REGISTER: Žižek adopts from Lacan the idea that the psyche is organized in terms of three sets of relations, termed 'imaginary', 'symbolic' and 'real'. These relations are often called 'registers', or 'orders'. The REAL differs from the other two in that it is what by definition resists, or is lacking in, them. Much of Lacan's early thought is devoted to distinguishing between the imaginary and the symbolic. Žižek is less concerned with exploring this distinction, but it retains a structuring value in his thought. The symbolic is the domain of structure, difference and gap, as realized, for example, in the SIGNIFYING CHAIN; whereas the imaginary provides the illusion of stability, content and wholeness. The symbolic is realized in the interaction between the BIG OTHER and the SUBJECT, whereas the imaginary informs the construction of all our objects, including the 'self'. In Lacan's algebra, capital letters usually denote symbolic constructs, and lower-case ones their imaginary correlates, a usage followed by Žižek.

S1, S2: see SIGNIFYING CHAIN, DISCOURSE.

$: see SUBJECT.

SIGNIFYING CHAIN: Lacan's account of signification differs importantly from Saussure's, on which it is based, in that it posits a fundamental imbalance between the two planes of signifier and signified, whereas Saussure saw them as related to one another like two sides of the same piece of paper. Accounts of how this imbalance arises differ in different parts of Lacan's teaching. Žižek is less interested in the earlier account, which identifies the missing signified as the maternal phallus, and draws more on Lacan's distinction between a unary signifier and the binary one, schematically represented as S1 and S2 respectively. Minimally, the opposition between the two represents the capacity for difference within the order of signification. S1, when termed the 'unary trait' (*Seminar VIII*, session xxiv), is the element in signification involved in the formation of the subject's symbolic identity ('the ego ideal'). It is also referred to as the master signifier, and as such is for Žižek a key support of ideology.

SINTHOME: see SYMPTOM.

SUBJECT: The psychoanalytical account of the subject on which Žižek draws is that associated with Lacan's teaching from 1957–8 (*Seminar V*) onwards and presented in the 'graphs of desire'; these are explicated in *Sublime Object*, chapter 3. This is not the S or Es of the early seminars, but the barred $, an empty structure which results from the subject being, at base, no more than a disruption of the SIGNIFYING CHAIN. 'The "subject" itself is *nothing but* the failure of symbolisation, of its own symbolic representation' (*Contingency*, 120). This empty structure is filled out ('subjectivized') in a variety of ways – for example, by the misrecognition of interpellation – but the most basic filler is the OBJET *a*, 'which is merely a positivisation/embodiment of this failure' (ibid.) and which supports the fundamental FANTASY, a relation expressed in the formula $ ◊ *a*. The key Lacanian reference point here is the relation of alienation and separation described in *Seminar XI*: the subject alternates between sliding under the BIG OTHER and thus being alienated in it, and separating from it in such a way as to expose the lack in both of them that is held open by the *objet a*. The purpose of analysis is to restore the $ in its emptiness (a process known as 'subjective destitution'). Thus revealed as a deadlock in the process of signification, the subject can also be defined as 'the answer of the real' (e.g. *Sublime Object*, 178). Following Lacan's lead in *Seminar XI*, Žižek sees a continuity between $ and the subject of Cartesian philosophy, but he goes further than Lacan by arguing that the split subject of psychoanalysis continues and illumines the philosophical tradition of Kant, Hegel and Marx (*Tarrying with the Negative*, chapter 1), and that the formula of fantasy equates to the Hegelian relation of subject and substance.

SUBLIMATION: see PERVERSION.

SUPEREGO: Žižek's clearest accounts, which are based closely on Lacan, are in *Metastases*, 67–8, and *The Ticklish Subject*, 268–9. The superego is a malign agency, the internalized reflex within us not of the Oedipal FATHER but of the father in Freud's *Totem and Taboo* who commandeered all the women of the tribe for his own use, and was then murdered by his sons. This father is imaginary, in that he represents an imagined refusal of 'CASTRATION'. However, just as in Freud's text the sons became inhibited by the pressure of their dead father and drew up laws to restrict their own behaviour, so we too are haunted by his agency. Although, unlike this dead father, we have submitted to 'castration', his voice persists as an object-remainder in the symbolic fabric, exhorting us to derive ENJOYMENT from the LAW. Žižek gives the example of a child who not only must go and visit her granny, she must go because she wants to, and she must enjoy it (*Ticklish Subject*, 268). The superego is thus the agency that provides us with surplus enjoyment. This makes our relationship to the law perverse, and indeed the superego is also referred to as the *père-vers*, or 'perverse father'. Žižek frequently describes the superego as 'a ratchet' or a 'vicious cycle', whereby the more we submit to the law, the more we sacrifice ('castration'), so the more enjoyment we feel we have given up and the more compensatory surplus enjoyment we obtain from the superego which makes us submit even more to the law, etc.

SURPLUS ENJOYMENT: see ENJOYMENT.

SYMBOLIC: see REGISTER.

SYMPTOM: The symptom is a form of communication which is delegated to the body, and so remains unknown to the subject. As a communicative act, the symptom belongs in the REGISTER of the symbolic and is designed to be interpreted by the Other. It thus presupposes a relationship of transference and a belief in the efficacy of the BIG OTHER. Initially, Lacanian therapy was aimed at the symbolic dissolution of the symptom: once it was interpreted, its message would have been heard and it would go away. However, the symptom is also the mechanism whereby the subject, unbeknownst to himself, organizes his ENJOYMENT; the subject 'loves his symptom more than himself' (*Sublime Object*, 74), and it is thus almost impossible for him to give it up. The expression 'enjoy your symptom' refers to this condition (*Sublime Object*, 21). Therapeutic attention was then turned to the FANTASY, as the dimension of the symptom in which enjoyment was articulated. Later, Lacan recast the notion of symptom as *sinthome*. Shorn of the symbolic dimension that shapes the symptom, the *sinthome* is concentrated in the imaginary and the real, and can be represented by the phallic signifier Φ. It is 'a terrifying bodily mark which is merely a mute attestation bearing witness to a disgusting enjoyment, without representing anything or anyone' (*Sublime Object*, 76). The subject is enjoined to identify with the symptom as his link with the real of his enjoyment. See *Sublime Object*, 71–9, for Žižek's account of the development of Lacan's thinking about the symptom.

THING: Žižek adopts the term from Lacan's *Seminar* VII. Lacan's usage is indebted to Heidegger's essay 'The Thing', which describes the way in which a seemingly humdrum object can reveal itself from outside the structure of representation and disclose its cosmic relevance. The Thing, for Lacan, is the point just outside the scope of symbolization where the sense that the symbolic has a limit concentrates itself into a threat of what might lie *beyond* that limit. The Thing is, in language, what the blind spot is in our vision: it can be present in its very absence, as the point from which some invisible menace threatens. At the point of the Thing, the DRIVES, especially the death drive, seem to press upon us. Sublimation takes place when an object is 'raised to the dignity of the Thing' (*Seminar* VII, 112) and thus both communicates and wards off the real of the drive beyond it (see PERVERSION AND SUBLIMATION). Žižek's use of the term 'Thing' reactivates its Kantian implications. For him, the Thing is transcendental in the Kantian sense; that is, it lies outside the reach of phenomenology. But, as he explains in *Metastases*, 181, it differs from the OBJET *a* in that the Thing belongs outside language, whereas the *objet a* is a hitch or gap within the signifying order.

VOICE: see SUPEREGO.

Notes

Chapter 1 Introduction: Thinking, Writing and Reading about the Real

1 This and the immediately following paragraphs are based on the 'Introduction' by Wright and Wright to the *Žižek Reader*; Laclau, 'Preface'; scattered references in Žižek's works; and the various collaborative volumes he has edited or co-edited. In the English-speaking world the best-known Slovenian Lacanians are Mladen Dolar, Renata Salecl and Alenka Zupančič. Others are Miran Božovič, Raho Riha and Ždravko Kobe.

2 Sometimes whole passages are repeated from one book to another. About 30 per cent of *The Abyss of Freedom* is lifted verbatim from *The Indivisible Remainder*, and there are extensive overlaps between *The Fragile Absolute* and *The Art of the Ridiculous Sublime*.

3 Here are just three examples of the many errors of fact that litter his pages. In film, Spielberg is named as the director of the Star Wars movies (*Plague*, 75). In literature, the Marquise de Merteuil in *Les Liaisons dangereuses* becomes the Marquise de Montreuil (*Metastases*, 100). And even in Lacan, the discs on the prisoners' backs in Lacan's essay on 'Le Temps logique' become hats (*Indivisible Remainder*, 133–5).

4 I have translated this from the French version of Lacan's 'Seminar on "The Purloined Letter"'; see *Ecrits*, 25. The English translation (55) runs 'glued to its heel'.

5 e.g. Derrida says of it: 'Lacan's "style" was constructed so as to check almost permanently any access to an isolable content, to an unequivocal, determinable meaning beyond writing' (*Post Card*, 420). See also Malcolm Bowie, who e.g. describes the style of *Seminar* XX as 'lurch[ing] between catechism, riddle-book and Pindaric ode' (*Lacan*, 150).

6   Other techniques of composition which can be difficult to decipher include implicit dialectical reversal, and writing in conformity with an unacknowledged model such as Lacan's seminars (see n. 8 below).

7   This chapter is also reproduced in abridged form in *Mapping Ideology*, 296–331.

8   Analogously, the influence of Lacan's *Seminars* is perceptible on the structure of several of Žižek's writings, notably in the progression which they often show from the registers of the imaginary and the symbolic to the real.

9   The masculine variant runs 'I am, therefore it thinks'.

10 In Freud's early accounts of the psyche, the major division is between the conscious and preconscious parts of the mind, on the one hand, and the unconscious on the other. But when he realized that a large part of the ego was unconscious, he resorted to a different topography in which the three elements are *ego*, *superego* and *id*. The *id* is thus a part of what is unconscious, and is identified with the drives; this means that it is, for Lacan, a psychic manifestation of the real. See DRIVE in the Glossary.

11 For good analyses of Žižek's style, see the articles in the Bibliography by Eagleton and Gigante.

12 Such formulations, endemic to Žižek's writing, may be a pastiche of Hegel's pedagogical style in his *Encyclopaedia*.

13 See e.g. *Plague*, 24–5, 53–4; *Indivisible Remainder*, 2–3; *Ticklish Subject*, 268–9.

14 See e.g. *Fright*, 5–6.

15 See DISCOURSE in the Glossary, and Žižek's 'Four Discourses, Four Subjects', in *Cogito and the Unconscious*, 74–113, for a fuller account.

16 I use the feminine pronoun because the hysterical subject, for Žižek, is feminine and the only true subject, a point I shall discuss in chapter 4.

17 *Seminar* XVII, 41.

18 Laclau, 'Preface', x; Wright and Wright, 'Introduction' to *The Žižek Reader*, 1.

19 See Glynos, 'Grip', 199–203, for an examination of the clinical categories used in Žižek's political analyses.

20 This suggestion is made, *à propos* of *Did Somebody Say?*, by Hatzopoulos, 'The Wrong Book'.

Chapter 2   Dialectic and the Real: Lacan, Hegel and the Alchemy of *après-coup*

1   Of the various initiatory guides, the most relevant to Žižek's reading of Lacan is Hill, *Lacan for Beginners*; another elementary introduction is Leader and Groves, *Lacan for Beginners*. M. Bowie, *Lacan*, is more demanding. Indispensable accompaniments to reading Lacanian

psychoanalysis are Laplanche and Pontalis, *Language*, and Evans, *Introductory Dictionary*. For Hegel, see especially Singer, *Hegel* and Mure, *Philosophy*. An extremely helpful handbook is Inwood, *Hegel Dictionary*. Lacan's *Seminars* are easier to read than the *Ecrits*, and Hegel's teaching on logic is more easily accessed through his *Encyclopaedia Logic* than his *Science of Logic*.

2 Although Žižek refers to a wide range of Lacanian texts, he concentrates on those from the late 1950s onwards. The 'essential' Lacan, where he is concerned, comprises books VII, VIII, XI, XVII and XX of the *Seminar* plus a few essays – principally 'Subversion of the Subject' and 'Kant with Sade' – from the *Ecrits*. Žižek's Hegelian repertoire is also selective, consisting mainly of *The Phenomenology of Spirit* and *The Science of Logic*, although he also repeated quotes from the *Jenaer Systementwürfe*; see below.

3 See the entry APRES-COUP in the Glossary and the entry on 'time' in Evans, *Introductory Dictionary*.

4 e.g. his practice of expounding a body of thought in a way which anticipates his intended critique of it; see p. 6.

5 Eagleton, 'Enjoy!', 47; Dews, 'Tremor'.

6 See M. Bowie, *Lacan*, 80–2.

7 Inwood, *Hegel Dictionary*, 250.

8 *Ecrits: A Selection*, 292–324; earlier published as 'Subversion du sujet et dialectique du désir' in *Ecrits*, 793–827. My references to this dense and important paper, first read at a conference on dialectic, cite the pagination of the English translation but provide some crucial terms from the French. Dews ('Tremor') cites Lacan's critique of Hegel in his 'Réponses à des étudiants en philosophie', questions that responded to 'La Science et la vérité' but are not included with it in the French *Ecrits*; they can be found in the *Cahiers pour l'analyse*, May–June 1966.

9 *Phenomenology*, §§178–96. Hegel's dialectic is between a (feudal) lord and his serf or bondsman, whereas Lacan's terminology relocates it in a Greek context, suggesting he was relying not on Hegel's text but on its mediation by Alexandre Kojève.

10 See his stress on the materiality of the signifier, e.g. in *Seminar* XI.

11 Hegel himself does not refer to the stages of the dialectic in this way, and Lacan's usage here again suggests that his knowledge of Hegel is not firsthand; cf. n. 9.

12 My translation. An English translation of *Seminar* XVII by Russell Grigg is in process.

13 '[I]n almost all my books', as he confesses disingenuously in *The Ticklish Subject*, chapter 1, n. 33.

14 Cited, with slight modifications from *The Ticklish Subject*, 29–30, and *Enjoy!*, 50, from Verene, *Hegel's Recollection*, 7–8; Verene translated the passage himself from the *Jenaer Systementwürfe*, iii. 187.

15 Hegel has indeed played into Žižek's hands by providing this exemplary definition of *après-coup*: 'We must hold to the conviction that it

is the nature of truth to prevail when its time has come, and that it
appears only when this time has come, and therefore never appears
prematurely, nor finds a public not ripe to receive it' (*Phenomenology*,
§71).

16 Žižek's use of emphasis is so frequent that henceforth I will draw
attention only to emphasis that I have added myself.

17 Žižek's understanding of this passage from the *Phenomenology* is
influenced by Lacan's reading of the skull in Holbein's painting *The
Ambassadors*, in *Seminars* VII and XI.

18 The first two chapters of *For They Know Not* offer a difficult, sustained
analysis of identity as always either multiple or lacking.

19 There is also a clear account of a similar position in Kant in *The
Ticklish Subject*, 304.

20 Hence the title of Žižek's thesis, *Le Plus Sublime des hystériques: Hegel
passe*.

21 'Preface' to *Philosophy of Right*, 10. The translator notes that 'actuality'
here does not mean simply 'really existing', but refers to 'the synthesis of essence and existence' which comes about when something
realizes its true nature.

22 'Who *is* this idiot who is claiming that *there is* an Other of the
Other, that the desire of the analyst is a pure desire, and so on? There
is, of course, only one answer: *Lacan himself a couple of years ago*.' The
'idiotic' position which Žižek is attacking in *The Indivisible Remainder*
looks, for example, like the one he has just been quoted as holding in
Enjoy!.

23 *Encyclopedia Logic*, §163, add. 1.

24 Laclau points out the anti-Althusserian thrust of Žižek's argument in
his useful introduction to this passage ('Preface', pp. xiv–xv).

25 See e.g. Inwood, *Hegel*, 372: 'Hegel is clearly prepared to assign concrete universality to actual things for a variety of reasons. The expression has hardly any meaning at all independently of the context in
which it occurs.'

26 *Encyclopaedia Logic*, §163: 'The *Concept* as such contains the moment of
universality, as free equality with itself in its determinacy; it contains
the moment of *particularity*, or of the determinacy in which the Universal remains serenely equal to itself; and it contains the moment of
singularity, as the inward reflection of the determinacies of universality and particularity.'

27 On the need stringently to oppose *objet a* and S1 as the forms taken by
the singular and the particular in relation to the universal, see also
Contingency, 239ff.

28 This is a recurring theme in Žižek. See also e.g. *Ticklish Subject*, 313ff;
Fragile Absolute, 90.

29 All the thinkers in *Contingency* are engaged in a somewhat comic
struggle to appropriate Hegel and distance themselves from Kant.

30 See *On Belief*, 29–31, and chapter 6.

31 The formulation 'elevate . . . to the dignity of' echoes Lacan's definition of the sublime as 'elevating to the dignity of the Thing', and
resonates with Lacan's own identification of Hegel as sublime. The
notion of sublimation will be addressed in chapter 3; see also
Glossary, PERVERSION AND SUBLIMATION and THING.

Chapter 3   'Reality' and the Real:
Culture as Anamorphosis

1 De Quincey's sally (from 'Murder Considered as One of the Fine Arts')
runs: 'If once a man indulges himself in murder, very soon he comes
to think little of robbing; and from robbing he comes next to drinking
and Sabbath-breaking, and from that to incivility and procrastination.'
Žižek offers another amusing deformation of the same passage at the
beginning of *Enjoy!*: 'How many people have entered the way of perdition with some innocent gangbang, which at the time was of no great
importance to them, and ended by sharing the main dishes in a
Chinese restaurant!' (p. ix).
2 On the collision of discourses see Miklitsch, 'Going Through'.
3 This is how the term has been understood in Wright and Wright, *Žižek
Reader*.
4 'The Seminar on "The Purloined Letter"'; already quoted (from the
French version, *Ecrits*, 25) in my Introduction, p. 4 and n. 4.
5 The chief target of this polemic is Bordwell and Carroll, *Post-Theory*,
which is anti-psychoanalytic and pro-cognitivist. 'A cognitive analysis', as stated in their Introduction (p. xvi), 'seeks to understand
human thought, emotion, and action by appeal to processes of mental
representation, naturalistic processes, and (some sort of) rational
agency.'
6 The term, introduced by Melanie Klein, was taken up by Lacan. The
contrast is between a body part that functions as organ for a particular drive (= partial object) and the whole person (e.g. as the object of
love).
7 Žižek stresses how the psychoanalytical account of these objects
differs from Derrida's account (e.g. *Indivisible Remainder*, 99–103).
Derrida sees the look and the voice as trading on the presumed
immediacy of the seen and the heard, as nostalgically attached to
the myth of presence, and thus as prime targets for deconstruction.
But for Žižek, far from assuring our sense of reality, these objects
trouble it.
8 Chion, 'Impossible Embodiment'; Dolar, 'Object Voice'.
9 See also *Enjoy!*, 116–20, and the collection *Gaze and Voice*.
10 Dolar, 'Hitchcock's Objects', 34–6. Žižek's examples in *Everything*
summarize this article.

11 Žižek is thinking of 'it' as the *ça*: Lacan's translation of Freud's *Es*, English *id*, as a way of referring to the unconscious.

12 The Courbet painting, *L'Origine du monde*, was owned by Lacan, on whose walls is was usually hung masked by another painting by Matisse.

13 This is the only interpretation envisaged in *For They Know Not*, 197; it is thus amusing to see it swept aside as inadequate in the later essay.

14 Though the recycling of material between *Art*, 30–1 and 33–5, and *The Fragile Absolute*, 73–8, is among the most disreputable in Žižek's *oeuvre*. What in the one is 'absolutely crucial' about Lynch turns out, in the other, to be 'absolutely crucial' about Schelling: the point is identical in both cases.

15 See also Flieger, 'Has Oedipus Signed Off?' and Watson, 'Tamagochi'.

16 Or, 'The more that "simulacra" (images beyond which nothing real can be found) are pursued, the more "appearance" (symbolic fictions invested with visionary promise) is impaired', as the Wrights put it in their introduction to 'Is it Possible?', *Žižek Reader*, 103.

17 See e.g. Adorno and Horkheimer, 'The Culture Industry', in *Dialectic*, 120–67. When Žižek critiques Adorno in *Metastases*, chapters 1 and 2, it is as though the Slovenian School was seeking to replace the Frankfurt School as the leading psychoanalytical interpreters of politics.

18 See also 'There is No Sexual Relationship', in *Gaze and Voice*, 221–2, where Žižek discusses the similarity between Wagner's scores and Hollywood sound-tracks.

19 See *Ticklish Subject*, 289–90; *Fright*, 1–68 *passim*; *Did Somebody Say?*, chapter 5.

20 Homer, 'It's the Political Economy', 7.

21 Especially vehemently opposed to psychoanalysis are the essays by Prince, 'Psychoanalytic Film Theory', and Smith, 'Unheard Melodies?', both in *Post-Theory*.

Chapter 4 The Real of Sexual Difference:
Imagining, Thinking, Being

1 Indeed, I have already experienced it in the reactions of various readers to earlier drafts of this chapter. One is pro-Butler, another against; one maintains that there is absolutely nothing heterosexist about Žižek; another finds emphasis on terms like 'phallus' and 'castration' seriously off-putting. Writing or reading about sexuality graphically demonstrates how we all are partisan.

2 See e.g. Kay, 'Desire'.

3 Žižek draws here on Deleuze, *Sacher Masoch*, who stresses the link between masochism and the law of contract.

4 For more on the two fathers, see *Enjoy!*, 124–5.

5 Lacan, *Seminar XXII*, session of 21 January 1975.
6 *For They Know Not*, 122–4; *Enjoy!*, 2nd edn, 223; *Tarrying*, 56–8, but also all of chapters 2–4; *Metastases*, 154–60; *Indivisible Remainder*, 155–67 and 217; *Fragile Absolute*, 143–9; *Fright*, 91–2.
7 Elizabeth Wright provides a good explanation of the meaning of the symbols in *Lacan and Postfeminism*, 23–32.
8 Žižek gets this point from Chion, *David Lynch*; see Žižek's essay 'The Lamella', 211.
9 See the whole of chapter 2 of *Metastases* for a brilliantly clear exposition of causality and the subject.
10 My thanks to the press's reader for most of this paragraph.
11 See Dolar, '*Cogito*', and the *Cogito and the Unconscious* volume generally.
12 However, Žižek points out elsewhere (*Ticklish Subject*, 294) that Miller has shown that female patients are more readily treatable through the fantasy and male ones through the symptom (or *sinthome*), so there remains some correlation between psychic pathology and anatomy.
13 Butler is also influenced by Žižek, or at least by the nexus of thinkers with whom he works. Her work shifts between *Gender Trouble* and *The Psychic Life of Power* from a primarily Foucaldian-Derridian orientation to one more engaged with Althusser and Lacan, whom she identifies (*Bodies that Matter*, 188) as Žižek's reference points.
14 Mitchell and Rose, *Feminine Sexuality*.
15 Brennan, *Between Feminism and Psychoanalysis*.
16 Neither Butler nor Žižek in his review of her arguments comments on the term 'foreclosure', despite the fact that it is smuggling in concerns other than those associated with repression. Foreclosure is associated with psychosis, whereas repression, leading to the founding of Oedipus, is linked with perversion and neurosis.
17 Although they ended by all falling out with one another (personal communication from Žižek).
18 Butler's misreading is, in itself, of course strategic.
19 See in particular Lacan's *Seminar IV*.
20 The reference is to Freud's Wolfman analysis in 'From the History'.
21 e.g. Brennan, *Between*, Introduction; Irigaray, 'Psychoanalytic Theory'.
22 Also in *Gender Trouble*, 57–72. The essay in *The Psychic Life of Power* began as a lecture to the American Psychological Association, and is perhaps more a strategic challenge to its audience than a meticulously constructed argument.
23 For the sake of simplicity, I have left out the other major strand of Žižek's argument with chapter 3 of *The Psychic Life of Power*, where Butler asks why we embrace subjection.
24 Žižek has often referred to the lamella before; see particularly 'The Lamella', reworked in chapter 5 of *Metastases*. But the account of it in *The Ticklish Subject* in relation to the fundamental fantasy is new.

25 See e.g. Freud's essay 'On Femininity' in his *New Introductory Lectures*, 112–35.

26 See chapter 1 of the *Anti-Oedipus* for the association between a 'body without organs' and the body as a series of machines.

Chapter 5   Ethics and the Real: The Ungodly Virtues of Psychoanalysis

1 The most sustained arguments with Derrida are in the early books, especially *Sublime Object*, chapter 5, and *For They Know Not*, 72–91; but see also *Did Somebody Say?*, chapter 4.

2 Of course Kierkegaard and Schelling could now be said also to be in some ways 'post-modern' philosophers; see e.g. Andrew Bowie's *Schelling*.

3 'In a word, there are three things that last forever: faith, hope, and love, but the greatest of them all is love' (1 Corinthians 13: 13; this and subsequent biblical quotations are taken from *The New English Bible*).

4 Especially for my section on Pascal. *On Belief* and *Did Somebody Say Totalitarianism?* appeared after Moriarty's article was written; and his argument is addressed to questions of faith rather than freedom, so he does not discuss Kierkegaard or Schelling.

5 Mannoni, 'Je sais bien'. Žižek draws extensively on this paper in his early writings.

6 Althusser, 'Ideology', 130–1.

7 Žižek's argument is paralleled and developed in Dolar, 'Beyond Interpellation'.

8 *Pensées*, 152–3 (fragment 418).

9 My translation is from the French, *Ecrits*, 768–9. The same passage is cited in abbreviated form in *Seminar VII*, 79.

10 See Žižek's dissections of this 'Kant with Sade' theme in *For They Know Not*, 229–41; *Everything*, 219–23; *Plague*, appendix III, and 'Kant with (or against) Sade'.

11 See e.g. *Indivisible Remainder*, 115–19. A particularly extended account of the opposition between sacrifice and renunciation is to be found in *On Belief*, 68–80.

12 Žižek's thinking on Kant and the ethics of the real benefits from being read in conjunction with Zupančič, *Ethics of the Real*. Zupančič's account, which is extremely lucid, has both been influenced by Žižek and, in turn, influences him (see e.g. his acknowledgement in *Fragile Absolute*, n. 105).

13 See Gigante, 'Toward a Notion', for a critical assessment of Žižek's reading of Schelling. Dews, 'Eclipse', is also critical; see Žižek's rebuttal of Dews in 'From Proto-reality'.

14 Schelling's term, cited in *Indivisible Remainder*, 24, underlines the analogy with the Lacanian *jouissance* of the drive.

15 Žižek cites from a different translation in *Indivisible Remainder*, 21.
16 This is also explained in *Fragile Absolute*, 71–3.
17 Cf. *Plague*, 78–9, where Žižek's interest in Malebranche revolves around his excommunication by the Jesuits: proof, for Žižek, of the value of his insights. Malebranche's view of grace is discussed by Moriarty, 'Žižek, Religion and Ideology', but I have not had room to include it.
18 The term is also Heidegger's; see *Being and Time*, 32: ' "Being-ontological" is not yet tantamount to "developing an ontology". So if we should reserve the term "ontology" for that theoretical inquiry which is explicitly devoted to the meaning of entities, then what we have in mind in speaking of Dasein's "Being-ontological" is to be designated as something "pre-ontological".' Žižek's use of the term goes back to *The Indivisible Remainder* (62), where 'pre-ontological' designates what is not yet inscribed in the order of creation. The ground of God's existence is not 'a positive base'; rather, it is pre-ontological, 'it "is" only *sous rature*, in the mode of its own withdrawal'.
19 There are difficulties identifying what constitutes a truth-event which I'll discuss in chapter 6. However, both Badiou and Žižek concur that events come from the political Left and not from the Right, so that, for example, the October Revolution is an event, but not the advent of the Third Reich.
20 This suggestion is also made, *à propos* of *Did Somebody Say?*, by Hatzopoulos, 'Wrong Book'.

Chapter 6   Politics, or, The Art of the Impossible

1 See also Glynos, 'Grip', 199–203.
2 Žižek's Marxism has taken a Leninist turn in his most recent book, *Revolution at the Gates*, which appeared just as this one was going to press.
3 See also Homer, 'Psychoanalysis'. For a more sympathetic reception of Žižek's Lacanian politics, see Glynos, 'There is no Other', and Miklitsch, 'Going Through'.
4 The reference Žižek gives is to Jacques-Alain Miller, 'Paradigms of *Jouissance*', an essay published in the New York journal *Lacanian Ink*, 17 (2000). I have not included it in the bibliography, as I have not been able to consult it myself or verify the reference.
5 This theme of ideology and its critique continues throughout Žižek's *oeuvre*. Most recently, the notion of hegemonic appropriation is developed through discussion with Laclau in *Contingency, Hegemony, Universality*. The antagonistic nature of political life opens up a potential space, and hegemony is effected when this space is colonized in the interests of the ruling class. Hegemony is thus 'a universality contaminated by particularity' (Laclau, *Contingency*, 51), whereby a group

within society succeeds in promoting itself to the status of universal and commanding the submission of others. Thus, for instance, a bourgeois hegemony obtains in the Western democracies which purport to be egalitarian and in the interests of all, whereas in reality they favour the wealthy and rely on an unbridgeable divide between them and the poor. Žižek, following Laclau and Mouffe, *Hegemony*, is interested in democratic elections as moments when political parties compete for dominance of the symbolic codes, each hoping to impose its own particular version of universality on everyone else (see e.g. *Contingency*, 93–4).

6 Žižek still takes this view in his most recent publications; see *Did Somebody Say?*, 92.

7 Derrida in turn took the term 'spectre' from Marx's opening words in the Communist Manifesto: 'A spectre is haunting Europe . . . the spectre of Communism.'

8 See Homer, 'It's the Political Economy', for a critique of this chapter. Homer shows that earlier essays on which it is based were more outspokenly Marxist, but were here tempered for an American readership.

9 There is a very useful analysis of this in Glynos, 'There is no Other', and it is also touched on by Moriarty, 'Žižek, Religion and Ideology'.

10 Giddens, *Consequences of Modernity*, and *idem, Modernity and Self-Identity*. The term was pioneered by Ulrich Beck; see e.g. Adam et al., *The Risk Society and Beyond*.

11 'How to feed and educate a child, how to proceed in sexual education, how and what to eat, how to relax and enjoy oneself – all these spheres are increasingly "colonized" by reflexivity, that is, experienced as something to be learned and decided upon' (*Ticklish Subject*, 337).

12 As I said in chapter 2, these are terms which French expositors of Hegel, such as Kojève, made common currency in France.

13 The term 'deterritorialization' is taken from the Marxist psychoanalysis of Deleuze and Guattari, in *Anti-Oedipus*.

14 *Phenomenology*, §§632–71. This is one of Žižek's most frequently cited Hegelian themes.

15 On Holocaust studies see esp. p. 68; for a critique of academic fashions, see chapters 4 and 5 *passim*. There is a remarkable study of Stalinism in chapter 3.

16 There is much more to be said about Nazism in *The Ticklish Subject*, since the whole of the first chapter is a complex exposition of Heidegger, whose failure to think the pre-ontological is aligned with his politics.

17 See *Welcome to the Desert of the Real* (dated 17 September 2002, though published as delivered in November) and the interview, 'The One Measure of True Love Is: You Can Insult the Other' (which took place in October). The phrase 'Welcome to the desert of the real' is a quota-

tion from *The Matrix*, from the scene where Lawrence Fishburn shows Keanu Reeves the horrific post-nuclear wasteland that America now is, by contrast with the elaborately crafted digital world people *think* they inhabit.

18 Grigg is especially critical of the way Žižek treats Antigone as a fable he can narrate in any way he chooses, rather than respecting Sophocles' text.

19 *Tarrying*, 92 and chapter 5, *passim.*

20 On the contrast between 'activity' and 'act' see e.g. *Enjoy!*, 156.

21 Thus Evans, *Introductory Dictionary*, s.v. 'act', p. 2: 'Neither ACTING OUT nor a PASSAGE TO THE ACT are true acts, since the subject does not assume responsibility for his desire in these actions.'

22 *Enjoy!*, 61, n. 5. Since *Enjoy!* was reissued, with an additional chapter, in 2001, Žižek's *On Belief* may well be clearing up an area of confusion in the earlier work. Examples of such self-correction are very common in his work.

Bibliography

Works by Slavoj Žižek

(These are the works I have referred to. The list of books is complete at the time of going to press, at least for publication in English. A more complete list of short works in English can be found on the web at http://www.lacan.com/bibliographyzi.htm.; see also the web page devoted to Žižek at http://www.mii.kurumeu.ac.jp/~leuers/zizek.htm)

Books in order of date of publication

Le Plus Sublime des hystériques: Hegel passe (Paris: Point Hors Ligne, 1988).
The Sublime Object of Ideology (London and New York: Verso, 1989).
For They Know Not What They Do: Enjoyment as a Political Factor (London and New York: Verso, 1991).
Looking Awry: An Introduction to Jacques Lacan Through Popular Culture (Cambridge, MA: MIT Press, 1991).
Everything You Always Wanted to Know about Lacan (But Were Afraid to Ask Hitchcock), ed. Slavoj Žižek (London and New York: Verso, 1992).
Enjoy Your Symptom! Jacques Lacan in Hollywood and Out (London: Routledge, 1992; 2nd edn, London: Routledge, 2001).
Tarrying with the Negative: Kant, Hegel, and the Critique of Ideology (Durham, NC: Duke University Press, 1993).
Mapping Ideology, ed. Slavoj Žižek (London and New York: Verso, 1994).
The Metastases of Enjoyment: Six Essays on Woman and Causality (London and New York: Verso, 1994).
The Indivisible Remainder: An Essay on Schelling and Related Matters (London and New York: Verso, 1996).

Gaze and Voice as Love Objects, ed. Renata Salecl and Slavoj Žižek (Durham, NC: Duke University Press, 1996).

The Abyss of Freedom/Ages of the World by F. W. J. von Schelling (Ann Arbor: University of Michigan Press, 1997).

The Plague of Fantasies (London and New York: Verso, 1997).

Cogito and the Unconscious, ed. Slavoj Žižek and Renata Salecl (Durham, NC: Duke University Press, 1998).

The Ticklish Subject: The Absent Centre of Political Ontology (London and New York: Verso, 1999).

The Art of the Ridiculous Sublime: On David Lynch's Lost Highway, Occasional Papers 1 (Seattle: Walter Chapin Simpson Center for the Humanities, University of Washington, Seattle, 2000).

The Fragile Absolute – or, Why is the Christian Legacy Worth Fighting For? (London and New York: Verso, 2000).

Contingency, Hegemony, Universality: Contemporary Dialogues on the Left, with Judith Butler and Ernesto Laclau (London and New York: Verso, 2000).

Did Somebody Say Totalitarianism? Five Interventions in the (Mis)use of a Notion (London and New York: Verso, 2001).

The Fright of Real Tears: Krzystof Kieślowski Between Theory and Post-Theory (London: British Film Institute, 2001).

On Belief (London and New York: Routledge, 2001).

Opera's Second Death, with Mladen Dolar (London and New York: Routledge, 2002).

Revolution at the Gates, ed. Slavoj Žižek (London and New York: Verso, 2002).

Shorter works and interviews, in alphabetical order of title

'Chance and Repetition in Kieślowski's Films', *Paragraph*, 24 (2001), 23–9.

'From Proto-reality to the Act: A Reply to Peter Dews', *Angelaki*, 5/3 (2000), 141–6.

'Is it Possible to Traverse the Fantasy in Cyberspace?', in *The Žižek Reader*, ed. Wright and Wright, 104–24.

'Kant with (or against) Sade', in *The Žižek Reader*, ed. Wright and Wright, 283–301.

'Lacan in Slovenia'. Interview with Slavoj Žižek and Renata Salecl, in *A Critical Sense*, ed. Osborne, 21–35; first published in *Radical Philosophy*, 58 (1991), 25–31.

'The Lamella of David Lynch', in *Reading Seminar XI: Lacan's Four Fundamental Concepts of Psychoanalysis*, ed. Richard Feldstein, Bruce Fink and Maire Jaanus (Albany, NY: SUNY Press, 1995), 205–20.

'The One Measure of True Love Is: You Can Insult the Other.' Interview with Sabine Reul and Thomas Deichmann, October 2001. *Spiked Culture*, http://www.spiked-online.com/Articles/00000002D2C4.htm;

first appeared in German as 'Der Krieg und das fehlende ontologische Zentrum der Politik', *Novo Magazin*, 55/6, http://www.novo-magazin.de/55/novo5512.htm.

'Preface: Burning the Bridges', in *The Žižek Reader*, ed. Wright and Wright, pp. vii–x.

'Symptom', in *Feminism and Psychoanalysis*, ed. Elizabeth Wright, 423–7.

Welcome to the Desert of the Real (New York: Wooster Press, 2001) [text of a lecture].

Other Works

Adam, Barbara, Ulrich Beck and Joost van Loon, eds, *The Risk Society and Beyond: Critical Issues for Social Theory* (London: SAGE, 2000).

Adorno, Theodor W. and Max Horkheimer, *Dialectic of Enlightenment*, trans. John Cumming, Verso Classics 15 (London and New York: Verso, 1997).

Althusser, Louis, 'Ideology and Ideological State Apparatuses (Notes Towards an Investigation)', in *Mapping Ideology*, ed. Žižek, 100–40.

Badiou, Alain, *Saint Paul: la fondation de l'universalisme* (Paris: Presses universitaires de France, 1997).

Bordwell, David and Noel Carroll, eds, *Post-Theory* (Madison, WI: University of Wisconsin Press, 1996).

Bowie, Andrew, *Schelling and Modern European Philosophy: An Introduction* (London and New York: Routledge, 1993).

Bowie, Malcolm, *Lacan*, Fontana Modern Masters (London: Fontana, 1991).

Boynton, Robert S., 'Enjoy Your Žižek! An Excitable Slovenian Philosopher Examines the Obscene Practices of Everyday Life – Including His Own', *Lingua Franca*, 8 (1998), consulted at http://www.linguafranca.com/9810/zizek.html.

Brennan, Teresa, *History After Lacan* (London and New York: Routledge, 1993).

——ed., *Between Feminism and Psychoanalysis* (London and New York: Routledge, 1989).

Butler, Judith, *Bodies that Matter: On the Discursive Limits of Sex* (London and New York: Routledge, 1993).

——*Gender Trouble: Feminism and the Subversion of Identity* (London and New York: Routledge, 1990).

——*The Psychic Life of Power: Theories in Subjection* (Stanford, CA: Stanford University Press, 1997).

——with Ernesto Laclau and Slavoj Žižek. *Contingency: Hegemony, Universality: Contemporary Dialogues on the Left* (London and New York: Verso, 2000).

Chion, Michel, *David Lynch*, trans. Robert Julian (London: British Film Institute, 1995; first published, Paris: Editions de l'Etoile/*Cahiers du cinema*, 1992).

—— 'The Impossible Embodiment', in *Everything You Always Wanted to Know about Lacan (But Were Afraid to Ask Hitchcock)*, ed. Žižek, 195–207.

Copjec, Joan, 'Sex and the Euthanasia of Reason', in *Read My Desire: Lacan against the Historicists* (Cambridge, MA: MIT Press, 1994), 201–36.

Daly, Glyn, 'Ideology and its Paradoxes: Dimensions of Fantasy and Enjoyment', *Journal of Political Ideologies*, 4/2 (1999), 219–38.

Deleuze, Gilles, *Sacher Masoch: An Interpretation. Together with the Entire Text of 'Venus in Furs'*, trans. Jean McNeil (London: Faber and Faber, 1971; first published, Paris: Minuit, 1967).

—— and Felix Guattari, *Anti-Oedipus: Capitalism and Schizophrenia*, trans. Robert Hurley, Mark Seem and Helen R. Lane (Minneapolis: University of Minnesota Press, 1983; first published, Paris: Minuit, 1972).

de Quincey, Thomas *'On Murder Considered as one of the Fine Arts'; and 'On War': Two Essays* (London: Doppler Press, 1980).

Derrida, Jacques, *The Post Card: From Socrates to Freud and Beyond*, trans. Alan Bass (Chicago: University of Chicago Press, 1993; first published, Paris: Aubier-Flammarion, 1980).

—— *Resistances of Psychoanalysis*, trans. Peggy Kamuf, Pascale-Anne Brault and Michael Naas (Stanford, CA: Stanford University Press, 1998; first published, Paris: Galilée, 1996).

—— *Specters of Marx: The State of the Debt, the Work of Mourning, and the New International*, trans. Peggy Kamuf (London and New York: Routledge, 1994; first published, Paris: Galilée, 1993).

Dews, Peter, 'The Eclipse of Coincidence', *Angelaki*, 4/3 (1999), 13–23.

—— 'The Tremor of Reflection: Slavoj Žižek's Lacanian Dialectics', *Radical Philosophy*, 72 (1995), 17–29; repr. in *The Limits of Disenchantment* (London and New York: Verso, 1995), 236–58.

Dolar, Mladen, 'Beyond Interpellation', *Qui Parle*, 6 (1993), 73–96.

—— 'Cogito as the Subject of the Unconscious', in *Cogito and the Unconscious*, ed. Žižek and Salecl, 11–40.

—— 'Hitchcock's Objects', in *Everything You Always Wanted to Know about Lacan (But Were Afraid to Ask Hitchcock)*, ed. Žižek, 31–46.

—— 'The Object Voice', in *Gaze and Voice as Love Objects*, ed. Salecl and Žižek, 7–31.

—— With Slavoj Žižek. *Opera's Second Death* (London and NY: Routledge, 2002).

Eagleton, Terry, 'Enjoy!', *Paragraph*, 24 (2001), 40–52.

Evans, Dylan, *An Introductory Dictionary of Lacanian Psychoanalysis* (London: Routledge, 1996).

Flieger, Jerry Anne, 'Has Oedipus Signed Off (or Struck Out)?: Žižek, Lacan, and the Field of Cyberspace', *Paragraph*, 24 (2001), 53–77.

Freud, Sigmund, *The Standard Edition of the Complete Psychological Works of Sigmund Freud*, trans. under the editorship of James Strachey, 24 vols (London: Hogarth Press, 1953–74), abbreviated in the following as SE.

—— 'A Child is being Beaten', *SE* XVII, 179–204.

—— 'From the History of an Infantile Neurosis', *SE* XVII, 1–122.

——*Moses and Monotheism, SE* XXIII, 7–137.

——*New Introductory Lectures on Psycho-Analysis, SE* XXII, 5–182.

——*Totem and Taboo, SE* XIII, 1–162.

Giddens, Anthony, *The Consequences of Modernity* (Cambridge: Polity, 1990).

——*Modernity and Self-Identity* (Cambridge: Polity, 1991).

Gigante, Denis, 'Toward a Notion of Critical Self-Creation: Slavoj Žižek and the "Vortex of Madness"', *New Literary History*, 29 (1998), 153–68.

Glynos, Jason, 'The Grip of Ideology: A Lacanian Approach to the Theory of Ideology', *Journal of Political Ideologies*, 6/2 (2001), 191–214.

——' "There is no Other of the Other": Symptoms of a Decline in Symbolic Faith, or, Žižek's Anti-Capitalism', *Paragraph*, 24 (2001), 78–110.

Gould, Stephen Jay, 'Phyletic Size Decrease in Hershey Bars', in *Hen's Teeth and Horse's Toes* (London and New York: Norton, 1983), 313-19.

Grigg, Russell, 'Absolute Freedom and Major Structural Change', *Paragraph*, 24 (2001), 111–24.

Hatzopoulos, Pavlos, 'The Wrong Book Written for the Right Reason', review article on *Did Somebody Say Totalitarianism?*, *Journal of Political Ideologies*, 7/1 (2002), 117–22.

Hegel, Georg Wilhelm Friedrich, *The Encylopaedia Logic*, trans. T. F. Geraets, W. A. Suchting and H. S. Harris (Indianapolis: Hackett, 1991).

——*Jenaer Systementwürfe*, in G. F. W. Hegel, *Gesammelte Werke*, vol. 8 (Hamburg: Meiner, 1976).

——*Phenomenology of Spirit*, trans. A. V. Miller, analysis and foreword by J. N. Findlay (Oxford: Oxford University Press, 1977).

——*Philosophy of Right*, trans. T. M. Knox (Oxford: Clarendon Press, 1942).

——*The Science of Logic*, trans. A. V. Miller (London: Allen and Unwin, 1969).

Heidegger, Martin, *Being and Time*, trans. John Macquarrie and Edward Robinson (Oxford: Blackwell, 1978).

——'The Thing', in *Poetry, Language, Thought*, trans. with an Introduction by Albert Hofstadter (New York and London: Harper & Row, 1975), 165-82.

Hill, Philip, *Lacan for Beginners* (New York and London: Writers and Readers Publishing, Inc., 1997).

Homer, Séan, 'Psychoanalysis, Post-Marxism and the Subject: From the Ethical to the Political', *PS: The Journal of the Universities Association for Psychoanalytic Studies*, 1 (1998), 18–28.

——'It's the Political Economy, Stupid! On Žižek's Marxism', *Radical Philosophy*, 108 (2001), 7–16.

Inwood, Michael, *Hegel: The Arguments of the Philosophers* (London and New York: Routledge, 1983).

——*A Hegel Dictionary* (Oxford: Blackwell, 1992).

Irigaray, Luce, 'Psychoanalytic Theory: Another Look', in *This Sex Which Is Not One*, trans. Catherine Porter with Carolyn Burke (Ithaca, NY: Cornell University Press, 1985), 34–67; first published, Paris: Minuit, 1977.

Kant, Immanuel, *Critique of Practical Reason*, ed. Mary Gregor, Introduction by Andrews Reath. Cambridge Texts in the History of Philosophy (Cambridge: Cambridge University Press, 1997).

Kay, Sarah, 'Desire and Subjectivity', in *The Troubadours: An Introduction*, ed. Simon Gaunt and Sarah Kay (Cambridge: Cambridge University Press, 1999), 212–27.

Kierkegaard, Søren, *Fear and Trembling; Repetition*, ed. and trans. with Introduction and Notes by Howard V. Hong and Edna H. Hong (Princeton, NJ: Princeton University Press, 1983).

Lacan, Jacques, *Ecrits* (Paris: Seuil, 1966).

——*Ecrits: A Selection*, trans. Alan Sheridan (London: Tavistock, 1977).

——'Kant with Sade', *October*, 51 (1989), 55–75; in French in *Ecrits*, 765–90.

——'Position of the Unconscious', trans. Bruce Fink, in *Reading Seminar XI: Lacan's Four Fundamental Concepts of Psychoanalysis*, ed. Richard Feldstein, Bruce Fink and Maire Jaanus (Albany, NY: SUNY Press, 1995), 259–82; in French in *Ecrits*, 829–50.

——*The Seminar of Jacques Lacan*, ed. Jacques-Alain Miller:

Book III. The Psychoses. 1955–6, trans. with notes by Russell Grigg (London: Routledge, 1993; first published, Paris: Seuil, 1981).

Livre IV. La Relation d'objet. 1956–7 (Paris: Seuil, 1994).

Livre V. Les Formations de l'inconscient (Paris: Seuil, 1998).

Book VII. The Ethics of Psychoanalysis. 1959–60, trans. with notes by Dennis Porter (London: Routledge, 1992; first published, Paris: Seuil, 1986).

Livre VIII. Le Transfert. 1961–2 (Paris: Seuil, 1991).

[Book XI] *The Four Fundamental Concepts of Psycho-analysis* [1964], trans. Alan Sheridan, Introduction by David Macey (Harmondsworth: Penguin, 1994; first published, Paris: Seuil, 1973).

Livre XVII. L'Envers de la psychanalyse. 1969–70 (Paris: Seuil, 1991).

Book XX. Encore. On Feminine Sexuality, the Limits of Love and Knowledge, trans. Bruce Fink (London and New York: Norton, 1998; first published, Paris: Seuil, 1975).

Livre XXII. RSI. 1974–5, Ornicar? 2–5, 1975.

——'Seminar on "The Purloined Letter"', trans. Jeffrey Mehlman, *Yale French Studies*, 48 (1972), 38–72; in French in *Ecrits*, 11–61.

——'Subversion of the Subject and the Dialectic of Desire in the Freudian Unconscious', in *Ecrits. A Selection*, 292–325; in French in *Ecrits*, 793–827.

Laclau, Ernesto, 'Preface' to Slavoj Žižek, *The Sublime Object of Ideology*, pp. ix–xv.

——with Judith Butler and Slavoj Žižek. *Contingency, Hegemony, Universality: Contemporary Dialogues on the Left*. (London and New York: Verso, 2000).

Laclau, Ernesto and Chantal Mouffe, *Hegemony and Socialist Strategy: Towards a Radical Democratic Politics* (London: Verso, 1985).

Laplanche, J. and J.-B. Pontalis, *The Language of Psychoanalysis*, trans. Donald Nicholson-Smith (London: Hogarth Press and the Institute of Psycho-Analysis, 1973).

Leader, Darien and Judy Groves, *Lacan for Beginners* (Cambridge: Icon Books, 1995).

Mannoni, Octave, 'Je sais bien, mais quand même', in *Clefs pour l'imaginaire ou l'Autre Scène* (Paris: Seuil, 1969), 9–33.

Miklitsch, Robert, ' "Going Through the Fantasy": Screening Slavoj Žižek', in *Psycho-Marxism: Marxism and Psychoanalysis Late in the Twentieth Century*, ed. Robert Miklitsch, *South Atlantic Quarterly*, 97 (1998), 475–507.

Mitchell, Juliet, and Jacqueline Rose, *Feminine Sexuality: Jacques Lacan and the Ecole Freudienne* (London: Macmillan, 1982).

Moriarty, Michael, 'Žižek, Religion and Ideology', *Paragraph*, 24 (2001), 125–39.

Mure, G. R., *The Philosophy of Hegel* (Oxford: Oxford University Press, 1965).

Osborne, Peter, ed., *A Critical Sense. Interviews with Intellectuals* (London and New York: Routledge, 1996).

Pascal, Blaise, *Pensées*, trans. with an Introduction by A. J. Krailsheimer (Harmondsworth: Penguin, 1966).

Prince, Stephen, 'Psychoanalytic Film Theory and the Problem of the Missing Spectator', in *Post-Theory*, ed. Bordwell and Carroll, 71–86.

Schelling, F. W. J. von, *The Ages of the World*, trans. Judith Norman, in Žižek, *The Abyss of Freedom*, 107–82.

——*Of Human Freedom*, trans. with Introduction and Notes by J. Gutman (Chicago, IL: Open Court, 1936).

Singer, Peter, *Hegel*, Past Masters (Oxford: Oxford University Press, 1983).

Smith, Jeff, 'Unheard Melodies? A Critique of Psychoanalytic Theories of Film Music', in *Post-Theory*, ed. Bordwell and Carroll, 230–47.

Torfing, Jacob, *New Theories of Discourse: Laclau, Mouffe, and Žižek* (Oxford: Blackwell, 1999).

Verene, Donald Phillip, *Hegel's Recollection. A Study of Images in the 'Phenomenology of Spirit'* (Albany, NY: SUNY Press, 1985).

Watson, Ben, 'The Tamagochi and the *objet a*', *Radical Philosophy*, 97 (1999), 42–4.

Wright, Elizabeth, ed., *Feminism and Psychoanalysis: A Critical Dictionary* (Oxford: Blackwell, 1992).

——*Lacan and Postfeminism* (Duxford: Icon Books, and Lanham, MD: Totem Books, 2000).

Wright, Elizabeth and Edmond Wright, eds, *A Symposium on Slavoj Žižek: Faith and the Real*, *Paragraph*, 24 (2001).

——*The Žižek Reader* (Oxford: Blackwell, 1999).

Zupančič, Alenka, *The Ethics of the Real: Kant, Lacan* (London and New York: Verso, 2000).

Index